The Wisdom of Listening

The WISDOM OF LISTENING

Edited by Mark Brady

Wisdom Publications • Boston

Wisdom Publications
199 Elm Street
Somerville MA 02144 USA
www.wisdompubs.org

Library of Congress Cataloging-in-Publication Data

The wisdom of listening / edited by Mark Brady.
    p. cm.
  ISBN 0-86171-355-9
  1. Listening. I. Brady, Mark, 1946– II. Title.
  BF323.L5W57 2003
153.6'8—dc21

                                    2003014468

07 06 05 04 03
5   4   3   2   1

Wisdom Publications' books are printed on acid-free paper
and meet the guidelines for permanence and durability of
the Committee on Production Guidelines for Book
Longevity of the Council on Library Resources.

Designed by Gopa & Ted2, Inc. Set in Fairfield LH light 10/16.
Cover designed by Christian Dierig
Printed in Canada

Table of Contents

Preface

Listening skillfully is difficult. To listen impeccably, with fixed, full attention is a discipline much like meditation. It requires practice, rigor, and resolve. And when our efforts slacken, it may require forgiveness, gentleness, and sometimes a bit of creative inspiration to get ourselves back on track.

In Western culture listening has never been a prized pursuit, the way, for example, teaching or preaching has been. There will never be a *Who's Who in American Listening.* To pursue the desire to become a master listener, a "listening warrior," requires turning away from the dominant culture to explore paths few have chosen.

This anthology has grown out of my own "countercultural" passion to become an increasingly skillful listener. Many years ago, a memorable college professor of mine, Jim Fadiman, encouraged an eager group of graduate students to "teach what you most want to learn." This continues to be sage advice. Teaching what I most want to learn has forced me to focus deeply, to research accurately, and to bring sufficient creativity to make the topic interesting to others.

I am still exploring those depths with respect to listening and learning—and the proof is in this anthology. In it I have followed another bit of advice from Dr. Fadiman: identify those teachers from whom you'd most like to learn and go to them directly. It is a mentor/apprentice model that has served a variety of crafts and disciplines well over many centuries, and I have adapted it to the practice of listening. The contributors to this anthology are all consummate teachers with important things to teach me—and I hope you as well—about listening. Some of the contributors to this collection I knew personally beforehand; some only through their published writings; others were identified by the self-posed question: "Who might teach me valuable things about listening?"

The list that resulted from posing that question was a long one and many of them are included here. All these essays have one theme in common: listening is vital to psychological and spiritual growth, and the skillful cultivation of it requires ongoing, disciplined practice.

The articles in this anthology are a collection of thoughtful, instructive words on listening. They are also wise words, true words, useful words. A diligent reader of these words will come away with many benefits. To mention but a few, such a reader will:

- uncover the skillful means to be more fully in the world, present and responsive, rather than distracted and reactive;
- realize that listening *is* a practice, and a practice that *takes* practice, and being skillful does not require being perfect;
- recognize and rectify the myriad ways in which the mind can close the ears;
- find that listening skillfully nourishes others, and that we can teach others how to return that nourishment to us;
- realize that unskillful listening has a variety of causes, and with practice we can learn to recognize and remedy them;
- discover how listening skillfully to others can facilitate hearing and deeply honoring our own tender hearts;
- recognize that there are ways to effectively listen in large groups, where distractions and competing agendas often make listening challenging;
- find confirmation of the truth that words have power; and that listening can be accomplished in ways that channel words optimally, positively, and cooperatively.

...and there are many more unnamed benefits an earnest reader will find in putting into practice the teachings in this collection of listening wisdom.

Finally, I assert that human maturation seems to significantly correlate with an increasing capacity for skillful listening. It is as if the years spent focused on speaking words and thoughts centered around one's own unique experience and personal worldview soften the adamant need to prove our own points, or to consign others' viewpoints to the background. There is more room available for the words and thoughts of others, space that can accommodate perspectives different from our own. Such maturity lends validity to the assertion that being able to fully hear and deeply respect *your* point of view, doesn't automatically require me to agree with you. The world is large enough to hold conflicting viewpoints, spacious enough for all of us to peacefully grow, learn and mature.

And so, it is my hope that this small collection of writings from wise teachers on listening will significantly contribute to the maturation of us all. According to Mother Teresa, listening is, after all, how God most frequently expresses his own spiritual maturity in the world.

Mark Brady
Los Altos, California
Fall 2003

PART ONE

The Promise of Listening

We do not believe in ourselves until someone reveals
that something deep inside us is valuable, worth listening to,
worthy of our trust, sacred to our touch.
Once we believe in ourselves we can risk curiosity, wonder,
spontaneous delight or any experience that reveals the human spirit.

~ e. e. cummings

We ourselves are arguably the most significant factor in any human exchange. More specifically: the quality of heart, wisdom, attention, and intention that we bring with us significantly impacts every exchange we conduct. In this contribution, hospice founder and longtime trainer of hospice workers, Christine Longaker provides ample evidence for the power of such heartfelt and attentive presence. In addition, she offers extensive possibilities for ways that regular meditation can shape, influence, and guide us both in the short term and, equally important, in the long term. As will quickly become evident, such presence cultivated wisely can produce transformative effects in virtually every area of our lives.

Listening with Presence, Awareness, and Love

Christine Longaker

EVERYTHING DEPENDS ON HOW WE ARE

WHEN A FRIEND is in tremendous emotional or physical pain, sometimes we're afraid to go and be with him or her, or afraid of communicating honestly when we visit. We think we should know how to relieve our friend's pain, or have just the right things to say. Yet what a person who's suffering most needs is our presence. The Greek word for one who comforts is *paraclete,* literally meaning "one who comes to walk alongside." What we bring to support a friend is our loving presence, with perspective. More than anything we do or say, what helps a person who is suffering is how we are.

"How we are" is a reflection of the unified perspective we have on the whole of life, which includes experiences of joy and adversity. Our presence is also an expression of our confidence, the profound love and unqualified respect for others we have come to embody through our spiritual practice. "How we are" is also connected to our awareness of our own suffering and the extent to which we have worked through our grief. And finally, our loving presence depends upon our ability to acknowledge and then release our fears and expectations, remaining compassionate and receptive toward the other person.

Cultivating a daily practice of meditation, and then training ourselves to integrate the mindfulness of meditation whenever we communicate, helps us develop these qualities of loving presence, authenticity, and confidence.

MEDITATION: CONNECTING WITH OUR TRUE NATURE

Meditation is more than a relaxation exercise; it is a practice designed to connect us to our innermost essence of wisdom. When our mind settles deeply in meditation, the conceptual mind and ordinary sense of self may temporarily dissolve. Then we experience a gap or space between our thoughts: a wakeful, clear, radiant awareness unstained by hopes, fears, or habitual projections. Pursued deeply and sincerely, spiritual practice enables us to purify and release the emotional conditioning and self-grasping ego that separate us from reality. Meditation connects us ever more reliably and profoundly to a natural, effortless awareness, in which there is a deep relaxation and spaciousness, an unbounded gratitude, and an all-embracing, joyful compassion.

INSPIRED OPENNESS AND PURE PRESENCE

> The Buddha sat in serene and humble dignity on the ground, with the sky above him and around him, as if to show us that in meditation you sit with an open, sky-like attitude of mind, yet remain present, earthed, and grounded. The sky is our absolute nature, which has no barriers and is boundless, and the ground is our reality, our relative, ordinary condition. The posture we take when we meditate signifies that we are linking absolute and relative, sky and ground, heaven and earth, like two wings of a bird, integrating the sky-like deathless nature of mind and the ground of our transient, mortal nature.[1]

The real meaning of "meditation" is to sustain the flow of pure awareness, free of duality—pure, simple, naked presence—awareness without commentary or reactions, a presence of profound peace and unbiased love, free of grasping after external things and free of our sense of self, the "grasper." And this is the ultimate relief from suffering—dissolving our habitual identification with the selfish ego and arriving at the profound peace and bliss of our true nature. As Sogyal Rinpoche describes:

Meditation is bringing the mind home, releasing any tension or struggle, and relaxing into the clarity and peace of your true nature. In meditation, you can allow all the scattered energies of your mind to settle, like sediment in a glass of turbulent muddy water. What happens when you set the glass down on a table? The mud swirls for awhile, but eventually it settles to the bottom. The clarity of the water, which was always there— only temporarily obscured—naturally begins to manifest.

To arrive at this state of pure presence in your practice, there are many methods of meditation which can slowly tame and settle your agitated mind, disarm your negativity and fear, and help you make friends with yourself, and thereby the world around you.[2]

When we connect with our true nature in meditation, we are connecting with our essence, which is the union of wisdom and boundless love— and this is the inspired "presence" we can be while listening to those who are suffering or dying. As Sogyal Rinpoche wrote:

All of us need to give our love to a dying person, but if we have come in touch with the nature of our mind, stabilized it through our practice of meditation, and integrated it into our lives, then the love we have to give can only be deeper, because it comes from a different source: from our innermost being, the heart of our enlightened nature. It has a special quality of freedom. This kind of love, beyond all attachment, is like divine love. It is the love of all the buddhas, the love of Christ, of God.

In that state, without contriving, and even without thinking, we can feel the presence of the Buddha or of Christ. It's as if we become their ambassador, their representative, our love backed by their love, and infused with their blessing. Love that springs truly from the nature of the mind is so blessed that it has the power to dispel the fear of the unknown, to give refuge from anxiety, to grant serenity and peace, and to bring inspiration in death and beyond."[3]

THE THREE NOBLE PRINCIPLES FOR HEALTH CARE PROFESSIONALS

How can you keep your meditation practice alive in a busy hospital or nursing home when there is nothing in the environment to support it? Training yourself daily to rely on the Three Noble Principles—establishing a motivation of profound compassion; sustaining the attitude of non-grasping; and sealing the practice through dedication—will shift your perspective on everything you encounter at work. The next step is to sustain your effort until your compassionate motivation and your spiritual practice become part of your flesh and bones. Once you have changed the attitude in your mind and heart, then no matter how distressing your work environment, you can be happy.

ESTABLISHING A MOTIVATION OF PROFOUND COMPASSION

Generating a deep compassion can make our spiritual practice and prayers more potent in their ability to help those in distress. Before beginning your daily meditation, spend some time reflecting on the suffering in the world, or on your friends' or patients' suffering, and as their suffering touches and opens your heart, let your compassion grow even deeper, and your intention to help even stronger. Dedicate your meditation and prayers to those who are suffering terribly. You could even imagine that they are gathered around and practicing with you, and that you are all receiving the blessings together.

Each day, then, re-establish your sacred intention for your spiritual path and your entire life: recognizing the many degrees of suffering that all beings everywhere experience, pray that they all may have happiness and become free of suffering, and that all attain liberation. Inspired with this intention, you might eventually decide that the best way you could benefit others and free them from suffering is to dedicate your life toward attaining enlightenment.

You might pray, "May everything I do today be beneficial. Through remembering my spiritual practice throughout the day, may I gain more confidence in the wisdom and compassion of my true nature. And through this realization, may every contact I have with others bring us both benefit, relieving suffering, bringing healing and happiness, and furthering us along the path to freedom. May kindness and wisdom increase in the world, and through my efforts today, may I contribute to the betterment of life for all."

BLESS ME INTO USEFULNESS

Arousing this motivation at work creates a sacred atmosphere for all our activities. When difficulties arise, we will be able to welcome them as reminders to transform our perspective once again. Instead of always trying to change others or judge them, we will learn how to see the pain and fear behind their actions and generate compassion for them.

Of course, sometimes we make mistakes. In caring for others we may get feedback that we have said or done something unhelpful. Or we may feel regret or frustration when forced to do something we don't agree with. Instead of getting lost in our reactions, we must remember our motivation—to be of immediate and ultimate service to all beings—since it is the motivation behind our actions that counts. As soon as we recognize our error, we can ask for forgiveness, let go of the mistake, and train ourselves in keeping our heart and mind pure. Each day we can make a fresh start, gradually training ourselves to become more aware, more compassionate, and more skillful.

Sustaining the Attitude of NonGrasping

Next, resolve to sustain the view of your true nature throughout your day. From the vast openness and clarity of your innermost essence, an unconditional love and compassion radiates toward all beings; allow this to resonate in your being as long as possible after meditating. Even if you do not directly connect with the nature of mind in meditation, by simply trusting it is there you can release your grasping and become more at ease with yourself.

Bring the clear awareness of your true nature to the way you perceive and relate to others. From that perspective, every moment is the flow of meditation, every activity is prayer, everyone you meet is a potential Buddha, worthy of respect. Train yourself to relate to each person with pure perception and a good heart, always from the intention of benefiting others.

You may have noticed how easy it is to fixate on one problem at work, leading you to feel tense, angry, or upset. Once you grasp onto and solidify the problem, then it becomes your whole reality, and you can no longer be present for anyone else. When you are tense, you might make more mistakes, and have misunderstandings and communication problems. Instead, contemplate Chagdud Rinpoche's advice: "Always recognize the dreamlike qualities of life and reduce attachment and aversion. Practice good-heartedness toward all beings. Be loving and compassionate, no matter what others do to you. What they will do will not matter so much when you see it as a dream. The trick is to have positive intention during the dream. This is the essential point. This is true spirituality."[4]

When you recognize that everything is impermanent, you take things a bit more lightly, with more humor. Resolve that whenever you find yourself falling back into emotional, grasping patterns, you will recall your fundamental sky-like nature, and allow changes to pass through you.

This is also how you can begin breaking down the artificial division between your spiritual practice and daily work. Allow the inspiration and spacious generosity of your meditation to transform your perception of those you meet; allow it to inform your choices and responses so that your life becomes a continuous and active expression of your deepest motivation.

SEALING THE PRACTICE THROUGH DEDICATION

As you conclude your practice and your work each day, reflect on the gift you have received: a spiritual path which can free you from suffering. With a deep wish that your patients, friends and family and all other beings become free as well, dedicate your practice and everything you do, all of your work and even your difficulties, to the benefit of all beings. Dedicating at the end of each work day ensures that the goodness of what you've done is never lost.

Through spiritual training, you are reducing your selfishness and territoriality. After you've done something good, however, your ego may react: "Wasn't that a great and noble thing! I hope someone will notice and thank me for it!" To free yourself of this subtle grasping, think instead: "May every kindness I do be unseen by others. May I share with all others the merit and positive power of my practice and my work, so that everyone enjoys good circumstances in their life and is free of suffering. May all my positive efforts contribute to the enlightenment of all beings."

YOUR OWN SUFFERING FORMS A BRIDGE TO THE OTHER PERSON

You can obtain valuable insights for responding to another person's suffering from your own experience. Take some time to reflect on a period in your life when you went through a deep experience of suffering, loss or grief. Remember what it was you really needed during that time. Recall what helped you to face and heal your pain, and what resources—either internal or external—you called on for help. Or if you never received what you most needed, reflect on what you wished for to help you get through your painful distress.

Finally, you might ask yourself: What benefit did this suffering bring to my life? Did this experience of loss or suffering play a purposeful role in my development? Was I able to give a meaning to my difficulty by the way I chose to respond?

Reflecting on your own experiences of deep suffering will enable you to realize that you have the necessary skills for supporting others, the confidence that suffering is not hopeless, and an appreciation that suffering presents us with an opportunity to change or find meaning in the midst of our adversity.

Before meeting a friend who is experiencing physical or emotional pain, sit quietly for a few minutes. Become aware of any thoughts or fears that might impede your receptivity, and connect again with your inherent openness and love by reflecting on your friend's suffering. As you settle quietly in meditation and watch your thoughts, you might find that you have fear about the other person's anguish, or concern about your ability to make him or her feel better. Perhaps you're already trying to plan what you will say, to feel some control in the uncertain situation ahead. Acknowledge these thoughts and fears, and then allow them to dissolve. You might imagine setting your fears, plans and thoughts in a box next to you and leaving them behind, before going into your friend's room.

Reflect on your friend's situation, and let your friend's suffering touch your heart, awakening your compassion and love. No matter how painful the circumstances or how disturbing the physical appearance you will encounter, remember that your friend has, at the core of his or her being, an innermost essence of wisdom and compassion. Your role then is not to rescue or give your solutions, but to help you friend recall and turn toward his or her own inner resources.

After becoming aware of yourself and compassionately opening your heart to your friend, you'll feel more ease in communicating authentically with him or her. You don't have to have all the answers or be perfect; you can simply be yourself.

LISTEN WITH YOUR WHOLE BEING

You might begin: "I'm at a loss here because I don't know what to do. And I can't even imagine how difficult this is for you. Still, I've come because I want you to know that I care about you, and you are not alone. No matter what happens, or what you're feeling, I love you. Please tell me what is happening for you now." Then listen as your friend expresses who he is and how he is feeling. And you must listen with your whole being, not just your ears. Listen with your body, your heart, your eyes, your energy, your total presence. Listen in silence, without interrupting. Fill any spaces of silence between you with love, with silent permission for the other person to go on and to go deeper. Once in a while, perhaps, ask a question to draw your friend out even further: "What else are you going through; what else is happening in your life right now? What are you thinking about as you go through this difficulty? What's the hardest part of this for you? What is your biggest fear?"

Give space for answers and acknowledge pain. Don't immediately jump in with your stories or brilliant ideas. Silently acknowledge your rising thoughts and feelings, and continue to be there for him. Focus on what he is communicating on every level—through his body, his expression, the tone of his voice, his energy, and his words. Listen to what is said and also to what was not said, yet implied. Validate the feelings he has expressed, and through your intuition and questions, slowly draw out even more of his thoughts or needs.

You might reflect back to your friend: "This must be very hard. You are going through a great difficulty right now, do you realize that? As I listen to you, I feel your distress, your sorrow, your frustration or fear. This must be really, really hard. Whatever you are feeling is perfectly understandable, given the circumstances you are facing."

After encouraging your friend to describe his deepest fears, angers, regrets or sadness, you can acknowledge his pain and let him know that it may take a while for it to diminish. By fully listening to and accepting your friend's pain, you help him accept himself and his present condition, thus alleviating a great deal of the emotional suffering that can result from guilt or harsh self-judgment.

While it's good to reveal yourself at times, be aware of how much you reveal, and when, and most importantly, why. When you do speak, communicate clearly, with honesty and kindness.

At a later time, when the person's emotional suffering has somewhat lessened, you may see an appropriate opportunity to expand your friend's awareness beyond his immediate situation. You could choose words and images of hope which come from phrases your friend has already used; or, you might express something like the following:

"I hear your pain and confusion and I understand how very bad things are for you right now. I know you may feel lost in the dark sometimes, or fear this suffering will never end. But even though it won't go away quickly, your pain won't last forever.

"Your suffering might seem like a heavy cloud covering up every trace of hope at the moment, yet remember that there is another aspect of your being that is always whole, peaceful and loving. This aspect of you has known joy and happiness, and can experience happiness again. Remember this and please do not judge or abandon yourself as hopeless. No matter what happens, I am going to stay in contact with you, and keep visiting. I love you."

HEALING RELATIONSHIPS: DISSOLVING YOUR POSITION

When your motivation in communicating is to "win" the discussion or change the other person, you are doomed to fail. If you truly want to heal the conflicts in a relationship, first you need to sit quietly and become aware of your own thoughts and feelings, the hopes and fears that are operating behind your perceptions and communications. In your previous communication, what were your expectations of this person? That he would admit he was wrong, or promise to change? That he or she would never make another mistake, or would promise never to hurt you again? That he would extend his love to you in the exact way you think it should be shown?

Similarly, you must become aware of your fears about communicating with the other person. Are you afraid of being rejected or misunderstood, of feeling ashamed or foolish? Afraid of having your feelings hurt once again? The hope that another person will never hurt you, or will always love you perfectly is unrealistic, as is the expectation that the other person must change in order for you to be happy. The only freedom you have is to change yourself.

Thus, you need to become aware of your habitual identification with the "selfish ego" and realize you can identify instead with your true nature: a clear and fundamental goodness, or "good heart." Meditating and connecting with this highest aspect of your being will help you tap into your own wellspring of love and meet the other person without fear.

The next step, before actually communicating face to face, is to establish your motivation. In meeting someone with whom you normally have a problem, imagine that your intention now is simply to listen to the other person's feelings and experience, and to express your natural self. That's all. See if you can be willing to "meet" the other person as he is. If you've been holding onto old judgments that would make this difficult, then first do the following reflection, which may help you understand the other person's experience in a new way, and thus have more compassion for him. There are two steps to this reflection: Seeing the Other as Another You, and Exchanging Places.

SEEING THE OTHER AS ANOTHER YOU AND EXCHANGING PLACES

Instead of seeing this person in their usual role—parent, sibling, or boss—see him or her in your mind's eye as just "another you." Consider that this person is just like you, with the same desires for happiness and with the same fears of suffering.

Once you have established this feeling, then imagine changing places with the person. Now you are in his life, standing in his shoes. Imagine you have this person's history—with his possible past experiences of rejection, grief, trauma, or fear. Consider that you have whatever constitutes his or her present suffering as well: feelings of being misunderstood and unfairly judged, deep experiences of pain or fear, or hidden insecurities and frustrated cravings which give rise to constant states of unhappiness. Imagine and consider the suffering this person may yet face—the physical deterioration and pain of aging or illness, the grief of future losses, the loneliness of dying or feeling abandoned.

From this perspective of seeing the world through the other person's eyes, now imagine seeing "you" enter the room to have a talk. Ask yourself: What would I most want from this person coming to see me? What would I most need from him or her?

Marisa, a vibrant and pretty doctor in her mid-thirties, asked me how to deal with an angry, demanding patient. I suggested that she try the compassion practices described above. "When I exchanged places with my patient, suddenly I was this old woman who had constant pain, who felt ugly, helpless and unwanted," recalled Marisa. "And when I saw this attractive young doctor coming into my room full of smiles, I hated her more than anything."

The next time Marisa went into her patient's room, she wasn't smiling cheerfully. Feeling genuine understanding and love for the old woman, Marisa was able to meet her gaze, even while the woman continued to scream in anger at her. "I knew just how she felt. In my heart,

I told her that I understood her anger, and that it was all right. She continued to be demanding, but after she saw I wasn't reacting anymore, her tone grew quieter. When I left her room and walked down the corridor, my mind was peaceful and calm as though the meditation was still continuing."

I asked Marisa what happened when she went to see the next patient. "That man was very sweet and kind, and immediately I reacted with pleasure." She laughed. "That's when I realized I had lost my equanimity, and how important it is to keep my meditation going in every situation, whether it is difficult or pleasant."

CONNECTING WITH THE COGNITIVELY IMPAIRED

It's extremely difficult to relate to someone who is comatose or suffers from brain disease or dementia. Normal dialogue is impossible, and most of us have no experience with other means of communication.

Two common temptations are to treat the person condescendingly, like an infant, or to speak as if he or she is no longer in the room—already dead, for all intents and purposes. We must, in all circumstances, treat the dying or cognitively impaired person with respect and kindness, the same way we would wish to be treated in his place. Whether or not the confused or comatose person can speak with any clarity, or even speak at all, he is nonetheless aware and present in the room.

When a person has severe brain damage due to disease or aging, close family members experience that on one level, they have "lost" this person, for the personality they've long known is disintegrating. Loved ones will naturally grieve this loss, as they let go of their attachment to the old form of the relationship. Even so, they don't have to let go of their love, or abandon him as though he were already dead. By continuing to give the cognitively impaired person their love, speaking to him genuinely and sharing their lives with him, loved ones are giving his life meaning.

So how can we communicate with a confused or unresponsive person? First, we should never let his condition keep us from seeing who he really is. Remember, the fundamental nature of every being is a pure awareness and "good heart." This innermost essence or wisdom nature is the indestructible ground of our being; therefore it's always present, irrespective of the functions of the brain or sense organs. Since the confused or comatose person never loses this deepest level of awareness, we can always communicate and connect with him or her on that level. And this is why we must always treat him as a living person, respecting him in the same way we would if we were meeting him at the prime of life.

Our next task is to acknowledge and release our own fear of or aversion to the person's condition. Then we can connect through deeper types of communication:

- Touch
- Eye contact
- Humor and play
- Music or singing
- Resolving our side of any unfinished business
- Offering prayers or spiritual practice
- Sending loving, positive thoughts

If communication is both giving and receiving, how can we "hear" from those who are noncommunicative and understand them? Through meditation we can empty our mind of concepts, and connect with our clear awareness and loving receptivity. Then, after we express what is in our heart with sincerity and kindness, we can listen in silence, and learn to intuitively sense the other person's experience and needs. Coleman Barks translates a poem by the Sufi mystic Rumi in which a judge asks to determine which of three sons will inherit his father's fortune:

What if a man cannot be made to say anything?
How do you learn his hidden nature?"
And the third son replies,
"I sit in front of him in silence,
and set up a ladder made of patience,
and if in his presence a language from beyond joy
and beyond grief begins to pour from my chest,
I know that his soul is as deep and bright
as the star Canopus rising over Yemen.
And so when I start speaking a powerful right arm
of words sweeping down, I know him from what I say,
and how I say it, because there's a window open
between us, mixing the night air of our beings. [5]

When we speak genuinely to those who are non-communicative, even if they cannot respond verbally, they will respond to us in their hearts and minds. We must find creative ways to open a window between us which can help ease the person's suffering and loneliness.

We should always treat those who are confused or in a coma as though they are consciously present. Many people who come out of a short- or long-term coma report they were indeed fully aware of what others in the room did and said, sometimes even what they were thinking. Thus besides offering the best we can in terms of medical care, the greatest comfort and relief we can give is our respect, friendship, and love.

NURTURE A VAST PERSPECTIVE

What does it mean to find hope when we are facing suffering or death? Real hope comes as we begin discovering and nurturing a vast perspective on life—an outlook that views the whole cycle of life and death from the deeper dimension of our true nature.

When we cultivate such a perspective, we do what we can as we listen to and support those who suffer, but we don't look upon their situations as irrevocable tragedies. And we don't shoulder all their burdens ourselves. When another person's burden weighs too heavily, then we have lost this larger perspective, and are no longer able to help. As the Zen master Suzuki Roshi wrote,

> To live in the realm of Buddha nature means to die as a small being, moment after moment. When we lose our balance we die, but at the same time, we also develop ourselves, we grow. Whatever we see is changing, losing its balance. The reason everything looks beautiful is because it is out of balance, but its background is always in perfect harmony. This is how everything exists in the realm of Buddha nature, losing its balance against a background of perfect balance. So if you see things without realizing the background of Buddha nature, everything appears to be in the form of suffering. But if you understand the background of existence, you realize that suffering itself is how we live, and how we extend our life.[6]

Thus, cultivating a spiritual view which embraces all of life and death can transform our view of those who are suffering. A nurse working in a German hospice for many years put it this way: "I've learned to see and appreciate the real person inside of each patient, the true human being who is always there, underneath his physical appearance or emotional state."

Learning to acknowledge with compassion our own suffering will give birth to a limitless compassion in our heart for the suffering others experience and a reverence for all life. Through sustained spiritual practice and study, we cultivate a joy in developing our potential, and begin to appreciate the sacred potential within each person we provide care for. Don't let their appearance or their suffering ever make you forget who they truly are. In the essence of their being, no matter how they appear, each person is perfect, whole, and complete.

NOTES AND REFERENCES

This entire chapter is excerpted and adapted from various chapters in: *Facing Death and Finding Hope: A Guide to the Emotional and Spiritual Care of the Dying*, by Christine Longaker (New York: Doubleday, 1997).

1. Sogyal Rinpoche, *The Tibetan Book of Living and Dying,* 2nd ed. (San Francisco: HarperCollins, 2002), 58.

2. You can find instructions for how to meditate in many books, including Chapter 5 in my book, *Facing Death and Finding Hope.*

3. Sogyal Rinpoche, foreword to *Facing Death and Finding Hope,* by Christine Longaker. (New York: Doubleday, 1997), x.

4. Chagdud Tulku Rinpoche, *Life in Relation to Death.* (Cottage Grove, OR: Padma Publishing, 1987), 28.

5. Coleman Barks, trans. *The Essential Rumi.* (San Francisco: Harper Collins, 1995), 31–32.

6. Shunryu Suzuki, *Zen Mind, Beginner's Mind.* (New York: Weatherhill, 1970), 31.

*O*ur capacity for listening deeply and skillfully is affected by many things: our momentary energy level, emotional makeup, personal preferences, needs, and biases, as well as our developmental conditioning and the defenses we erect to protect against the pain of the losses we've suffered. One of the clearest and most elegant descriptions of how these various limiting conditions come into being is offered by the spiritual teacher, A.H. Almaas. Almaas posits that, over time, essential aspects of our being become lost, leaving vacant holes in their place (lacunae, *in the psychiatric literature*), and that these essential aspects must be restored in order for us to function fully. In the following article we discover the importance of kindred community, of sangha, *in providing the potential for that restoration to take place, for rediscovering and recovering our native wisdom, sometimes called "the pearl of great price"—and inevitably becoming more skillful listeners in the process.*

Listening Through the Holes

A. H. Almaas

A FUNDAMENTAL IDEA used in our work is called the Theory of Holes. People, as they are under usual circumstances are full of what we call "holes." Now, what is a hole? A hole refers to any part of you that has been lost, meaning any part of you that you have lost consciousness of. What is left is a hole, a deficiency in a certain sense. And what we have lost awareness of, is of course, our essence. When we are not aware of our essence, it stops manifesting and is lost. Then we feel a sense of deficiency. So a hole is nothing but the absence of a certain part of our essence. It could be the loss of love, loss of value, loss of capacity for contact, loss of strength, loss of will, loss of clarity, loss of pleasure, any of those qualities of essence. There are many of them. But when they are lost, they are not gone forever; they are never gone forever. You are simply cut off from them.

Let's take, for example, the quality of value, of self-esteem. When you are cut off from your value, the actual state of being cut off is a sense that there is a hole left inside you; it's empty. Then you feel a sense of deficiency, a sense of inferiority, and you want to fill it with value from the outside—approval, praise, whatever. So you try to fill the hole with fake value that comes from the outside.

Everyone walks around with lots of holes, but you usually aren't aware of them. You're usually aware of desires: "I want this, I want that, I want this praise. I want to be successful here, I want this person to love me. I want this or that experience." The presence of desires and needs indicates the presence of holes.

Of course, these holes originated during your childhood partly as a result of traumatic experiences or conflicts with your environment. You get cut off from one of those qualities at such times. Perhaps your parents did not value you, that is, they didn't treat you as if your wishes or presence were important; they didn't act in ways that let you know you mattered; they ignored your essential value. And because your value was not seen or acknowledged, perhaps even attacked or discouraged, you got cut off from that part of you, and what is left is a hole, a deficiency.

Later on, when we relate to someone else in a deep way—the deeper it is, the more this happens—we fill those holes with the other person. Some of our holes get filled with what we believe or feel we're getting from the other person. We feel valued because this person appreciates us, and this fills our holes. We don't know consciously that we're filling it with their appreciation, we just feel full when we're with them; we feel valuable. So, when I am with that person, I really feel I am valuable, but unconsciously I feel the other person has my value. The other person not only makes me feel valuable, but whatever the other person is giving me is a part of me, is part of that fullness that I experience.

So unconsciously, I don't see that part of the person that makes me feel my value as separate from me; I see it as part of me, as filling this hole. I don't know there is a hole, I only feel the fullness. If the person dies, or the relationship ends, I don't feel that I'm losing that person, I feel that I'm losing whatever is filling the hole. So, the loss of the person is not felt as a loss of a separate person. It is experienced as a loss of yourself, because unconsciously, you saw that person as filling part of you. In this way, he or she became a part of you, so that losing that person, you experience the loss of a part of yourself, and therefore you feel a hole. That is why it is so painful. It feels like you're being cut, and something is being taken out of you. Sometimes you feel as if you lost your heart; sometimes you feel you've lost your security, your strength, your will—whatever the person fulfilled for you. Sometimes the person gives you will, gives you strength, or support, or love, or value. So when you lose a person close to you, you feel whatever hole you had that the person had filled.

That's one thing people are talking about when they say that "we fit each other." Each person fits the other's holes. This fits into this hole; that fits into that hole; they feel like one thing. They no longer seem separate. But if you do separate them, you'll be left with a lot of holes. If these two people live together, they'll feel full and complete. They're complementary, they make a unified whole. But another person rarely fills all your holes. You have several people, many activities in your life, and still they don't fill all your holes. There will be some holes left, which keep the dissatisfaction going. And, of course, holes don't get filled completely and perfectly. The moment the other person changes a little, or says something that makes you feel bad, you feel the hole, the deficiency: "Oh, he doesn't think I'm worth anything after all." You feel angry, hurt, because the hole is getting exposed. So the dissatisfaction continues because the person is not always filling your holes perfectly, especially if he's wanting you to fill his holes.

With any change, there's a jiggling around of holes. Some holes become empty, some get filled. The person has to adjust, they have to fill their holes some other way, and this usually means they have to deal with some of these holes—feel their presence and maybe understand them.

So now we can understand more why the loss of somebody who has been very close to you, very intimate with you, is so painful. After being with this person a long time, you're so accustomed to the fit, you believe that other person is part of you. Losing the person is losing a part of yourself.

Another factor arises here: when you experience loss and separation, you have the possibility of seeing that what was filling you wasn't really you. If you stay with the hurt and the pain of loss without trying to cover this pain with something else, it is possible that you will feel the emptiness, feel the hole, see the hole. Then if you allow yourself to feel the deficiency, the emptiness, you may find the essential part of you that will really fill the hole, from the inside, once and for all. It's not even filling; it is just the elimination of the hole and the identifications with the deficiency. In that way, you regain part of yourself. You connect with the part of your essence that you lost, and that you thought only somebody else could provide for you.

It can be very painful. Most people feel a loss of self-esteem when a relationship ends, which is why I'm using this particular example of value. But if you stay with that feeling and pay attention, and ask yourself, "How come I feel so worthless, how come I feel like a nothing just because that person isn't around any more? Why do I feel I'm so much less valuable?" If you stay with that feeling without trying to fill it, and just pay attention and try to understand it, then you will experience the deficiency and the hole. If you understand that deficiency and its source, you might even remember the actual event or pattern of events that brought about your loss of value.

A hole is usually filled with part of our personality that has the memory of what was lost, the memory of the situation that brought about the loss, the memories of the hurts and conflicts. We have to go through the hurt at the deepest level, get close to the hole itself, and then we will see the memory of what was lost. When we see the memory of what was lost, the essence that was lost will start flowing again.

So any deep loss is an opportunity to grow, to understand more about yourself, to experience holes you believe can only be filled by someone else. But people usually defend like crazy against feeling loss deeply. This defense is primarily to avoid feeling the hole. People don't know that the hole, the sense of deficiency, is a symptom of a loss of something deeper, the loss of essence, which can be regained. They think the hole, the deficiency, is how they really are at the deepest level, and that there is nothing beyond it. They think something is wrong with them, something is basically wrong. The feeling that something is wrong is an unconscious knowledge of the presence of the hole, and people will do anything not to feel that hole, really feel the deficiency. They believe that if they get close to the hole, it will swallow them up. If their work is bringing them, for example, to the hole of love, they might feel threatened by a devastating loneliness, emptiness. Other holes will bring up what feels like a threat of annihilation. No wonder they don't want to go near it! But in our work we have seen a surprising thing: when we stop defending against feeling a hole, the actual experience is not painful. We simply experience empty space, a feeling that there is nothing there—but not a threatening noth-ingness—a spaciousness, an allowing. This spaciousness allows essence to emerge, and it is essence and only essence that can eliminate that hole, that deficiency from the inside.

You might have anger as a result of a deficiency, especially as a defense against feeling a hole. Most feelings, most emotions, specifically those that are automatic and compulsive, are the result of holes. When there are no holes, there are _____ ns. What are these emotions? There's ___ y, anger, hatred, fear. All these are the ___ you don't have any of those emotions. ___ uch emotions are sometimes called ___ elings.

___ h us that we should get our value, ___ onderful it is to do things for other ___ eaningful profession—things like ___ people to fill each other's holes. ___ filling holes. Civilization as we ___ ity. It is the product of the false ___ personality. It is what sustains

___ on in our own defenses: the ___ selves. So this is one way of ___ st holes.

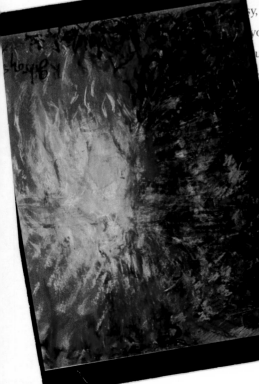

Allowing ourselves to tolerate the holes and go through them to the other side is more difficult now because everything in society is against this. Society is against essence. Everybody around you, wherever you go, is trying to fill holes, and people feel very threatened if you don't try to fill yours in the same way. When a person is not trying to fill his holes, it tends to make other people feel their own holes. So it's becoming more and more difficult to do the work. And the work is also becoming more and more needed.

That is why it is important to have a community of people involved in the same task of self-understanding. You have the support of many people who are allowing themselves to feel the holes instead of filling them. It is very difficult, almost impossible, for one person alone to do this because everything in his environment is against it.

Many people earn their living by filling other people's holes. Many businesses are there to fill people's holes. I have no moralistic attitude about filling holes. I don't think it is a sin, that it is bad. I don't think you should feel guilty about it, or punish yourself about filling holes. Sometimes you fill your own holes, sometimes you fill someone else's holes. So what? Let's talk about understanding things. I'm not building a religion around holes: "Thou shalt not fill thy holes." You can look at everything you do in terms of the work, in terms of holes or filling holes. You will see that all the time you're either filling a hole or you are tolerating a hole, or you are experiencing the real thing that was lost. This is going on all the time, at every moment. In this work the holes you deal with get bigger and bigger.

First, the smaller holes, and then the bigger holes, until you get to the biggest hole of them all, which is the loss of everything. It's called death. Right? When you die you lose everything. You have to accept that hole to get back everything. So one of the last holes is the loss of the body itself. To experience physical death is exactly like that. You experience a big hole, a black, dark, empty hole.

You try to fill that hole with the body. If you let the body go, at least in your consciousness—I don't necessarily mean that you die physically—

then you'll suddenly see the complete you, which is really you, the one you usually try to substitute your body for. Most people think they are their bodies.

One of our deepest identifications is with the body. That is one reason why we have desires and cravings for physical pleasures, pleasures of the body. I think the basis for the deepest craving, the craving for physical pleasure, is a hole. The hole is the absence, the cutting off from the real pleasures, the essential pleasures.

Of course, nobody wants to believe that one. "If I let go of that one, what will be left for me? If I don't eat cookies twice a day, have sex every other day, and do this and that, how am I going to enjoy myself?" But this is one of the last holes to be explored. In the beginning we need to experience the holes that have to do with love, compassion, value, strength, will, peace—things that we try to get from the outside.

In your life, you do whatever you do, and you just study what's happening. That's all you need to do, study it to understand it. One of the ways the work was done in the past was to retire into a monastery to renounce everything totally. The point was not really to reject everything, it was an attempt to experience holes. In time, of course, such practices took on a moralistic, religious sense—the idea that it's bad to have certain kinds of external contact. The purpose of such retreats is to allow yourself to feel the holes and not fill them, to see what they are all about.

One more thing about the theory of holes. As I said, the holes get produced when you're a child. When you're a baby, you have no holes, you're complete when you are born. As you grow up, because of your interactions with your environment and certain difficulties you encounter, you get cut off from certain parts of yourself at different times. Every time you get cut off from a certain part of you, a hole manifests. The holes then become full with the memory of the loss and the issues around the loss. After a while, you just fill in the holes. What you fill the holes with are the false feelings, ideas, beliefs about yourself, strategies for dealing with your environment. These fillers are collectively called the personality—the false personality, or what we call the false pearl.

So the false personality, as you see, is a result of losses of parts of the self. But after a time, we think that is who we are. Everybody thinks that's who they are, the fillers. The false personality is trying to take the place of the real thing. That's why we do a lot of work here on understanding our personalities. Our work leads to studying the history of the development of our false personality until we are finally able to experience the memory of the situation in which the particular hole formed. In this way you can regain your essence, part by part, until you're complete.

As you see, I'm saying these things in a very general way. We can be much more specific. We can look at each quality, see when it is lost, and what results. Sometimes combinations of qualities get lost. For instance, you might lose your strength, your will, and your love, and these would be a composite hole. So a whole psychological perspective can be built around this understanding—the psychology of holes which is the psychology of the personality, of the false pearl.

The false personality is mechanical in the sense that, after you lose an essential quality of yourself and there is a hole, your personality automatically tries to fill it with false qualities from the outside. Then that part of your false personality is formed. The actions of the personality are two-pronged. One prong is always attempting to avoid the hole, to avoid pain, and to experience pleasure. This is automatic. And the other prong of the personality is always attempting to fill the hole as soon as something happens to expose it. This is also automatic. We need to observe ourselves closely. Most people are so identified with their attempt to fill the holes that they don't think it's possible not to do it. A person who is trying to get someone to love them doesn't know there's an alternative. He thinks that's the best thing to do, and can't imagine anything else. Most people never question these things. It's so mechanical, they say that's the way they are, that is reality, that's how things are. When you're feeling low, get somebody to praise you. What else can you do? If you're feeling unlovable, find somebody who likes you. People usually identify with these patterns so completely that there is no chance of change. To begin to work on such a pattern, first you need to observe it happening over and over, and to see that it doesn't work, really. People generally don't come to work here until they have begun to see that their way doesn't work. Otherwise, they don't come. They believe in their strategies so completely that they think if they just get better at it and do it a few more years, it will work. Maybe they haven't found the right person, or they haven't found the right situation yet. If they just make a little more money, things will work out.

It takes a long time for people to understand this, that trying to fill the hole doesn't work. Even as you're listening to me now, you're trying to fill holes through some understanding. Some of you are already believing that the words I'm saying are going to fill the holes. "If I just know what the story is, then things should be better." What I'm saying is effective if you're starting to feel your holes, which means if you're starting to feel your emptiness. If you're filling it with words or ideas, you're just filling it again. I think this perspective helps us to see an overall view of society. The hole is taking over! Most of the work of our society is attempting to fill holes in people.

*A*nne and Charles Simpkinson were the founders of Common Boundary, *a magazine that explored the interface between mind, body, psyche, and spirit. In this article, excerpted from their book* Soul Work: A Field Guide for Spiritual Seekers, *the authors present a compelling case for the power of skillful listening to provide necessary daily psychological and spiritual nutrition. From their perspective, the dilemma is not that many Americans live on a regular regimen of psychological and spiritual malnutrition, but that so few recognize it and instead accept loneliness, isolation, alienation, and depression as the norm. It is through becoming a more skillful listener and receiving the benefits of being listened to that one can become nourished by and attuned to our world and the people in it in healthy, nurturing, and constructive ways.*

Feeding One Another

Anne Simpkinson and Charles Simpkinson

Listening and being heard are important
psychological nutrients that we need every day.

HAVE YOU EVER wondered why some conversations—even with close friends and family—are emotionally unsatisfying? Do you feel that hardly anyone is listening to you or understanding what you are saying? When you aren't heard, do you wonder if the other person cares about you? If you find yourself contemplating these things, you are not alone. As a nation, we have the technical expertise to create a vast web of communications using highly sophisticated technology, but as individuals our exchanges with each other are often primitive, unsatisfying—even unhealthy. Many people live every day of their lives in a state of chronic psychological malnourishment and don't even know it.

Such a condition results from not receiving enough recognition, validation, empathic understanding, and caring. In his 1990 best-selling book, *Dr. Dean Ornish's Program for Reversing Heart Disease,* Dean Ornish discussed the prevention of and recovery from severe coronary heart disease. Although most people think that his program is primarily about food and diet, Ornish says that the most significant factors in healing are love, intimacy, and relationships. In his most recent book, *Love and Survival: The Scientific Basis for the Healing Power of Intimacy*, Ornish pinpoints the real epidemic in our culture: emotional and spiritual heart disease stemming from a profound and prevalent sense of loneliness, isolation, alienation, and depression.

Without adequate amounts of psychologically nutritious communications, people cannot nurture love or develop intimacy. Instead they compensate for these things by becoming self-centered, acquisitive, and power-hungry, among other things.

This line of reasoning usually generates several questions: Did our grandparents or great-grandparents have this same need? Isn't it self-indulgent to want validation and acknowledgement? Can't a person supply all the psychological nourishment he or she needs without relying on others? These questions reflect our suspicious and guarded attitude toward the legitimacy of people's need for psychological nourishment and are based upon an unfounded faith in individualism and a general misconception about egotism. An overblown sense of self-importance, self-centeredness, and egotistical behavior result more from a lack of self-acceptance as a result of psychological malnutrition, than from a surfeit of self-esteem.

The result of these misunderstandings is that our need for adequate psychological nutrition often gets ignored or ridiculed as a form of self-indulgence. From today's perspective, our forebears were silent about these matters because their values and behavior were part and parcel of a sociological web made up of social role, status, and institutional identification. One could get along in the world without developing an awareness of one's inner self as the agent or organizer of experience because one's social grouping—one's tribe—provided the values, direction, principles, and code of behavior that formed one's identity and defined one's place in the world. Today the development of an inner self is necessary for providing direction because many of the old external supports no longer function as a compass and guide.

Psychotherapy as Food

Before the 1960s, psychotherapy and those who went to therapy carried a stigma. The average person considered psychotherapy a treatment for the insane and severely mentally imbalanced and thought that to see a psychiatrist was to be branded as crazy. Today psychotherapy is recognized not as an irrevocable sentence but as a tool for coping with distressing life situations and healing self-destructive or unhealthy patterns of behavior. Today people enter therapy because they want relief from stress, substance abuse, depression or anxiety brought on by a crisis such as the loss of a job, a divorce, or the death of a loved one, or from a pervasive sense that their lives are empty or out of control. Generally just a crack in the usual self-sufficient persona provides motivation to explore the source of the pain.

It is now commonly accepted that everyone to a greater or lesser degree has psychological difficulties that manifest as unresolved hurts and inhibitions from childhood, or as vulnerabilities that prevent or undermine full functioning. With these advances in understanding, psychotherapists have not only shed much of their negative image, but actually grown in numbers and stature. One reason for their increased numbers is the fragmentation of the family and the loss of our sense of geographical community. The Census Bureau indicates that we have become a highly mobile society, with 19 to 20 percent of us moving each year. Mary Pipher points out in her book, *The Shelter of Each Other,* that in 1990 "72 percent of Americans didn't know their neighbors." An extraordinary and painful loss is buried in that statistic. Gone are the days of porch-sitting and greeting neighbors on their way home from work; gone too are the days of unlocked cars and houses.

As extended family networks break apart, their members relocating geographically, and as divorce splinters nuclear families, we lose a powerful traditional support system. No longer can a child who has difficulties with one or both parents form an attachment with a grandparent, aunt, uncle, or cousin, because physical distance may prevent it. The nuclear family is under siege, and the complications of single parenthood, joint custody, and blended families stress individuals in these systems. Most of us do not remain in one community long enough to grow histories with nearby families. And managed care notwithstanding, how many physicians today dance at the weddings of babies they delivered? Torn from the fabric of family and community, we have turned to professionals for help. And although some critics may argue that we are too reliant on psychotherapy, the fact of the matter is that emotional support—talking about and having someone listen to what's really bothering us—is more important than ever.

As family and communal ties are weakened, we lose a major source of our identity. For the most part, the Depression-era and World War II generation did not need to "find themselves." They were not lost. They were for the most part securely embedded in social structures that told them who they were and where they came from. Today, however, we are forced to carve out our roles as well as to develop a set of values, a moral code, and a life purpose. The hardest part of this task is constructing a coherent, independent personality and a sense of personal worth.

What Makes a Healthy Ego?

Simply stated, if a child is responded to positively, she will develop a positive evaluation of herself, which will allow her to meet life tasks and challenges with self-confidence. If, however, a child receives mostly negative responses, she will evaluate herself negatively and not feel confident in the face of life's tasks. Even where she might see the adults' faults and follies, as a child she is unable to counteract the impact of these negative messages and actions by herself. One example of this dynamic was evident in the late Princess Diana. When she failed to receive love in her marriage or support for her new role in England's royal family, she responded as if it were her fault. She struggled painfully with self-doubt, bulimia, and

self-mutilation, even attempting suicide. Eventually, however (we assume with psychotherapeutic support), she was able to recognize that her lack of love and support was more a statement of Prince Charles and his family's dynamics than it was a result of a personality defect on her part. She went on to defend herself publicly, to maintain a connection with her sons, and to mature into a warmhearted and gracious spokesperson for a variety of charitable causes.

Children form their sense of self from what they see reflected in their parent's eyes and facial expressions. For example, the British psychoanalyst D. W. Winnicott has written that a mother's face, especially in the early weeks of an infant's life, serves as a mirror for the tiny new person. It is less important for a mother to actually look at her child, and more important that she reflect the child's expressions. If the mother (or father) does not mirror back the child's expressions, the child will not receive validation of its existence. As Winnicott explains: "When I [the infant] look, I am seen, so I exist." With that basic ego groundwork in place, the child can then look out again and see the world and interact with it.

Psychologist Daniel Goleman, in his best-selling book *Emotional Intelligence,* cites the research of psychiatrist Daniel Stern, who found through the study of videotaped parent-child interactions that the small, repeated exchanges that took place between parent and child laid down the most basic lessons of emotional life. Stern discovered that the most critical moments were those in which the child's emotions were met with empathy and acceptance, indeed reciprocated in a process he labeled attunement. Attunement basically means that the mother and father accurately reflect back to the child what the child is feeling. The countless repeated movements of attunement or misstatement between parent and child form the basis for the kind of emotional relationships that adults create later in life.

Goleman goes on to observe that "prolonged absence of attunement between a parent and child takes a tremendous toll on the child" and can have devastating effects. If a parent isn't attuned to the child's emotions—

to delight, sadness, distress, need for security—then the child will begin to avoid expressing, or possibly even feeling, these emotions. Thus, if the parent does not reflect back a caring, valuing, accepting view of the child as she is, the child will develop a similar set of noncaring, nonvaluing eyes with which to view herself. Accordingly, the child will begin to believe she is unacceptable, unlovable, of no value, and will cover up her real self in an attempt to become whatever she believes will gain her love and acceptance, thereby reducing her fear of abandonment. She will adopt a false face or "mask" that she hopes will appear more pleasing and therefore earn more positive responses.

Introducing Psychological Nutrition

As a culture, we are all suffering from an attention deficit disorder, but not necessarily of the neurological kind. More and more frequently, our social institutions, organizations, and government are losing their responsiveness.

Despite what mental-health professionals know about psychological and emotional needs, few people outside the profession recognize that the way you feel about yourself depends in part on how others respond to you. We all have a need to be acknowledged and appreciated for who we are and what we do. But our interactions with other people may be more or less nourishing to us depending upon the quality of the exchange.

Take this example: You tell a friend how excited you are that you have received a promotion. Instead of showing interest and asking what you will now be doing, your friend deflects your statement and tells you about some kudos he or she has recently received. In terms of your need for a certain amount of attention and recognition, this exchange offers neither person any nourishment.

Only recently have we recognized that we have a daily minimum requirement of psychological needs, and that the level of psychological nourish-

ment we get has an effect on our physical and mental health. Some people downplay the fact that they have such needs, convincing themselves (and trying to convince us) that they are self-sufficient. In reality, they probably have indirect ways of getting these needs met. They may, for example, strive for fame, power, or wealth in lieu of personal connectedness. However, it is not the real person who is getting attention but his or her image, status, prestige, or money. Such indirect attention simply covers up the need.

Causes of Psychological Malnutrition

Individuals who are not getting their daily minimum requirement of recognition tend to compensate by substituting superficial interactions for real contact. The following list of strategies describes the various styles of behavior through which we may try to get our needs met indirectly without admitting we have them. Note that the level of sophistication increases as you move up the scale.

1: **Doormat:** You find yourself accepting abuse in a relationship because you don't feel you deserve anything better. This indirect method is not the road to sainthood; it's the road to the hell of abuse.

2: **Valiant Caretaking:** You take care of everyone else as a way of never having to ask anything for yourself. You hope that someone will see your need and offer to meet it. Perhaps you are afraid that if you ask, you will meet with disappointment or rejection. If you thought better of yourself, you would realize that you deserve to get your needs met too.

3: **Eat Your Heart Out:** You find yourself willing to settle for the envy of others (e.g., by bragging about your children's accomplishments, name-dropping, etc.) because you don't feel that you deserve their love. In this regard, envy compared with respect and appreciation is as satisfying as a cup of instant coffee and powdered dairy creamer compared with an aromatic, freshly prepared cup of coffee.

4: **Super Self-Absorption:** You don't really listen to what others are saying unless it refers directly to you. You become irritated and bored when the conversation moves to a topic other than yourself. Others may think that your outrageous egotism is a sign that you think too well of yourself. You and they need to think again.

5: **Trumping:** You view every conversation as a competitive match in which you must prove your importance. Thus you must "top" everyone's story. To make sure you are ahead, you silently keep score.

6: **Subtle Trump:** Instead of seeking ways to establish direct connection or communication with another, you find yourself secretly thinking about how to promote yourself in ways that are subtle enough so that your hunger for self-importance won't be detected. This requires great imagination, and some of us have taken it to the level of an art.

Sadly, these strategies are hollow in that they really don't add to your overall sense of self-worth; indeed, they prevent you from feeling your unmet needs and confronting your feelings of inadequacy. Like drugs or alcohol, they merely cover up the problem without addressing the source of the discomfort. If you recognize your use of any of these indirect ways of meeting your psychological needs for recognition and attention, don't be embarrassed. You are not selfish, egotistical, or narcissistic. You use these ploys because your interactions with others are nutritionally deficient. You are resorting to indirect means to get your needs met. Take your behavior as a message that you need more nourishment than you are getting. One way to "feed" one another is through a form of Stern's attunement. For the sake of discussion, let's say that the nutritional richness of attunement can be measured in units—minimum daily psychological nutrition requirements (MDPNRs). Though the precise number of MDPNR units has not yet been researched or established, we recommend at least one daily exchange containing six units of nutritional attention. The following scale provides you with a way of estimating the value of the attention you are receiving and giving. Remember: A person needs to be empathically "mirrored" in order to maintain a strong and healthy sense of worth. Here are some guidelines for measuring the nutritional value of the responses you give or get from others. If your score for any one day remains under six, you will no doubt find yourself resorting to indirect methods for fulfilling your needs.

SCALE OF PSYCHOLOGICAL ATTUNEMENT

-1 **Beyond Unresponsive:** The person you are talking with interrupts you in the middle of your sentence and shifts to a different topic. Subtract one unit.

0 **Unresponsive:** The person obviously isn't listening, only waiting for you to stop talking. When you finish, the person shifts to an entirely different topic.

1 **Indirectly Unresponsive:** The other person says or implies, "Well, you shouldn't feel that way...."

2 **Self-Referential Free Association:** The person says something like, "Oh, yeah, that reminds me of the time when I..." or "Well, you think you had it bad—listen to what happened to me," and makes no other reference to anything you have said.

3 **Free Association:** The person responds to your statement by going off on a tangent and making only an indirect reference to what you said.

4 **Impersonal/Nonnurturing:** The person indicates she has heard you but offers no sympathetic or empathic response. Basically, her stance is: "That's the way the cookie crumbles."

5 **Superficial:** Although the person responds by saying, "Yeah, I know what you mean," she does not sound sincere or empathic.

6 **Adequate:** The person shows evidence that he heard what you said but does not show interest or follow up your statement by encouraging you to expand upon it.

7 **Responsive:** The person not only hears what you said but also inquires further so that you can elaborate. He asks questions that demonstrate interest.

8 **Resonant:** The person indicates that she emotionally resonates with what you have said by responding with statements that show she is trying to imagine what you are experiencing (e.g., "I can imagine that you feel terrible about losing your favorite pair of earrings").

After reading this scale, you may be wondering if you can nourish your self-worth without depending on others. There are, of course, ways of doing so. For example, when you attend a film, play, or concert, you may sense that something is resonating with you and is satisfying. Some people who relate to nature feel nourished by contact with the outdoors. When you achieve one of your goals, you can celebrate your accomplishment. You can also give yourself attention by writing daily in a journal or diary, or by periodically reflecting on your own feelings and thoughts—in other words, listening to yourself. By giving yourself time to pursue a hobby or avocation—knitting, playing the piano, or hiking—you are recognizing the things you enjoy, choosing to spend time on them, and ultimately renewing and refreshing yourself. You may also have the satisfaction of seeing aspects of yourself reflected in what you create, whether it be a plush sweater or a three-course dinner for friends. But remember, you can't do it all by yourself. The positive or negative responses that you get from others affect the way you feel about yourself, whether you like it or not.

People can learn to give one another the attention they need. For example, psychologist Eugene Gendlin has developed forms of interaction that he calls nourishing partnerships and nourishing-partnership groups.

In the 1950s, clinical psychologist Carl Rogers developed a therapeutic approach entitled client-centered psychotherapy. It was different from classical Freudian analysis in that Rogers believed clients could come to know more about their problems than their therapists did. So he developed a way to encourage clients to trust what they knew about themselves, then to articulate it. He encouraged this process by repeating back to clients the gist of what they had just said so they would be able to track and go deeper into their thoughts and feelings. One of Rogers's students at the University of Chicago was Eugene Gendlin, who, after conducting research that Rogers designed, realized that the clients who made the most progress were the ones who knew how to "focus," that is, how to detect and give words to what they felt in their bodies, what Gendlin termed their "felt sense." From this research and his philosophical background came the focusing technique, which consists of small steps of bodily attention that move beyond the level of feelings that most people are aware of. By attending to the "felt sense" in the stomach or chest, we at first get only an unclear sense. But with steady attention, the body sense opens up and we find how different the information is that comes from the center of the body. We have the sense of being talked to by something deeper, something that is not infected by fears and conditioning. A few people focus naturally; most do not. The method is not the same as being in touch with emotions or the usual gut feelings. It literally involves a body sense, feeling how your body is carrying a particular life situation, problem, or concern. Once contacted, this sense leads to small steps of physically felt change and new actions. Gendlin combined Rogers's method of repeating the essence of what someone had said with the concept of focusing to create focusing partnerships. In this partnership, two people split a period of time, with one of them the focuser and the other the witness. The focuser can, but need not, say what the focusing is about. The witness repeats back the gist of what the focuser says. This partnership provides both support for venturing inward and a validating connection to the outer world.

Some will argue correctly that we need a lot more than just attention to have good mental health. Psychologist Abraham Maslow maintained that there was a hierarchical scale of psychological needs. According to Maslow, once basic physical needs (food, safety, shelter) are taken care of, other needs (a sense of belonging, meaning) come to the forefront. We agree, but see attention as the principal ingredient in the alchemical process of connecting to self, others, and the Divine.

*M*uch of the downside of not being fully heard, understood, and received deeply is readily evident in modern culture. But what of the other side, the positive, beneficial, deeply healing experience of being loved in ways that include being heard, fully understood, and welcomed in all our glorious differentness? In this selection, interfaith hospice chaplain Margaret Truxaw Hopkins calls on her experience of being on both the giving and the receiving ends of such life-affirming experience. Out of these direct encounters she offers us valuable insights that hold the potential to significantly transform not only our own interpersonal relationships, but the relationships between families, communities, and nation-states as well.

The Healing Power
of Being Deeply Heard

Margaret Truxaw Hopkins

May we all be free from suffering and the root of suffering.
May our practice of listening release the illusion of separation.
May it heal the listener, heal the one who is heard, and bring
healing forth in an ever-expanding circle that knows no boundaries.
May the words here manifest this sacred intention.

W HAT IS SO SPECIAL about being heard? What happens to us when someone listens deeply to us? What does it take to be spiritually healed and psychologically transformed in the process? How does healing feel in body, mind and heart? Who can do it? Is it difficult? Is listening simply remaining silent? Are there any limits to the benefits being heard can provide? Does the listener get a turn? What if the listener has reactions? Is paraphrasing or mirroring important? What is the best way to handle judgments? In thinking about listening deeply, all of these questions and many more may arise. In this essay, I want to explore the power of being heard as I have encountered it, especially within chaplaincy training. I see the healing power of being heard from three perspectives: from the perspective of the person who is heard, from the perspective of the listener, and also from the wider perspective in which we see that listening can effect a global transformation. It is my own experience that being heard nurtures, heals, and transforms. In an action-oriented world where the focus is often on fixing problems, the transformational benefit of simply being heard may not seem sufficient—but very often, it is.

Allowing Wholeness

Imagine you are walking along a creek with someone you love. The weather is mild, a gentle breeze is blowing. You can hear the soothing sound of the creek. You notice a bird in the reeds on the bank. The path is dappled with the shade of oak limbs and sycamore leaves. Your friend turns his/her attention to you and invites you to talk. Your friend's eyes are soft as they rest upon you. You know your friend is interested and open to you. You begin awkwardly, tentatively speaking what's on your mind. You fumble through the thoughts and feelings that arise. You recognize them, honor them, and express them. Your friend hears and accepts what you say. There seems to be room for any feelings that arise. You are not judged and you release your own judgments. You are encouraged to continue. You believe in the sincerity of the listener's attention. As the top layer of words and feelings finds expression, another layer begins to emerge. It bubbles to the surface and breaks into the bright morning air. Then, another layer of feelings bubbles up, painful at first, then freeing. You feel the breeze enter the open spaces in your body where tension has been released. A sigh of relief escapes and your muscles become noticeably more relaxed. Something has changed in you. A knotted place, where an old hurt has held you in check, melts into healing. A block to the flow of life energy releases. A long-dormant interior pathway gently reopens. Healing is happening.

Healing is a word that is often used synonymously with the word *curing*, but it can mean something more. *Curing* is associated primarily with removing physical ailments. Without minimizing the value of curing a physical ailment, I contend that healing takes place at a more inclusive level. It is coming back into wholeness. Deep healing makes no distinction between body and soul. Healing can produce measurable clinical changes as part of a more integrated process. It often does. Healing, however, is not reserved for illnesses of the body. In fact, it can take place in profound ways even while the physical body is dying. Our essential nature begins as and remains one of wholeness and oneness. Then, we incarnate into the illusion of separation. As we go along through life, insults and injuries can accumulate to deaden, or disconnect us from, parts of the original wholeness. Unskillful or absent parents may play a part. Poverty or family crisis can leave scars. Threats to survival can upset the balance, as can experiences that are perceived as threats. Many forms of oppression, abandonment, or trauma cut off parts of our authentic whole selves from the optimal flow of our life energy, our wholeness. The deadened parts of ourselves may fester and draw off energy we otherwise would use to live more fully. These deadened, blocked, hidden parts can be reclaimed when they are brought into consciousness and acknowledged with care.

The process of bringing conscious listening to the service of wholeness is central to the work of the hospital or hospice chaplain. Learning to listen effectively takes skill and self-awareness.

SIMPLE LISTENING

Listening skillfully requires us to get out of our own way. This isn't always easy to do. Listeners frequently have emotions within them touched by what they are hearing, and these emotions distract them from what is being conveyed by the speaker. The listener may be planning how to respond or rehearsing a reply at the cost of concentrated focus. Especially if the listener and speaker share a personal relationship, the content can overlap the personal history of both and present itself as a source of potentially tangled communication. Conflicting needs can derail the intention to offer a compassionate ear. So how does one listen skillfully? As one teacher summarizes it bluntly to his students: "Shut up and learn to manage your own reactivity."

One part of learning to listen is to simply stop talking and focus your attention on the speaker. Another part is to take responsibility for the thoughts and feelings that arise reactively and hold them in silent awareness, without judgment, while returning again and again to the intended focus on the speaker. It is much like a meditation practice. I watch my monkey-mind try to get control of the conversation. I breathe. And I gently bring my awareness back to the focal point of the speaker. I notice when I stray from this intention. I come back again to the focus. And then I do it again…and again.

It really is this simple, at the heart of it. However, as one develops the practice of placing focused attention on the speaker, a series of skills grow in the service of that attention. One becomes interested in confirming that communication has been well understood. This stimulates curiosity and prompts mirroring or paraphrasing: "This is what I understood from what you said. Did I get that right?" Active listening can include other ways of drawing forth the authentic self and the deepest truth of the speaker, ways which can be developed as skills.

SPECIALIZED LISTENING IN CHAPLAIN TRAINING

In the Clinical Pastoral Education programs in which I trained, the styles of communication, or core dynamics, were divided into three general categories of spiritual assessment. There were several different structures for naming these categories. Identifiable patterns are likely to emerge when an individual is acutely stressed, as one typically is during a hospitalization. In *Promise of the Soul*, Dennis Kenny names these categories *Giver*, *Wanter*, and *Searcher*. Following the principles of this structure of core dynamics provides a framework that allows a listener to tune in with a customized response, depending upon the pattern of the speaker. For example, the category characterized by the label *Wanter* includes people who can tolerate feedback that is more blunt, or at a higher volume than people whose styles more closely match the other two categories. In abbreviated and simplified form, the Giver and Searcher respond more openly to support and clarification than to confrontation. Ways of listening can be customized to perceived individual need. To the extent that we are able to discern the style of the speaker, these concepts can apply to listening in a professional or informal context. The skills of active listening are also useful when we are listening to someone we know very well.

In the process of "growing a group of chaplains," the work is divided between time spent ministering to patients and families and time spent working formatively in an interdenominational group of chaplain residents. The group time is used largely to explore the personal and interpersonal dynamics of the group members. It is a practice of growing self-awareness and practicing ministering skills.

Consider self-awareness. When one becomes increasingly aware of one's own tender spots, quirks, and general patterns of reactivity, it becomes easier to manage anxiety as one listens to another person, whether an intimate partner or client. It is also easier to recognize and customize one's responses in ways most likely to be received by the partner as constructive and healing. This is the edge for developing skills.

One of the components of effective listening as a tool for deep healing is the willingness of the sharer to be self-disclosing. In the context of the chaplain residency group, where each group member is alternately listener and sharer, I was invited to consider a paradoxical idea regarding vulnerable self-disclosure and the safety of the group container. My initial expectation was to be shown that the group could be trusted to keep me safe in my self-disclosure before exposing myself. I wanted proof of safety first; only then would self-disclosure follow. The paradoxical reality was that the vulnerability of self-disclosure within the group was key to growing the trust, safety, and skillful responses of the group members. Though I found this a radical idea, in retrospect I can see the paradox. There is a certain mystery, terror and wonder in participating in a group as it becomes increasingly compassionate, authentic, and skillful in listening, in proportion to the increasing boldness and vulnerability of the sharing. The process is dynamic and interactive, with mutual growth the inevitable result.

LISTENING TO YOUR LOVE

Managing one's own reactivity is especially crucial when the conversation takes place between people who share a close, caring relationship, whether in intimate partnership or within a facilitated peer group. In the container of such a relationship, there is potential for great healing, when listening is skillfully practiced with loving-kindness. When there is a breach in the intention and the attention, the opposite can occur, and there is potential for eliciting further suffering. Sometimes it is difficult to tell the difference. The process of releasing what has long been held tightly can hurt even as it heals. It requires a conscious choice and a disciplined practice on the part of the listener and the sharer to make the most of the opportunities a relationship generates. We are often drawn to a partner whose complementary issues offer us the most challenging, but most potentially rewarding, mirror for our own growth. Relationship built on a foundation of trust and deep listening is not for the faint of heart. But the rewards are worth the work.

When I am listening to my partner with skill, I can see more clearly which elements of a conflict belong to him and which belong to me. If I feel a strong emotional reaction to what he says, it is almost certain that something tender and vulnerable in me has been touched, and it is useful to note that for when it is my turn to be the speaker. When I am in a conversation without consciousness and care, my subjective reactions can spill out with little control, and the listening temporarily comes to an end. When I can tune my attention with awareness to his core dynamic, there is a better chance that the container will be strong enough for deeper healing work to begin. I can see my own needs and wants as well as his.

Freedom from Judgment

When I am deeply heard without judgment, tender heartfelt truths are allowed to emerge. As you listen quietly, or mirror my truth to me for confirmation and clarification, I ease into letting go of my attachment or aversion. The knots of energy stuck to my thoughts and feelings become loosened. The illusion that appears to separate me from you, from the community, and from the universal divine, begins to dissolve.

Judgment can be tricky. It is simplistic to imagine that judgment will be entirely excluded from a listening practice. Mindful awareness of one's own reactions helps the listener to avoid the interference of judgment. In our personal and professional listening roles, there are times when it is useful and compassionate to go beyond silent and reflective listening into that murky territory where responses may indicate judgment. Or so it seems from the process of chaplain training. When the sharer is capable of receiving and using feedback in the service of wholeness, the mirror of truth can be bolder and more direct. When incorporating confrontation in a listening practice, it is crucial to maintain vigilance about one's own internal experience and motives.

In my own experience of the Clinical Pastoral Education residency, making use of the full potential of being deeply heard was a gradual process. When I joined the group, I was hesitant, defensive, and easily bruised by feedback of any kind. My tendency was to polarize to opposite ends of a spectrum of self-judgment. I was either someone set apart in my specialness or someone set apart in my unique woundedness or unworthiness. When the experience of sharing in the group cast light on anything that was inconsistent with the momentary polarization, I would find myself hurtling through mental space toward the opposite pole. These frequent, violent jolts often left me feeling abused and battered, and inhibited any forward movement.

As time went by, the tendency to stay separate by inhabiting the alternating extremes of self-judgment began to soften. The trip back and forth between opposite poles slowed and even paused in the middle more often and for longer periods of time. The middle ground between the extremes holds the potential for accurate self-assessment, freedom, growth, and forward movement. My defensiveness in the face of feedback quieted. The container of the group and individual sessions allowed growth toward wholeness. The essence of the healing process involved choosing to express my deepest truth and being deeply heard in response.

FORGIVENESS

Our spiritual wounds are the parts of ourselves that have become disowned or cut off from awareness. When we disown ourselves, we become cut off from the universal whole.

Shorthand for the road home to wholeness is forgiveness, or reconciliation. To return to wholeness, I must find a way to embrace and reconcile the disowned parts back into myself. I can then allow myself to be embraced back into relationship, community, and universal wholeness. The tools of forgiveness or reconciliation lay in listening and in being heard. Forgiveness has many sides. I can ask forgiveness. I can forgive another. I can witness and facilitate the processes of another in reconciliation work. I can rage at God, or the universe, or fate, and I can forgive the object of my rage. And I can forgive myself. What remains unforgiven binds up my energy and cuts me off from the fullness of life. In the work of listening, the opportunities arise for the work of forgiveness to come forth. When I wrestle with blame and shame, being heard can transform my struggle into release.

In spiritual care, reconciliation can refer to a set of interactive steps designed to restore broken relationships. The Catholic Sacrament of Penance, also know as Reconciliation or Confession, has historical seeds in the healing practice of listening. The confessor, or listener, in the current formal Roman Catholic rite, must be an anointed priest, though the community can be included in the celebration. Up until the middle ages, laypeople also participated together in the reconciliation process, calling the estranged member to confession, and assisting in the return to the community. Whether in a formal rite, a conversation between lovers, or a therapy session, the process of conscious forgiveness offers a form of significant and powerful healing.

Reconciliation is a practice and it takes practice. It may take a long time and many iterations of speaking the truth before old wounds are closed and absolution and healing are complete. I may resist some part of the process. I may acknowledge what hurtful things I have done, but remain defensive and emotionally aloof. When listening in the service of forgiveness, one need not create an agenda for a particular outcome and force an issue. That would depart from the central task of listening. One must only listen well and remain open to what unfolds. However, in some schools of thought there is a pattern in the process of confessing a transgression and seeing it through to reconciliation. The pattern, modeled after the sacrament, requires speaking the truth with sincere contrition and with a penitential act, followed by forgiveness, and healing of the breach in the relationship. A skillful listener can facilitate the progress through this process. When the person whom I have wronged is not available, the listener can stand in for that person and respond. In the case of a chaplain, who may hold a representational presence for a deity or spiritual authority, there is a responsibility to bring skillful, conscious awareness to the healing potential of the reconciliation process.

LISTENING AT A GLOBAL LEVEL

Finally, there is the idea of the healing power of being heard as it touches the planet in a universal way. If individuals and groups grow toward wholeness and reconciliation of broken relationships as a result of skillful listening, why not apply the same approach to world problems and relationships between nations? Suppose a dialogue were to begin on a spiritual level between nations. Suppose defensiveness were tempered with sincere and skillful attention devoted to understanding the experience of the other. Suppose the world's powers became open to receiving the authentic story of the way of life of third world peoples. Suppose the lip service paid to diversity grew into robust mutual listening to the values of other cultures. Suppose the scars of injury were allowed a place in the light to heal, responsibility for transgressions was claimed, and atonement was made. Suppose the need to define one another as other melted away.

If the world were deeply heard, what potential do you imagine there would be for healing across the globe? Stop now. Take a breath. Attend to your disquietude. And listen.

*W*orking *for reform all around the world for more than twenty years, Fran Peavey has been a fearless activist with an atti-tude—one in which humor predominates. A longtime collaborator with activists such as Joanna Macy, Katy Butler, Claude Whitmyer, and John White, her personal commitment as the founder of Crabgrass, a community-based, nonprofit organization in San Francisco, is to environmental and social jus-tice and human rights. She has personally organized groups to clean up the Ganges River in India and has worked with refugees in Bosnia and South Africa. In a period when America's stock in the world may be at an all-time low, this article is particularly fitting. In this compelling piece from her book* Heart Politics, *Fran details the adventures resulting from her one-person social action plan—standing in various locations around the planet with a simple sign reading: "American Willing to Listen."*

American Willing to Listen

Fran Peavey

INTERNATIONAL TOURISM has never appealed to me. I just can't picture myself staying in a luxury hotel in Rome or Tokyo or Cairo, visiting museums and monuments, scouring gift shops for souvenirs. So for many years, I traveled abroad very little.

But the more I studied the nuclear threat, the more I became consumed with a desire to learn what was happening on this endangered planet, to talk with people around the world and find out how they felt about the future and the nuclear situation. I wanted to enlarge the context of my work to prevent nuclear war. Although theoretically I was fighting for the survival of every human being on the planet, I didn't actually know many people outside the United States. And since I now realized how important it was for me to be connected to the people I was fighting for, my goal became finding people around the world to know and love.

So I sold my house, paid my debts, and bought one of those around-the-world airplane tickets. Actually, the ticket limited me to the Northern Hemisphere, but that was enough for a start.

At my request, friends sent me names of people to talk with and stay with. I planned to go only to cities and towns where I had four or more contacts. After interviewing these contact people, I would ask them to suggest others. But I also wanted to interview people at random. So I came up with the idea of sitting in a park or other public place with a cloth sign that said "American Willing to Listen." Maybe people would come talk to me. I didn't dare tell my friends about the cloth sign for fear that their disapproval, or even their enthusiasm, might crush this fragile, tentative idea.

Before leaving the United States, I drove down to Santa Barbara to test my plan. I interviewed a few contact people there and asked them to refer me to others. And I tried sitting on a park bench with a sign—"Willing to Listen." I felt shy, exposed, and embarrassed. But it seemed better to get a start on those feelings close to home. People did stop and talk, and some of the conversations had depth. This encouraged me.

But on the plane to Japan my doubts and fears resurfaced. What if my interviewing project failed? Perhaps it was a big mistake to try. I had never traveled alone in the world. What if I got sick? What if thieves fell on me? And at the same time I felt excited; I was doing something no one in my family had ever done.

The project began in Kyoto, Japan. First I met my contact people: a Buddhist priest, several environmental activists, and a women's studies class at Kyoto University. It was a few days before I made my "American Willing to Listen" sign and a few more before I got up the nerve to use it. Waiting for a train in Osaka, I said to myself, "If I'm ever going to do this, I should do it here where nobody I know will see me." Unfolding my two-by-three-foot cloth sign, I laid it on the floor in front of me and sat down. Time passed. People came over, sized me up, and walked away, I tried to smile pleasantly.

If I busied myself with reading or writing, I was sure that people would not talk to me for fear of interrupting. So I just sat and smiled, all the while thinking, "This is a bad idea. I've spent a lot of money on my plane ticket, and the plan isn't working. I'm making a fool of myself. How will I ever get to talk with ordinary people?"

It was thirty or forty minutes before someone finally stopped to talk—a man in his forties who worked at a shoe factory. He wanted to know what I was doing. I tried to explain but he didn't understand, and I began to fear that I didn't understand either. I was so busy answering his questions that I never managed to ask him any of mine.

After another few minutes, a man of about thirty stopped to chat. He discussed some of his concerns: the border war between North and South Korea over control of rubber trees; consumerism in Japan and the level of consumption in developed countries in general; the investment of massive amounts of Japanese capital in China (he felt a China-Japan alliance might be destabilizing in the region). Closer to home, he was thinking about relations between the sexes. His wife was part of a women's consciousness-raising group, and he and the other husbands had felt jealous of it. They'd tried to start their own group, but it hadn't worked. He was disappointed, and the issue seemed to be unresolved for him.

Boarding the train to Kyoto, I felt happy and relieved. The second man I'd talked with had understood what I was doing and thought it was a great idea. And he had shared a little of his life with me. My confidence grew as the process of meeting people gained momentum. I met people by arrangement and at random, in their homes, schools, and workplaces, as well as in cafés, train stations, universities, and parks. I refined my interviewing technique, asking open-ended questions that would serve as springboards for opinions and stories—questions like "What are the biggest problems you see affecting your country or region?" and "How would you like things to be different in your life?" Being limited to English put me at a disadvantage, but people often volunteered to translate for me.

Early interviews showed me how little I knew about the world. There were countless issues I had never even heard about. For instance, nearly everyone I talked with in Japan mentioned Kim Dae Jung, a South Korean opposition leader who had escaped to Japan and then been sent back to Korea. I had never thought about relations between Japan and South Korea. In the United States these issues had seemed unimportant and had received only minimal coverage in the news media. Now I was meeting people to whom they were very important. I began to see glimmers of the many ways in which non-Americans saw the world.

It was exhilarating but exhausting. The rapid succession of new issues nearly overwhelmed me—the homogenization of Japanese culture, women's gossip in an Indian village, the flight of capital from Australia to the Philippines and Korea, the aspiration to know God, the near-melt-down of a Japanese nuclear power plant, rural Indian mothers' fears that their children weren't getting enough protein, doubts about the tradition of arranged marriage, regional conflicts over resource and capital alloca-tion, and the frustration of people everywhere who sensed that their des-tiny was controlled by the superpowers. It occurred to me that I might have to go on interviewing full-time for the rest of my life to get any sense of what was going on in the world.

Four years and hundreds of interviews later, I no longer feel quite so con-founded. I'm beginning to get a sense of social and historical currents around the world. On my first world trip I listened to people in Japan, Thailand, India, England, and Scotland. Subsequent trips have taken me to East Berlin, Israel, Palestine, Sweden, and India again. While traveling I've also met people from other countries in Asia, Africa, Latin America, and the South Pacific. My listening project has become a continuing prac-tice, both in the United States and abroad.

On the Punjab Mail, a train from Bombay to Hoshangabad, I inter-viewed the woman who shared my compartment. The wife of a retired railroad worker, she appeared to be in her mid-sixties, and she was trav-eling with a well-made wooden box that contained a cake for her nephew's wedding. As we rode along she spoke of her worries about her son, a drug addict who was now in Saudi Arabia. The woman's English was quite good, but she had trouble with my name. So I gave her my business card, which identifies me as a futurist. "What's a futurist?" she asked. When I tried to explain, her face lit up. "Oh, you mean a fortune-teller?" Preoccupied with getting ready for bed, I wasn't paying much attention. "Sort of," I said. She started asking me about her son. Was he still on drugs? Would he return to India? Or might he marry someone in Saudi Arabia and lose his religion? I said something mildly encouraging about parents and children.

Then she left the compartment. Twenty minutes later she returned, reporting that she had gone through the train announcing that a blue-eyed fortune-teller was on board. A group of people had gathered and were waiting to hear their fortunes. She would be happy to translate.

Discovering a line of twenty or thirty people outside our compartment, I tried in vain to convince them of my lack of talent or training in fortune-telling. But they replied, "You gave her a good fortune; you must give us one too." I was up most of the night giving friendly advice and encouragement.

A middle-aged farmer wanted to know about his cow. The cow had been sick, and her milk yield was poor. Would she get better? I asked a few questions and eventually suggested that he consult an animal specialist and get some help. He was grateful for my advice.

A couple came in and asked, "Will we find a husband for our daughter, and will she be happy in her marriage?" I said, "Yes, if they work hard at their marriage, I think they will be happy." They looked at each other with relief. "Will we be able to find her a husband close to our village? We want to have our daughter close to us." As they asked more questions, my translator explained to me about Hindu marriage arrangements. The bride lives with the husband's family, and difficulties can arise if the bride and the mother-in-law don't get along. I suggested to the couple that they interview prospective mothers-in-law to find a cheerful one for their daughter.

Another couple was traveling to visit their grandchild for her first birthday ceremony. Would the granddaughter grow up to be happy, healthy, and prosperous? I tried to get some hints. Was she a healthy baby? I said something mildly encouraging. They said: "In your country you beat children and treat them badly. That's because you don't believe in reincarnation." The woman explained that her beloved mother, who had died a year or two before, had been reincarnated as the baby. So of course this baby was very special to them.

After my stint as the blue-eyed fortune-teller of the Punjab Mail, I felt more at home in India. I'd begun to empathize with some of the problems Indians had in their lives. They were worried about their children getting married, just as I had worried about my younger sister's marriage. They were concerned about the health of their parents; I had been through that too.

Listening to people, I began to learn how each individual puzzled out large issues from her or his own vantage point. In Varanasi, India, a woman told me that when the Brahmans were thrown out of power in southern India, her husband could no longer find a satisfactory job there. So they moved north to Varanasi. She currently had no job, she said, because Varanasi was a place that didn't respect women. Now she feared that the lower castes would revolt in the north, as they had in the south. Already, she said, "Brahmans are unable to provide strong leadership because they feel so insecure." She expected people to become "more and more selfish, all thinking of themselves, no one thinking of society. And corruption has been getting worse and worse. Corrupt politicians are responsible for the misery in every sphere of life."

In Edinburgh, Scotland, a man who worked with the Scottish nationalist party told me that his country was a colony of England, and England would never grant them independence because the English wanted their offshore oil. The Scots for their part can't mount an effective independence movement, he said, because they are so fiercely individualistic that they can't work together.

In Darjeeling I met a thirteen-year-old from Bhutan who wanted to become a freedom fighter, to help his region gain independence from China. He earnestly told me about his desire to study hard, to become a strong man, to help his people. I was surprised to see such determination in a person his age.

Two Kyoto women in their twenties were thinking about why Japanese young people were so uninvolved in world affairs. The explanation they had developed was historical: Japanese people had been told that they would win the war against the materialist United States because Japanese spiritual values were superior. So Japan's defeat in World War II was considered a victory for materialism—which the Japanese then embraced. Materialistic, hedonistic values had taken over, they told me, and parents had neglected to give their kids the love and sense of security that would allow them to be involved in larger concerns.

I visited the Rasulia Center near Hoshangabad, where about thirty people, mostly from the Untouchable caste, live, farm, build bio-gas plants for energy, and work toward self-sufficiency. The leader of the community told me that India's culture used to be one of the greatest in the world— in the forefront in mathematics, art, and religion. India was no longer a leader, he said, because colonialism had squashed the Indians' initiative. In the cycles of history, civilizations rise and fall; India's will rise again. As petroleum becomes more expensive, he projected, societies that are not so dependent on oil (especially less-developed countries) can become a stronger force in the world. He didn't expect that trend to take hold for another hundred years or so, but he was very hopeful about the future and was preparing for it.

A conversation I had with a nuclear engineer in New Delhi lasted six hours. We started out at the YMCA, where I was staying; then he drove me to a fancy club he belonged to, and we ate dinner on the veranda there. We talked at length about nuclear power and his doubts about quality control in India's nuclear power industry. He also helped me understand the fear generated by the state of emergency declared by Indira Gandhi in 1975. Opponents of Mrs. Gandhi's regime were thrown in jail; so when she called an election, people were afraid even to admit to one another that they were planning to vote against her. "When I went into the voting booth," the engineer told me, "I hadn't asked my wife whom she was voting for, and she hadn't asked me. Nobody knew how anyone else was going to vote. Privately we were all afraid that if Mrs. Gandhi won, she would declare another state of emergency and refuse to hold elections in the future. Then we'd never be able to get rid of her." I could see how much he enjoyed being listened to, and how important it was for him to talk about things he hadn't been able to discuss with anyone else.

In all of my conversations, I would look directly at the person I was interviewing and at the same time observe the context we were in—the sounds around us, the birds, the wind, the way people nearby responded to my presence. I would listen to the person as open-heartedly as I could, trying to get a glimpse of the world through his or her eyes. Usually when the conversations lasted long enough, I would start to feel the soft stirrings of a connection—some uncovering of our common root system.

"Are things getting better or worse in your life? In the world?" These questions always got people talking. In Hoshangabad I began to notice that men tended to think things were getting better, while women were generally more pessimistic. A woman to whom I mentioned this observation responded: "That's because the men don't do the shopping."

When I asked about the future, many people went directly to the possibility of nuclear war. Near Kyoto, I spoke with a seventy-two-year-old farmer whose family had lived on the same land since the twelfth century. He feared that the population explosion had made nuclear war more likely. And nuclear war would make it impossible to grow things. "We in Japan are downwind from everyone," he told me.

A Tibetan businessman I met in an antique store offered to take me to "the wisest man in Darjeeling." I followed the businessman through an alley, up a dark staircase, and into a little room. There we met a Tibetan monk, a stout man who sat surrounded by his scrolls. On one side stood an intricately arranged altar; on the other, a window overlooked the Himalayas. The businessman translated as we chatted.

At one point the monk abruptly changed the subject. "What I really want to talk to you about is nuclear war." He reached in among his scrolls, brought out a world atlas, and asked me to show him where Hawaii was.

A friend from Hawaii had told him about nuclear war. Since then he had spent a lot of time thinking about it and had come to believe that the root of the nuclear threat was anger. Did I get angry often? he wanted to know. Did people often get angry at me? He advised me that this was an important area to work on. He looked out the window at the sacred Himalayas and mournfully observed, "Nuclear war would ruin these mountains."A scientist in Varanasi was more sanguine. Nuclear war might solve the population problem, he suggested.

In London, a political activist I met in a bookstore was concerned that the United States would provoke a war in Europe. "You think you can protect your own country by keeping the wars on our continent. Don't you care about us at all?"

I often encountered hostility toward the United States. A young doctor at the Rasulia Center said, "You Americans have so much and we have so little. Your aid comes with strings attached. You can't give a clean gift; you can't help without getting something out of it, even if it's only a slightly less guilty conscience." Foreign businesses come to India in search of cheap labor, he said. For every dollar they invest in India, they take out three dollars' worth of goods. "That is how you get things cheaply in your country." By now he was yelling. "We don't want your help, your charity, your money! Get your ships out of the Indian Ocean, and get out of our lives!"

Listening to him, I felt personally attacked. I wanted to tell him that I wasn't one of those industrialists. Yet I wasn't wholly divorced from the situation either—I ate cashews from India, and I'd never felt good about food being exported from a hungry country to the United States. So I kept listening, and noticing my own defenses.

A woman in New Delhi said her daughter wanted to know why American protesters did not continue to care about the Vietnamese people after the U.S. troops had gone home. How could we cut the connection so easily? The question stung. As she spoke, feeble excuses ran through my mind. Once our troops had left Vietnam, we no longer had much information about what was happening there. Anyway, hadn't we done our part by forcing our government to withdraw the troops? Wasn't it time to divorce ourselves from that situation? Even as these defenses arose, I could see I was struggling to convince myself of my own righteousness. But finally I inwardly admitted that there was no justification for my own fickle attention to the plight of the Vietnamese people.

One day I stumbled into the Nonaligned Nations Conference in New Delhi. I stepped into the Oberoi Hotel to make a phone call and then sat down at an unattended desk to write some notes. A woman wearing a brightly-colored dress came up to ask directions. I found out she was from Tonga and asked her to tell me what world issues concerned her most. She expressed outrage about the expansion of the U.S. military base on Diego Garcia, an island in the Indian Ocean. Other delegates I talked with at the conference shared that concern. They were sure that the base would be used for surveillance of southern Asia, northern Africa, and the South Pacific, and could potentially be used as a springboard for military intervention. The woman from Tonga was alarmed that I had no knowledge of any of this. She wanted to know whether my ignorance was typical of the American people. How could I consider myself well-informed and yet know nothing of this important global issue that involved my government?

She offered to bring other people from the conference to talk with me if I would come back in the next few days. So every afternoon I sat down at "my desk" at the Nonaligned Nations Conference. Delegates and others at the conference came to talk with me. The hotel staff began to recognize me and bring me stationery and water.

These conversations gave me a sense of how powerful a force the United States is in the lives of people in Third World nations. They envy the comforts we take for granted and long for a fair share of their own resources and the fruits of their labor. They are afraid of being devastated in a nuclear war they never agreed to take part in. They are bewildered that the American people don't seem to know or care about what is happening in the rest of the world.

I developed two rules for listening to people talk about my country. First, I do not explain or defend the United States. My goal is to see how we look to others and to let that understanding inform my being. Although I continue to feel defensive when my country is criticized, I try to keep listening. Second, I do not divorce myself from criticisms of America and Americans. I do not say or imply, "Yes, some Americans or some parts of our country are that way, but I'm not." I try to take the criticisms to heart.

But it's not only criticisms I encounter. I've also heard out-and-out adoration of the United States. In a park in East Berlin, I met a young couple out for a Sunday stroll. Right away I noticed the American flag pin on the man's shirt. The woman was noticeably pregnant, and both of them had high hopes for the future. They had already applied once for permission to emigrate to the United States, but it had been denied. They had heard all about America from the man's sister, who lives in California, and they longed for the freedom she had told them about. They wanted to work hard, advance in their careers, and be free to buy all sorts of things.

In Varanasi, two women students—one from Iran, the other from Bahrain—told me they knew all about the United States from watching *Dallas* on television. They especially admired the kitchens in *Dallas,* and all the electrical appliances. I told them that not everyone in my country had such a high standard of living—that some people didn't even have electricity. I could see they were struggling to believe what I said.

Throughout my travels I met people who had studied in the United States, including many of the delegates at the Nonaligned Nations Conference. Many people spoke of the inequality of the cultural exchange. A woman in Tokyo who had studied at the University of Chicago put it forcefully: "We send our smartest people to your universities to learn from you. But you don't send your students to learn from us. When you come to our country you stay in fancy hotels, go on shopping trips, and travel around in tour buses. There's a lot you miss. Yours is a young society, and you have a lot to learn from us."

I have found people to be grateful and excited that an American has come to learn from them. In Tokyo, Bangkok, Varanasi, and New Delhi, people lined up and sometimes waited for hours to talk with me. Around midnight on the night before I left Varanasi, I was busy packing my suitcase when I heard a knock on the door. It was a Bangladeshi man whom I'd met briefly at the university. He had heard that I was about to leave and he wanted to be interviewed. An engineering student, he was also very interested in international cooperation and wanted to make sure that Bangladesh was represented in my listening project.

I often ask people: "What have you learned in your life?" Some had learned about time's constant movement. Others spoke of sorrow and suffering. A revolutionary in Bangkok had learned that "you have to be very careful." He had helped start a people's credit union, but government agents had infiltrated it, shut it down, and confiscated all the money.

Several people said, "It was worth it." They seemed proud to announce that their achievements had been worth the costs. In New Delhi, a woman told me just the opposite. Once a doctor, she had given up practicing medicine. "What good does it do? I get them well but they get sick the next day. They don't have enough food. If I use my medical training, it only means that they are going to suffer longer." So now she makes decorative plaques. I felt threatened by her depression and sense of futility.

On my second day in Bangkok, I took a taxi driver's recommendation of a place to eat breakfast. The restaurant was a large room with about thirty tables, all but two empty. The only people in the place were two European men at a booth in front, and six or seven Thai women who were sitting or standing around tables nearby. They all looked up as I walked in. I sat in the booth behind the two men and soon got the sense that they were the owners. From a nearby table, a woman looked at me and mouthed the words "I love you." I was so confused I felt like a block of wood. I had come here for breakfast! She gestured to ask if she could join me; I shrugged my shoulders. Another woman came up behind me and started rubbing my shoulders. She said softly, "You want a massage? You want to come up to my room for a massage?" I said, "No, thank you." The first woman scooted around and sat next to me. I tried to carry on as meaningless a conversation as possible. What's your name? Where do you live? I ordered ham and eggs. It was about seven o'clock, so I said to the woman next to me, "You're here early this morning."

She said she'd been here late last night too, until 1:00 A.M. She was a short woman, not over thirty years old. She touched my arm with a cold hand—she must have been as scared as I was. Rubbing my arm suggestively, she asked if I'd like to come up to her room. "I can make you very happy." I could no longer escape the conclusion that she was a prostitute who thought I'd come looking for her services.

Putting my hand on hers to stop her from rubbing my arm, I remembered my interview book! I whipped it out and told her I was traveling to learn what was going on in the world. Would she be willing to talk with me? Yes, she would. She told me her job was to sleep with men and let them touch her. She had to work hard to feed her two children. It cost too much to send them to school, so they stayed with her mother during the day. The woman's husband had been killed recently when the truck he was driving turned over.

By this time my ham and eggs had arrived, bathed in grease. I couldn't bring myself to eat the food. The other women started coming over to my table, trying to get me to go upstairs with them. I realized what a mystery I must seem: I hadn't eaten my food; I'd just been talking to this woman; perhaps there was something else I wanted that they could give me. Soon, all the women were sitting with us, talking about husbands and children and work and life in Thailand. They spoke of their envy and fear of the American and Japanese business and military men who used their services. Americans are very friendly and have a lot of money, one woman told me, but sometimes when you get them upstairs they're awful.

The women had mixed feelings about the Thai government. A big problem was that houses were being torn down and people were being thrown out of their neighborhoods. The threat of eviction was terrifying. But they did have electric power and lights—that was an improvement over past years.

We talked about children. The women all wished they could send their kids to school, but they couldn't afford the tuition. When I spoke of schooling provided for free by the government, they all started talking at once. What a great idea! I mentioned the school I'd visited the day before in Bangkok, where poor people could send their children for one baht (about five cents) a day. They hadn't heard of it.

Before leaving I offered the woman who'd first sat with me some money for her time and her teaching. She refused, but I insisted, suggesting she use the money to send her children to the One Baht School.

Still feeling the effects of jetlag, I returned to my hotel room and tried to sleep. But I was too excited. I kept thinking about the Thai women, about how much fun it had been to chat with them, how lively our discussion had been. I thought of what I'd learned about the impact of widowhood. Several of the women I'd talked with had turned to prostitution because they had children to take care of and no husband or other source of support. I could understand their decision, but I fervently wished they had other options. I remembered how an idea that was familiar to me— free public education—had seemed thrilling to them. And I wondered why I had been so afraid in the first moments at the restaurant. What had been so threatening? Of course I had never been propositioned by prostitutes before. What does a decent person do in that situation? I had been unprepared. And yet even in the midst of my fear I had known I was in no real danger. I had to laugh at myself and my fear.

The next day, I returned to the One Baht School to talk more with its founder, Prateep Ungsongtham. A tall, graceful woman in her late twenties, she had founded the school at age fifteen. At the time she had been a childcare worker, and she began to be concerned about the children who brought their younger siblings to her but couldn't afford to attend school themselves. So although she had little schooling herself, Prateep began teaching the older children to read. In exchange they paid her one baht each and helped out with the childcare. Now the school had grown; there were two buildings and a basketball court. Prateep had finished college, and some of her former students who now had college degrees had returned to teach.

The One Baht School is in the middle of Klong Toey, a community of forty thousand squatters. Built on stilts over a canal, their dwellings are made mostly out of found wood but are very clean inside. I found myself wondering: In such terrible situations, where do people get the ideas, the will, and the drive to make things better, not only for themselves but for others? The land is owned by the Port Authority, which at the time was taking steps to evict six thousand slum-dwellers in order to build a container port. The school had been a focal point for the efforts against eviction. Prateep said, "To feel secure, we need to know that we can stay here for thirty or forty years."

When Prateep found out that I'd had some experience fighting eviction, she called in the other teachers. It was a Saturday, so there were no classes. Ten of us sat together, and I talked about the International Hotel, the American Indian struggle against uranium mining, and other land struggles. Every now and then our discussion would have to stop because someone would come in with a problem: an old man was dying or a woman's electric bill was forty times what it should be. The teachers were also community workers, and with each interruption one would leave to help resolve the problem.

I dredged up everything I had learned at the I-Hotel about fighting eviction—resistance tactics and techniques from England, China, Japan, the Philippines, and all over the United States. Each idea seemed to suggest others to them, and they would take off in their own language, talking excitedly. They had dreamed of defying the eviction order but had thought of their struggle as an isolated one. Hearing that others around the world had the same dream was exhilarating to them. I had never shared information with a more eager and intensely curious bunch.

During my time in Japan, it slowly dawned on me that I had not seen any slums or poor people there. I began asking the people I interviewed where the poor people lived. "We don't have poor people in Japan," I was told again and again. "We are all middle class." Or occasionally, "Oh yes, we have some but I don't know where. Maybe in Tokyo." These answers seemed implausible, so I continued my inquiry. Finally I heard about a district in Osaka called Kamagasaki, where day laborers and poor people lived. Church people from Osaka and Kyoto had organized a night patrol in the area so that people who fell asleep on the street would not freeze and those who were injured could be cared for. Each night of the week a different group was responsible for the watch.

I tagged along with a visiting group from Friends World College. We arrived at a small church in a bleak part of Osaka about 9:00 P.M. Our first job was to check the log books for news of the previous shift. Then the eight of us doing the watch that night gathered our supplies—gloves, first-aid kits, lanterns, and click-counters—loaded them into two pull-carts piled high with quilts, and walked to a nearby public building. I was amazed at what I saw there. More than a hundred people were sleeping on cotton mattresses covered with colorful quilts. It was an open-air sleeping center, a 25' x 75' area sheltered by the overhang of the building.

We picked up two containers of warm rice balls, put them in our carts, and set out in search of other people who needed a place to sleep. We divided into two teams of four and headed in different directions. As we walked, we found men sleeping in little hidden places. We kept track of how many we came across and where they were sleeping. My partner approached each sleeping person and checked on him. "Good evening.

How are you? Are you warm enough? Would you like some rice?" If he was cold, we would give him directions to the sleeping center. If he couldn't walk, we would put him in our pull-cart and take him there.

A toothless old man came up to greet us. His dog followed. The man reminded me of some of my Sixth Street Park friends. To make a place to sleep, he had leaned sheets of plywood against two ramen-noodle carts. He accepted a warm rice ball and chatted with us awhile.

Who are the twenty thousand people who live in Kamagasaki? Most are Koreans (the target of much discrimination in Japan). Others are poor Japanese. Many are men who have left their families. In Japan when you apply for a job, the company looks up your family name in the books of family history. If you do not come from a "good family," or if you are Korean, you have a very hard time getting a job. There are no training programs to help these men. Many are alcoholics. If a man can afford it, he rents a tiny room for about 250 yen (one dollar) a night. At the time of my visit, the landlords had recently doubled their profit by splitting the rooms in half. They would build an additional floor to divide each room horizontally, yielding two cubicles just big enough to crawl into.

At midnight we returned to the sleeping center, where by now about one hundred eighty men were sleeping. Another crew arrived shortly after we did, carrying a man in their cart. They checked his eyes with a light. Each time a new man arrived, a member of the day laborers' union would carry a mattress and quilt to a spot on the ground and make up a bed for him. The worker would tuck the man in, make sure he was warm, and say good-night. I was moved by the physical contact and the personal care. Workers stay there all night, standing guard so that no one can rob or take advantage of the sleeping men, and covering them up if their quilts slip off. I thought again of the people on Sixth Street in San Francisco, wishing the same kind of care were available to them.

We went back to the church and slept until 5:00 A.M., when we returned to the day labor hall. By that time all the bedding had been put away, and a nearby alley was full of minibuses with signs in their windows advertising for workers—ditch diggers, dirt carriers, and so on. But there were not enough jobs, and two-thirds of the men were left milling around.

At breakfast I interviewed one of the regular watch volunteers. He told me that Koreans have always been badly treated in Japan. They were once slaves, and they still do the lowliest work. Counting the street people is important, he said, because the society doesn't want to acknowledge its poor.

On the train back to Kyoto I thought about poor people and tried to envision better ways to get the world's menial work done. If we had a society where everyone was treated well, who would dig the ditches, pick the crops, and clean the buildings? If the United States didn't have a constant stream of immigrants to do that sort of work, who would do it? Are there ways to distribute menial work more evenly, and to value that work?

Everywhere I traveled, there were aspects of the society that I found disturbing. I tried to notice these, and to see whether my discomfort changed over time. For instance, in Varanasi one of the predominant smells is that of burning cow dung. At first I really disliked it. I lost my appetite and wished I could turn off my nose. To put myself at ease with the smell, I studied the cow dung cycle. I watched people gather the dung, mix it with a little dry grass, and slap it onto a nearby wall. There is hardly a vertical surface that isn't adorned with dung patties clearly imprinted with the hand of the pattymaker. The dung is left to dry and later plucked off and either burned or sold. This is the fuel most poor people use to cook and keep warm. Some pattymakers have a design sense and cover the walls in an artistic fashion; others seem to slap it up without thought or plan. As I became better acquainted with the process, the people, and the city, the smell bothered me less and less until the discomfort finally left entirely.

To this day I cringe at the cultural faux pas I know I've made in my world travels: eating with my left hand in India, touching a Brahman friend on the shoulder as I bade him farewell, losing track of which slippers were for which room in the home of a Japanese host. There must have been dozens of blunders that I still don't realize I made. I have learned to ask my hosts to forgive me for any disrespect I may have inadvertently shown for them, their religious practices, or culture.

When I returned from my world trip, I also returned to my job at Sixth Street Park. In a staff meeting some of the guys asked me to tell them what I had learned. I said I had been struck by the poverty in Japan, Thailand, and India. I told them I had seen people in Bombay living like animals, and people with severe disabilities out foraging for food on their hands and knees. Bird, who was sitting directly across the table from me, looked at me squarely, with a tear in the corner of his eye. He said, "It broke your heart, didn't it?" I could tell that even though he was very poor by the standards of the society around him, he had seen poverty much worse—maybe in the service or the merchant marine—and it had moved him. The park staff talked of their relative good fortune and of the idea of starting an international union of down-and-out people that could go on strike for better treatment.

It used to be that when I thought of India, I'd imagine the outline of the country on a map. I'd think of hungry people, women in saris, wild animals, mysticism, gurus—just floating impressions. Now I know what India looks like, smells like, feels like. I know some Indian people and have seen how their lives work in their own environment. I have a sense of some of the unresolved issues in the lives of individual people there.

This perceptual shift reminds me of going on field trips with my college zoology professor, Dr. Stanford. He would take us to an open field that didn't look special or interesting to us. Then Doc Stanford would say, "Let's take a look at just this one square meter." We'd explore its ecology in detail—the grasshoppers and beetles, the lichens and grasses, the parasites growing on the stalks of plants. Three or four inches below the surface, we'd find worms and a new set of bacteria; further down there were fungi growing on the roots of plants. We'd measure the acidity of the soil and note the kinds of plants it supported. We'd study the wind patterns, the geology, how water percolated down through the soil. We could take hours studying a square meter.

And that's the way I feel about the world now. I used to picture the world as a globe with continents and oceans and countries painted orange, yellow, and pink. Then, when I saw photographs of the earth taken from space, I saw a living whole. Now I see life on that spinning ball: specific places, specific concerns, specific lives.

I'm continually thinking of the people I've met around the world. That couple on the Punjab Mail: Is their granddaughter growing up healthy and strong? How are the street people in Kamagasaki doing? Have the squatters near the One Baht School successfully resisted eviction? In August I think about the monsoons in India. I can see the waters of the Ganges rising.

My listening project is a kind of tuning-up of my heart to the affairs of the world. I hear the news in a very different way now, and I act with a larger context in mind. Conspicuous consumption has become more difficult now that I have met poor people around the world. I hold myself accountable to the people whose lives I have seen. And I work to keep nuclear war from happening to us all.

I carry with me the pain of some of my partners in the world, but it does not weigh me down. Much of my life and environment have been designed to isolate me from this pain, but I have come to see it as a kind of holy nectar. The more I drink, the more I can taste what is happening on this planet.

*I*t might come as a surprise to many people that paying attention is a skill that can be taught and honed. In this selection, Gurdjieff scholar Kathleen Speeth identifies some of the learnable aspects of paying attention and offers up possibilities for cultivating them. The results of such learning can create the ability to consciously shift the focus of awareness in ways that can be of great benefit both to the person who is attentive and simultaneously to the object of attention.

On Therapeutic Attention

Kathleen Riordan Speeth

ATTENTION of the finest quality is the fundamental instrument of the therapist. Given its basic importance, it is thus quite astonishing that so little explicit discussion of attention is to be found in the clinical literature, and so correspondingly meager is the training in attention available to would-be therapists in professional psychology programs.

Training programs do provide a conceptual framework which assumes that the candidate is already adept in the uses of attention. In addition to a great deal of psychodynamic theory, these programs promulgate technical admonitions, which differ depending upon the school involved, and yet always seem to coalesce, whatever their content, into a sort of professional conscience, inner perceptor, or judge. This inner critic may exhort the conscientious therapist to carry out such attentional maneuvers as maintaining unconditional positive regard; monitoring the countertransference; sustaining a complementary relationship; being authentic (or hidden); refraining from solving the client's problems (or solving them with well-timed, technically elegant interventions); etc. The typical psychotherapist enters private practice feeling ethically committed to giving attention to each client, establishing and maintaining rapport, and sustaining sensitive contact regardless of subject matter, emotional tone, or context. Without further training, such requirements are about as easy to follow as the esoteric "Love thy neighbor as thyself."

"Psychotherapy is an undefined technique applied to unspecified problems with unpredictable outcomes. For this technique we recommend rigorous training," quips one text (Rainey, 1950). Yet this is exactly correct. It is just because psychotherapists must work in the realm of the vague and ephemeral that they need to apply themselves most diligently to the exacting art of paying attention.

Attentional expertise arises in several traditions. The psychotherapeutic tradition from Freud onward may be seen as a massive undertaking designed to free the submerged, frozen, or fascinated attention of people suffering from unremembered reminiscences. Indeed, the basic attentional training offered therapists today is through personal psychotherapy. And to the degree that it is successful, therapy does render the attention available to what is happening in reality, here and now, so that the truth can be perceived and made the basis for right action.

Attentional techniques are also to be found within the sacred traditions from ancient times onward. Each of the great religions has incorporated a system of meditation with its own procedures, phases, and stages. And each meditative discipline begins with and depends upon techniques designed to tame, direct, and master human attention.

Although the aims and methods of these two traditions are different, psychotherapy and meditation have commonalities too significant to overlook. And although the clinical psychotherapy literature recognizes the need for skillful attentional deployment, only the meditative traditions systematically deliver the skills in any specific way. The following discussion is based on insights and experience derived from the practice of both traditions.

ANALYSIS OF PSYCHOTHERAPEUTIC ATTENTION

All therapists, regardless of their theoretical orientation, must draw upon essentially the same raw sensory data. As a therapist I have what I can

see, hear, or otherwise sense outside me (the client's words, postures, gestures, tones of voice, patterns of breathing, etc.), and what goes on inside
me (my own proprioceptive sensations, feelings, thoughts and associations, hunches and intuitions, etc.). Ordinarily, my attention is simply
invested, either in the outside or the inside world. To borrow from Martin
Buber (1958) and G.I. Gurdjieff (1973), it may be said that attention is
divided between I and Thou, like the double-headed arrow, as shown in
Figure 1.

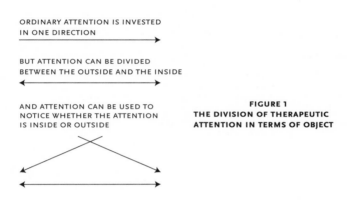

ORDINARY ATTENTION IS INVESTED
IN ONE DIRECTION

BUT ATTENTION CAN BE DIVIDED
BETWEEN THE OUTSIDE AND THE INSIDE

AND ATTENTION CAN BE USED TO
NOTICE WHETHER THE ATTENTION
IS INSIDE OR OUTSIDE

FIGURE 1
THE DIVISION OF THERAPEUTIC
ATTENTION IN TERMS OF OBJECT

The therapist, however, must learn to maintain attention in both directions. Both outer and inner worlds must be sensitively known for therapy
to be real therapy and not just a conversation. I notice, moment after
moment, what catches my attention out there and what it brings up in
me, in here. And what in the mind notices this? The attention is further
divided so that what the Sufis might call a "special organ of perception"
(Shah, 1964, p. 338) is formed in response to the necessity of the mind to
monitor itself. This witnessing, observing consciousness notes when I am
paying attention to you and when to myself. The division of attention
between my own inner process and what the client is doing, saying, etc.,
is a division according to the object of awareness.

But there is another contrast to be made, this time in terms of the *kind
of focus* of attention. Figure 2 shows attentional deployment in the psy-

chotherapeutic situation, this time with the witnessing function at the apex of a triangle in which a continuum of the kind of attentional focus forms the base. The impartial observer witnesses, as if from above, how focused the therapist's attention is, moment by moment. It notices how much investment, cathexis, or fascination there is with a particular element, whether the object be inner or outer. It also notices when the attention is not caught by anything specific but instead is broadly focused on the entire panorama of experience. The base of the triangle illustrates this continuum of focus. It ranges from the narrowly focused attention that we all know when entranced with a work of art, horrified at an accident, or even lost in reading the back of a cereal box, to the freely moving, evenly invested attention that notices the broad display of characteristics that compose the full range of inner and outer experience.

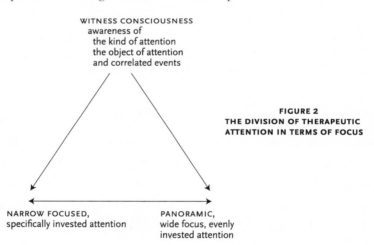

WITNESS CONSCIOUSNESS
awareness of
the kind of attention
the object of attention
and correlated events

FIGURE 2
THE DIVISION OF THERAPEUTIC
ATTENTION IN TERMS OF FOCUS

NARROW FOCUSED,
specifically invested attention

PANORAMIC,
wide focus, evenly
invested attention

As a psychotherapist I have a great deal of raw data with which I can fine-tune attention. There is information on what is going on outside of me and how much I am specifically focused on any particular aspect of it. There is information on what is going on inside of me and to what degree I am focused within. And there is meta-information that tells me how my attention is fluctuating from inside to outside and back again, and how the beam of my awareness is focusing narrowly or opening panoramically. Consciousness plays now on my client, now on myself. Now it is intensely caught by something, now even and free. It is the art and craft of psychotherapy to make full use of information from all these sources, detecting the forms and patterns that exist, and rendering them available for the benefit of the client.

The arrows composing the triangles in Figures 1 and 2 are in motion. At the apex, the witness is aware of awareness. Ordinarily this part of the mind is a noninterfering observer of the fluctuating focus of attention as it flits from outside to inside, from wide to narrow, and back again. With training it can also take control, intentionally directing the attention to focus on something, to maintain steady awareness of something, to stop focusing on something, or to play evenly over a field that encompasses everything without exception. For example, when my attention is fascinated by some portion of the client's story, I might want to stop being primarily content-oriented in order to pay attention to the client's wider spectrum of expression, which might include, for example body language or tone of voice. Or I might find it necessary to withdraw some of my attention to note my own discomfort triggered by the story. With practice comes skill in shifting the focus of awareness.

The two opposites of focused and panoramic attention must be seen as more heuristic than natural categories. These elemental forms of attention, like the pure elements of chemistry, probably exist rarely, if ever, in nature. The one-pointed concentration of the stalking lion or the bandit waiting in ambush lasts only until the prey is overcome or abandoned. The normal mode of attention in sentient beings everywhere seems to be a fluctuating panoramic awareness in which focus narrows upon significant objects and then widens again.

The distinction between narrowly focused attention and panoramic awareness is also made in the traditional division of meditation techniques in Buddhism, in which the novice is typically required to learn to interfere with the normal attentional flux by intentional focus on an object and, when this is more or less mastered, is taught how to expand the awareness to encompass all and everything. Nor is the distinction relevant only to Buddhist meditation practices. It seems to have universal value in understanding the array of attentional technologies within the world's religious traditions. In a review of meditation forms, Goleman (1977) categorizes the more familiar systems according to definitions given in the Buddhist classic, the *Visuddimagga*, into concentration methods (which are narrow-focus techniques involving identification), mindfulness methods (which involve panoramic attention), and methods hybridized from both. In Table 1, which is reproduced from Goleman's book, we can see the basis for the contrast between, say, the *Zikr* of a Helveti dervish who chants the name of Allah in total absorption, and the self-remembering of a Gurdjieff student who undertakes to witness self and environment with impartial awareness.

TABLE 1
AN APPLIED ATTENTIONAL TYPOLOGY OF MEDITATION TECHNIQUES

SYSTEM	TECHNIQUE	TYPE
bhakti	japa	concentration
kabbalah	karvanuh	concentration
sufi	zikr	concentration
raja yoga	samadh	concentration
transcendental meditation	transcendental meditation	concentration
kundalini yoga	siddha yoga	concentration
Tibetan buddhism	vipassana	integrated
Zen	zazen	integrated
Gurdjieff	self-remembering	mindfulness
Krishnamurti	self-knowledge	mindfulness
Theravada	vipassana	integrated

from Goleman 1977

These two practices illustrate the polarity shown in the triangle of therapeutic attention, where the base of the triangle represents the continuum ranging from narrow-/to wide-focus attention. The similarities that exist between the kinds of attention needed by therapists and those employed in meditation training appear to fit this model, at least in part. There have been other, more elaborate classifications of attentional processes (Naranjo & Ornstein, 1971; Speeth, 1978), but for our present purposes the ancient Buddhist contrast between narrow- and wide-beam attention will do nicely. Following the Buddhist tradition, we will begin with a consideration of the narrow-beam, tightly focused practices often described as concentration practices.

CONCENTRATION

Concentration is the fixation of attention on something to the exclusion of everything else. Typically, though not exclusively, the meditator is instructed to diligently require the wandering mind to become wholly occupied with one object, perhaps a *kasina*—a distinct colorful form like a light blue disk on a white background, or the reflection of the moon in a jar of water—or more commonly, the breath. In the Hindu practice of *trataka,* the meditator gazes one-pointedly at a candle flame until the eyes tear. In siddha yoga, the practice of *guru bhave* entails intentional identification with the spiritual teacher. The meditator systematically identifies each part of the body with the corresponding part of the guru's body: "This is my guru's right foot, this is my guru's left foot, this is my guru's right leg, this is my guru's left leg," etc. And all the religious traditions make use of concentration upon sacred syllables and formulas, from the "*Om mani padme hum*" and myriad other mantras of Tibetan Buddhism to the prayer of the heart, "Lord Jesus Christ, have mercy upon me, a sinner!"

All these practices involve the effort to limit the attentional focus and keep the mind steady upon this chosen object. Regardless of their religious affiliation, practitioners of such exercises report similar experiences when the attention is successfully focused in a steady way. In some forms of Sufism, there is an effort to attend only to God, regardless of whatever else impinges, so that, as Rumi sings, "Thou and I, with no 'Thou' or 'I' shall become one through our tasting" (in the experience of *Jana,* complete absorption with God). This state of being is exemplified in this story of Rumi's, as retold by Shah (1968, p. 189).

The Beloved

One went to the door of the Beloved and knocked. A voice asked: "Who is there?" He answered: "It is I." The voice said: "There is no room here for me and thee." The door was shut.

After a year of solitude and deprivation this man returned to the door of the Beloved. He knocked. A voice from within asked: "Who is there?" The man said: "It is Thou." The door was opened for him.

In the Tibetan tradition there is a teaching story that illustrates the relationship between narrowly focused, steady attention and identification. As is so often true with the Tibetans, it is somewhat more earthy and less ethereal than the Persian mysticism so poetically transmitted by Rumi. A Tibetan teacher, so the story goes, gives his disciple the assignment to go to the cowshed and meditate upon a bull. The student goes dutifully to the barn every day to contemplate the animal. After some period of time the teacher comes for a progress check. The student reports that his attention is wavering only a little now. "Good," says the teacher, "please continue!" After another while, the student reports that his attention is fully on the bull and nothing else, all the time. The teacher prescribes still more concentration. Finally, after many, many moons, the teacher comes for the usual ritual of evaluation. He calls through the cowshed door, asking about the student's progress in meditation. The only answer is a loud bull snort and a "Moo." Now the student has attained.

We have all experienced narrowly focused and concentrated attention when it is elicited by a strong enough pull from some aspect of the environment. When a movie is sufficiently engaging we forget to eat popcorn, even lose the sense of being in a theater. Subjects under hypnosis become oblivious to background stimuli when entering trance. Those newly in love can barely think of anything else, so fascinated is the attention upon one object. It is fundamental in developmental psychology that children learn early to attend to their primary caretaker, and in fact, the orientation to the caretaker seems to entail imitative identification.

Identification is a primitive and immediate attentional focus, familiar to anyone who has ever become caught up with the feelings of a character in a movie or play. Information is perceived at least in part by the process similar to that of concentrative, narrow-focus meditations, but different from them in being involuntary, temporary, effortless, and usually unconscious. For example, in the therapeutic situation, the therapist could learn what the client is feeling, at least in part, by experiencing the changes occurring within his or her own experience while performing an "imitative identification" with that client. But how is this done *voluntarily*, and not because the object is fascinating, i.e., due to our conditioning? One analyst (Greenson, 1967) describes a method thus:

Empathy means to share, to experience the feelings of another human being. One partakes of the quality of the feelings, and not the quantity. Its motive, in psychoanalysis, is to gain understanding; it is not used for vicarious pleasure. It is essentially a pre-conscious phenomenon; it can be consciously instigated or interrupted; and it can occur silently and automatically, oscillating with other forms of relating with other people. The essential mechanism is a partial and temporary identification with the patient on the basis of a working model of the patient within the analyst, which he has constructed from his sum of experience with the patient.

By shifting the working model of the patient into the foreground, and pushing all that is peculiarly or uniquely me into the background, I have let the patient's words and feelings enter this part of me. The model reacts with ideas, feelings, memories, or fantasies, etc.

Voluntary Control of Attention

Here we have a theorist of technique who explicitly employs empathy, consisting of identification that can be "consciously instigated or interrupted," implying a level of skill that, anyone who has seriously attempted to sustain a meditative focus to the point of identification will attest, is possible only with repeated, motivated efforts. It is in *voluntarily* instigating and interrupting this attentional activity that the methods and techniques of concentrative meditation might be most applicable for the psychotherapist. As for the involuntary sort of identification, this can be expected to arise from fascinating immediacies or from the therapist's countertransference (i.e. biases due to unfinished psychological business in the therapist's personal past; for a range of psychoanalytic explanations of identification in the countertransference, see Fliess, 1942; Fliess, 1952; Spitz, 1956; Reich, 1960; Kernberg, 1975).

Greenson indicates that in order to empathize one must hold the image or model of the other in the foreground, pushing what is oneself into the background. Presumably this is done in order that the identification that forms the basis for empathy can take place. By implication his method also suggests another key to the voluntary control of attention, a powerful method well known to masters of meditation. If I make what is "peculiarly me" foreground, the identification will stop. And what is uniquely me? My proprioceptive experience, certainly, and my thoughts and feelings and sense impressions. This is the fundamental practice given in the teaching of Gurdjieff, who saw the involuntary state of identification as the prison of mankind (Speeth, 1976). A student of Gurdjieff described this practice as follows:

Whether or not it be active in me, the possibility is given me to become aware, at certain moments, of my own presence: I, here, now. This, when I experience it, is accompanied by a strangely familiar taste, a particular sensation that might be called 'genuinely' subjective. It is quite simply, "I. I recognize myself. I remember myself. I" (Tracol, 1968).

Thus the interruption of identification by the therapist when it is no longer appropriate for empathy, or when it is contributing to therapeutic blocks because it is part of a counteridentification, can be effected by the practice of self-remembering, a particular form of attention in the family of mindfulness practices.

In therapy it is vitally important to get a taste of the client's experience, to know as if from the inside what it is like to live that life. Robert Heinlein (1961) coined a new verb for it: to *grok*. Grokking is a basic human way of knowing that is immediate, noncognitive, and deeply identified. Grokking is the sort of identification with another in which we temporarily match their inner experience. Upon this base, true empathy can be built. But grokking can be involuntary when the attention is focused narrowly and steadily because of patterns of countertransference. In this situation we have a potentially dangerous analog to concentrative meditation, which, like concentrative meditation, can entail certain risks.

It is widely known in the various meditation systems that fixed attention techniques are the most risky. In putting someone or something in the foreground while putting all that is peculiarly me in the background, and while so doing limiting the natural fluctuation of attention, I may lose touch with my own sense of self. I may become ungrounded, unbalanced, without the firm foundation of proprioception and inner mental perception that is a figured base in ordinary life. Concentration methods are thus ecstatogenic, quickly and reliably producing altered states of awareness, feelings of oceanic union, and other novel experiences that may be seized upon for their presumed significance by unbalanced minds. They may account for the majority of meditation casualties.

Countertransference may pin the therapist's attention upon one client in a manner not dissimilar to these concentrative meditations, and then similar phenomena of identification may occur, giving rise to the strange exhaustion that haunts so many people helpers, an occupational hazard currently known as "burnout." After all, therapists not only grok, but they have to grok fellow humans who are anguished, defeated, and often at their wits' end, or at least, certainly not at their best. Thus therapists are doubly at risk: they stand a chance of losing a feeling of being securely grounded in their own being, and they are in danger of unknowingly bearing the heavy burdens of many others who are presumably less fortunate than they in terms of the sheer weight of suffering in their lives. Should countertransference glue their attention, they will be in the position of the Tibetan novice with the bull, but with an entirely different conscious intent, and with success being the limited identification that is a normal part of human empathy, not a union without boundaries.

Mastering identification in psychotherapy involves three attentional skills. First, the therapist must be able to hold the attention steady on one object so that identification can ensue, not only when transference dictates, but voluntarily. Second, the therapist must be able to withdraw from a concentrated focus at will, so that if for some reason the attention has become fixed in an inappropriate way, it can be redirected or opened up. And third, the therapist needs the ability to let the attentional focus wax and wane without interference. This is the function of witness consciousness. It is most important technically because of the abundance of information it provides.

PANORAMIC ATTENTION

One-pointed attention—in which there is no felt difference between the observer and the observed, in which boundaries vanish into confluence and separate individualities blend in communion—gives mystical meaning to some, and, as an ingredient in the countertransference, problems of therapeutic effectiveness to others. Panoramic attention, in which awareness is invested evenly in all things, moment after moment, has no less importance or relevance for the therapeutic setting, but adds quite another flavor. There is a feeling of impartiality, of spaciousness, of breadth of vision. One is mindful of whatever is the case, moment by moment. The idea is not to be fascinated or fixed upon any one thing, but to allow the attention to be flexible and to stay with whatever is in the field of perception. There is no possibility of disturbance or distraction in this form of meditation because there is no attempt made to keep any object in the foreground, neither is there anything to oppose. Awareness is all-encompassing. As the ancient *Salayatana Vagga Samyutta* states:

> Bikkhus [monks], the all is to be fully known. What all is to be fully known? The eye is to be fully known, visual objects are to be fully known, eye-consciousness is to be fully known, eye contact is to be fully known, that weal or woe or neutral state experienced, which arises owing *to* eye contact—that also is to be fully known. Ear is to be fully known...nose...scent...tongue...savors...body is to be fully known, tangibles are to be fully known, mind is to be fully known. (Sayadaw, 1972).

The mind's capacity to register everything impinging upon it is brought into play in this practice. Attention is panoramic. The avoidance of selection of any one object makes it the antithesis of the practices which focus maximally. Achieving nonselective, nonpreferential attention is an art in itself. Nyanaponika Thera, the great contemporary Theravadan master, put it this way:

> Bare attention consists in the bare and exact registering of the object. It is not as easy a task as it may appear, since it is not what we normally do,

except when engaged in disinterested investigation. Normally man is not concerned with disinterested knowledge of "things as they truly are" but with "handling" them and judging them from the viewpoint of his self-interest, which may be wide or narrow, noble or low. He tacks labels to the things which form his physical and mental universe, and these labels mostly show clearly the impress of his self-interest and his limited vision. It is such an assemblage of labels in which he generally lives and which determines his actions and reactions. Hence the attitude of bare attention—bare of labels—will open a man to a new world (Nyanyaponika Thera, 1962).

This new world of things as they actually are is discovered through the cultivation of "choiceless awareness." This trend is rare in other religions but runs through Buddhism like a red thread connecting the original Buddhism of the Theravadan or Southern school with the continuous awareness practice of *shikan taza* in Soto Zen and even the nonpractice that is called *mahamudra* at the pinnacle of Tibetan Buddhism (Chang, 1963).

Zen meditation practice is typically a composite and counterpoint of concentrative and panoramic attention, a hybrid form. One of its most eloquent proponents, Suzuki Roshi, described the process of renouncing the tendency to maneuver an object into the foreground:

> When you are practicing zazen meditation, do not try to stop your thinking. Let it stop by itself. If something comes into your mind, let it come in and let it go out. It will not stay long. When you try to stop your thinking, it means you are bothered by it. Do not be bothered by anything. It appears that something comes from outside your mind, but actually it is only the waves of your mind, and if you are not bothered by the waves, gradually they will become calmer and calmer.... Many sensations come, many thoughts or images arise, but they are just waves from your own mind.... If you leave your mind as it is, it will become calm. This mind is called big mind (Suzuki, 1970).

Freud's "basic rule" of free association is to some degree a similar practice. Compare this version with Buddhist mindfulness.

> For the purpose of self-observation with concentrated attention it is advantageous that the patient should take up a restful position and close his eyes. He must be explicitly instructed to renounce all criticism of the thought formations which he may perceive. He must also be told that the success of the psychoanalysis depends upon his noting and communicating everything that passes through his mind, and that he must not allow himself to suppress one idea because it seems to him unimportant or irrelevant to the subject, or another because it seems nonsensical. He must preserve an absolute impartiality in respect to his ideas (Freud, 1900).

Freud described the inner work of free association as the twofold effort of paying attention to the process and content of the mind and simultaneously of eliminating all criticism or censorship of what arises. The requirement for lack of censorship makes this practice akin to Buddhist mindfulness. Of course, the psychoanalytic process, especially in its emphasis on communicating to the analyst, is directed toward different ends. It is expressive and interpersonal. There is a listener, the therapist. This is in contrast to mindfulness meditation where the practice is silent, often solitary, and intrapersonal.

Freud precisely defined how this method of listening was to take place, instructing the therapist that the appropriate attentional gesture simply consists

> in making no effort to concentrate the attention on anything in particular, and in maintaining in regard to all that one hears the same measure of calm, quiet attentiveness of "evenly hovering attention," as I once before described it. In this way a strain which could not be kept up for

several hours daily and a danger inseparable from deliberate attentiveness are avoided. For as soon as the attention is deliberately concentrated in a certain degree, one begins to select from the material before one; one point will be fixed in the mind with particular clearness and some other consequently disregarded, and in this selection one's expectations and one's inclinations will be followed. This is just what must not be done, however; if one's expectations are followed in this selection, there is a danger of never finding anything but what is already known, and if one follows one's inclinations, anything which is to be perceived will most certainly be falsified (Freud, 1900).

Panoramic attention, floating free of preconceptions and heeding everything equally, is the therapist's counterpart of the patient's free association of thought. Ideally, in analysis both participants are flexibly and spontaneously noting whatever is occurring to them; one is expressive, the other receptive.

Freud blithely remarked in the first chapter of *The Interpretation of Dreams* that most patients learned how to follow the basic rule for free association the first time it was taught them. He had more than three decades of practice to modify this view, for, as everyone who has attempted to follow his or her own mind knows, there may be distractions and obstacles which can be formidable. Although he admitted that he himself was quite expert at panoramic inner awareness of the kind we have been describing, Freud was astonished and disappointed to realize that others were not as immediately adept. He began to recommend a personal analysis for all practitioners of the psychoanalytic art in order that they might develop the ability to attend evenly and appropriately to patients. This is more obvious to therapists today who learn that widened attentiveness exists to the degree that there is no competing personal agenda (i.e., countertransference) within the therapist to capture his or her attention. Suppose, for example, that the therapist is concerned and worried about whether he or she is a good enough person, intelligent enough, or whether things are happening according to a textbook sequence. Such concerns are distracting and, at the very least, preclude evenly hovering, poised attention.

In order to relax the focus, neither directing the mind toward a goal nor grasping at clues to solve a mystery, the therapist must at least temporarily suspend the effects of the inner judge and critic. As a situation inviting the maximum creativity in patient and therapist alike, classical psychoanalysis can be seen as two people practicing procedures which are similar, in part, to mindfulness. Here, each sensitively notices whatever is taking place, moment by moment. The client follows the basic rule of free association of thought, while the analyst "oscillates between observer and participant" (Reik, 1948); that is, between panoramic and concentrated awareness, ever mindful of where and how the attention is. Glancing back at Figure 2, it will now be clear that this is what is schematized.

There has been very little mention of attention in psychotherapy outside of the psychoanalytic tradition, although the Gestaltists are a notable exception. Anyone experienced in mindfulness meditation practices will easily recognize some counterparts in the Gestalt awareness exercises, for example, the continuum of awareness. One set of instructions from an early work is given here.

(1) Maintain your sense of actuality—the sense that your awareness exists now and here. (2) Try to realize that you are living the experience; acting it, observing it, suffering it, resisting it. (3) Attend to and follow up all experiences, the "internal" as well as the "external," the abstract as well as the concrete, those that tend toward the past as well as those that tend toward the future, those that you "wish," those that you "ought," those that simply "are," those that you deliberately produce and those that seem to occur spontaneously. (4) With regard to every experience without exception, verbalize: "Now I am aware that ..." (Perls, Hefferline & Goodman, 1951).

That this exercise has elements which appear to parallel the mindfulness family of meditation practices is not surprising since Perls had not only the psychoanalytic lineage of Freud (Reich was his therapist), but sat Zazen meditation as well.

WITNESS CONSCIOUSNESS

If the therapist is to know when and how attention is being used, a certain amount of awareness must be withdrawn from the therapeutic interaction to watch the process. This is far from the more archaic and confluent forms of perception. As Nietzsche (1885) knew, "The thou is older than the I," which might be further translated as, we are interested in the outside world before we are interested in ourselves. The act of observing our inner world is less natural, more effortful and convoluted. When "The I observes the *Me*," as William James (1927) expressed it, human awareness is turned upon itself and psychological self-study begins.

In real psychotherapy, as opposed to a sympathetic conversation that merely looks and sounds like psychotherapy, the therapist sustains the inner stance of impartial observation, as if from outside the interaction, or above. While allowing most of the attention to play freely upon what the client is saying and doing, and what associations I have to it, how interested I am and how empathetic, I reserve just a little attention to notice all this flux. I allow my attention to play freely or to zoom into deep identification, yet I sustain a bit of myself above it. When I am immersed I watch my almost total immersion; when I am engaged in evenly hovering attention I watch that.

The ability to sustain such attention is acquired by skilled efforts of will, according to James (1927, p. 95), and "the longer one does attend to a topic the more mastery of it one has. And the faculty of bringing back a wandering attention over and over again is the very root of judgment, character, and will. No one is *compos sui* if he have it not. An education which should improve this faculty would be *the* education *par excellence*."

THERAPEUTIC ATTENTION APPLIED

We have now had an introduction to concentrated, focused attention; panoramic mindfulness; and the sustained impartial witnessing of attentional flux that observes the play of consciousness as if from the zenith. We can therefore consider problems of using these forms of attention in actual practice.

Concentrating on what is outside is the basis of identification; being mindful of what is outside is panoramic attention to outside events. In order to use the capacity for identification to its fullest extent, the therapist must be willing to participate deeply in the experience of another human being. Putting oneself in another person's shoes involves the ability to permit confluence to happen and in so doing to be temporarily absorbed, allowing all that is peculiarly me to recede into the background.

Certainly the individual pattern of character and level of personality organization will affect the depth of identification a therapist can experience. But a more serious impediment can be an insufficient capacity for regression. In order to allow regression into archaic forms of thinking and feeling, one must feel confident in domains beneath the rational strata of the mind. Perhaps only good mothering can provide a person with the wherewithal to make the dive into primary process, or perhaps courageous contact with deep truths about oneself is quite enough. In any case, without the ability to tolerate regression, protective mechanisms within the psyche may effectively prevent full empathy.

Those who are unable to break the bond of identification may be worn down by the burdens of others, losing effectiveness, sensitivity, and zest. Part of the problem may be the therapist's superego that dictates a caring and concerned attitude at all times and implies that it is superficial, overtechnical, or downright mean to voluntarily redirect one's attention toward one's inner world. The requirement so often found in humanistically oriented programs that the therapist must maintain a warm, caring stance may cause a reverse reaction. Knowing how to voluntarily connect or withdraw emotionally can provide the self-pacing skill necessary to go deep with another, and most particularly with another who suffers.

To attend fully to what is outside in a mindful, nonidentified way, one must, first of all, be relatively aware of one's own theoretical admonitions. Although some theoretical orientation is necessary to organize impressions and data, the therapist has to be sufficiently free from the compulsions of theory so that all information can be considered more or less equally. Otherwise, attention may be caught by what *should* be relevant to the problem and much goes by unnoticed. To believe unreservedly in the truth of a theory is to risk discovering exactly or approximately what one expected. For the client, the danger lies in detecting and producing just what a person who is seen as an authority (the therapist) seems to want. This is a commonly observed effect in psychotherapy: Freudian analysts report that their analysands have dreams about caves and projectiles; Jungians report that *theirs* produce dreams about wise old women and mandalas. Reinforcement theory would possibly account for the phenomenon, since a little "uh huh" or other minor affirmative expression demonstrably increases the probability of any word or behavior on which it is contingent (Greenspoon, 1955). The Freudian may hear one key word, the Jungian another—and both show, by the subtlest changes in posture, breathing, or facial expression that they are especially interested. Clearly, unassimilated preconceptions are a hindrance in the use of attention in clinical work.

The notion of maintaining complementariness in the relationship between therapist and client is relevant here. As Haley (1963) pointed out, it is necessary for effective therapy that the therapist be in an emotionally independent position with respect to the client. Certainly maintaining an observing, open attention is prerequisite to a complementary relationship. Further, maintaining even attention regardless of content permits the client to express negativities, talk about taboo issues, and report unpleasant reactions to the therapeutic situation that would be hidden if the therapist showed by the subtlest of reinforcing communications that these topics were hurtful or unwelcome. That the therapist can allow the client great freedom of expression is illustrated by the case of Pietro, presented by Erickson (Erickson & Rossi, 1979), who permits and encourages months of twice-weekly insults from a client, his graceful acceptance finally effecting a successful therapeutic outcome. Such skill in letting the attention hover evenly while being the object of negative (or positive) transference reactions is attained not through heroic acts of self-control, but through an understanding of the nature of transference and resistance in the human predicament.

Attending to What Is Inside

To become deeply absorbed with the contents of my own mind I must have considerable self-acceptance. In a situation where I am being paid to attend to another, how can I in good faith attend to myself? Of course, what is actually called for in the therapeutic situation is sensitive attention to everything, including deep feelings that arise in the therapist. Paying attention to myself, even to the degree of being immersed for a while in my own inner process, involves a tolerance for being in the foreground. This may prove difficult because of the therapist's superego described earlier, and it may also be difficult because of characterological biases requiring the therapist to stay in the background.

Related to the issue of allowing myself to feel strongly while functioning as a therapist is the question of whether and how these feelings are manifested. Effective therapy requires both the ability to feel deeply and give those feelings no expression at all, as well as the ability to feel deeply and express it genuinely and spontaneously. In fact, Rogers (1951) and others have recommended theater training for therapists, who need to develop these subtle skills.

But not all inner attention is of this concentrative, specifically focused kind. To be mindful of inner process without becoming immersed in any one aspect, the therapist must be able to acknowledge whatever arises in the mind without editing, judging, or getting unduly alarmed. In actual practice, an appropriate method might be to hold myself in unconditional positive regard, i.e., truly without conditions, so that whatever arises from the depths of me will not jeopardize my sense of worth and goodness. This necessarily applies to anything: memories of forbidden acts and ideas, trivial tunes, fragments of experience that might better be forgotten, sexual, aggressive, or unethical fantasies, private associations that are shocking—anything. To the degree self-acceptance is present, attention can range freely over the contents of the mind, allowing whatever is there to bubble up in reaction to the ever-changing situation. Within those bubbles are very often found the keys to the mysteries human beings bring to therapy. All depth psychotherapy is presumably conducted with the ideal of some sort of unconditional positive regard for the client, but what is not often said is that the therapist's unconditional positive regard for his or her own inner life is a wholesome and necessary component of therapy as well.

ATTENDING TO THE KIND OF ATTENTION BEING USED

In order to correctly perceive just how my attention is being used at any moment, I must, first of all, be able to tell the difference between the inner sensation of focused, invested attention and that of panoramic, impartial attention. I must have experienced both to do this. And I must have comprehended what was happening when I did. With regard to attending to my attention when it is concentrated, there is a seeming paradox. How can I watch myself when I am totally absorbed in something about myself or my client? The answer is that I cannot. I have, therefore, at least two choices: I can renounce full investment, retaining just enough consciousness to notice how and with what I am identified, or I can renounce knowing exactly what is happening during intense emotional investment, "coming to" again and realizing in retrospect that for a moment I had been "swept away." Personal preferences in this matter will probably be based on each individual's character structure. On the other hand, noticing when I am using panoramic, evenly hovering attention is much easier. There is no pull of fascination to work against the act of self-observation. I simply experience my mind softly registering whatever occurs, within and without.

To tolerate full awareness of my degree of focus or freedom of attention, I must be relatively independent of self-criticism. When my attention is deeply invested, or as soon as I realize that it was, then there is no point in placing a value judgment on that event, even though parents, professors, supervisors, or gurus might disapprove of that identification at that time. More is to be learned by bare attention. In the same way, it will be more helpful to my client and myself when I notice that my attention is wandering inadvertently if I simply note the fact and do not add evaluation to the event.

The therapist who is thoroughly conversant with both narrow-focus and panoramic modes of attention will be able to move from one to the other at will—a skill required of every psychoanalyst who practices according to Freud's indications, but equally important for other therapists as well. It is here that meditation practice can be relevant, although of course there is a psychodynamic aspect too. To be willing to withdraw a little attention from what I am doing and thinking to monitor the process, I must have somehow reduced the need to be immersed in my life experience. I must have lost some of the addiction to the thrills of identification, and awakened a little from the dream in which most of life is conducted.

REFERENCES

Buber, M. *I and Thou.* New York: Scribners, 1958.

Chang, G. *Teachings of Tibetan yoga.* New Hyde Park, N.Y.: University Books, 1963.

Erickson, M. & Rossi, E. *Hypnotherapy.* New York: Wiley, 1979.

Fliess, R. "The metapsychology of the analyst." *Psychoanal. Quart.,* 1942, 11: 211–27.

Fliess, R. "Countertransferences and counteridentification." *J. Am. Psychoanal. Assoc.,* 1952, 1: 268–84.

Freud, S. *The interpretation of dreams.* (1900) Standard Edition. London: Hogarth Press, 1955.

Goleman, D. *The varieties of the meditative experience.* New York: Irvington, 1977.

Greenson, R. *The technique and practice of psychoanalysis.* New York: Intl. Universities Press, 1967.

Greenspoon, J. "The reinforcing effects of two spoken sounds on the frequency of two responses." *Amer. J. Psychol.* 1955, 68: 409–16.

Gurdjieff, G. *Views from the real world: Early talks with Gurdjieff.* New York: Dutton, 1973.

Haley, J. *Strategies of psychotherapy.* New York: Grune & Stratton, 1963.

Heinlein, R. *Stranger in a strange land.* New York: Putnam, 1961.

James, W. *Principles of psychology.* New York: Henry Holt, 1927.

Kernberg, O. *Borderline conditions and pathological narcissism.* New York: Aronson, 1975.

Naranjo, C. & Ornstein, R. *On the psychology of meditation.* New York: Viking, 1971.

Nietzsche F. *Thus spoke Zarathustra.* (1885) New York: Penguin, 1961.

Nyanyaponika Thera. *The heart of Buddhist meditation.* New York: Weiser, 1962.

Perls, F., Hefferline, R. & Goodman, P. *Gestalt therapy.* New York: Julian Press, 1951.

Rainey, C. (Ed.). *Training in clinical psychology.* New York: Prentice Hall, 1950.

Reich. A. "Further remarks on countertransference." *Mt. J. Psychoanal.,* 1960, 41: 389–395.

Reik. T. *Listening with the third ear.* New York: Grove Press, 1948.

Rogers, C. *Client-centered Therapy.* Boston: Houghton Mifflin, 1951.

Sayadaw, M. *Practical Insight Meditation* (Series 2). San Francisco: Unity Press 1972.

Shah, I. *The Sufis.* Garden City, N.Y.: Doubleday, 1964.

Shah, I. *The Way of the Sufi.* London: Jonathan Cape, 1968.

Speeth, K. *The Gurdjieff Work.* Berkeley: And/Or Press, 1976.

Speeth, K. On the healing potential of meditation. In *The Holistic Health Handbook (Edward Bauman, ed.).* Berkeley: And/Or Press, 1978.

Spitz, R. "Countertransference: Comments on its varying role in the analytic situation." *J. Am. Psychoanal. Assoc.,* 1956, 4: 256–65.

Suzuki, S.D. *Zen Mind, Beginner's Mind.* New York: Weatherhill, 1970.

Tracol, H. *George Ivanovitch Gurdjieff: Man's awakening and the practice of remembering oneself.* Bray, Ireland: Guild Press, 1968.

PART TWO

The Practice of Listening

All things, animate and inanimate,
have within them, a spirit dimension.
They communicate in that dimension to those who can listen.
~ Jerome Bernstein

*A*ny attempt to improve our listening skills must find some effective way to deal with what I call the "Central Impediment." The Central Impediment arises from the fact that human beings speak at an average rate of 250 words per minute—and easily process speech at speeds more than triple that rate. How do we manage our minds during this time lag? Learning to work with this Central Impediment makes a tremendous difference in our ability to listen skillfully. In the following article, excerpted from their book How Can I Help?, Ram Dass and Paul Gorman offer a broad perspective on the nature of the listening mind. Out of their discussion emerges the possibility for training the mind to become calm, sharply concentrated, intuitive, and widely aware—and thus able to creatively kindle the space created by the Central Impediment. A practice results, as the authors point out, that produces an intimacy of attention that can deeply affect our lives.

The Listening Mind

Ram Dass and Paul Gorman

MUCH OF OUR CAPACITY to help another person depends upon our state of mind. Sometimes our minds are so scattered, confused, depressed, or agitated, we can hardly get out of bed. At other times we're clear, alert, and receptive; we feel ready, even eager, to respond generously to the needs of others. Most of the time it's really not one extreme or the other. Our minds are…well…they're just our minds. Like old cars, type-writers, or appliances, we put up with their idiosyncrasies with a shrug. What can we do about it anyway?

Perhaps we settle for too little. Our mind, after all, is potentially our most powerful tool. With it we have harnessed fire, devised technology, extended our ability to grow and process food, developed ways to protect ourselves from the elements, discovered means to cure illness and extend our life span.

Our mind is not only the source of ideas, a tool for gathering data, an instrument of training and technique, or a repository of experience and memory. Because the mind's capacity to think is so brilliant, we tend to be dazzled by it and fail to notice other attributes and functions. There is more to the mind than reason alone. There is awareness itself and what we sometimes think of as the deeper qualities of mind. Most of us know how supportive it is merely to be in the presence of a mind that is open, quiet, playful, receptive, or reflective. These attributes are themselves helpful. Moreover, there is something we frequently experience—perhaps we can call it intuitive awareness—that links us most intimately to the universe and, in allegiance with the heart, binds us together in generosity and compassion. Often it leaps to vision and knowledge instantaneously. "My understanding of the fundamental laws of the universe," said Albert Einstein, "did not come out of my rational mind."

This resource of awareness can give us access to deeper power, power to help and heal.

I had been meditating for a number of years. My progress, in terms of increased concentration and a more peaceful, quiet quality in my mind, was noticeable, though not dramatic. In the ancient texts I'd read accounts of monks who through meditation had gained great powers, and I kept wondering if the stories were true.

Then, I visited the wife of the former American ambassador in Thailand, and she told me about a monk who had built a monastery in which heroin and opium addicts were cured in ten days…for fifteen dollars. These kinds of statistics are unheard of in the West. Possibly this was one of those monks with the meditation powers. I prevailed on her to take me to meet him.

The monk had previously been a Thai "narc," something like our federal drug enforcement agency. He had an aunt who I was told was a Buddhist saint, whatever that means. One day she apparently said to him, while he was still a narc, "What are you doing? If you don't watch out you're going to end up killing people in this job. Why don't you help these people instead of hurting them?" He said that he didn't know how. She apparently told him to clean up his act and she'd show him.

So he left government service and became a monk. Now the Buddhist monks in Thailand are part of the Theravadin tradition which requires very severe renunciation in order to purify your mind so that you can do deep meditation. There are some 218 prohibitions, all of which he adopted.

Then he even added ten more on his own, such as never driving in automobiles. This meant that when he had business in Bangkok, about a hundred and fifty miles away, he'd just pick up his walking stick and start walking.

This rigorous training prepared him to do very intensive meditation practice which allowed him to tune to the deeper and more powerful parts of his mind. When his aunt felt he was ready, she instructed him in the preparation of an herbal diuretic which she instructed him to give to the addicts, and he started his monastery.

When we met him, my most immediate reaction was that I was shaking hands with an oak tree. His presence was immensely powerful and solid. He had us shown through the monastery where some three hundred addicts were undergoing treatment.

You could really see who was which. The first-day arrivals all looked like strung-out junkies. They were in one room. Then, further on, by the time they had been there for four days you could really see a change. And by eight days they seemed cheerful, were bumming cigarettes from me, and seemed really friendly—not particularly like addicts at all. And then after ten days they were gone. And their statistics showed 70 percent remained free of addiction afterwards. Amazing.

When I interviewed the monk, I asked him, "How do you do it?" He said, "Well, it's simple. I tell them that they can only come for ten days and they may never come again, and that the cure will work." I asked him if a lot of religious indoctrination was included in the ten-day program. "No," he said, "none of that. These people aren't suitable for that." I had heard that many drug experts, media people, and even some congressmen had come from the West, but that none of them could figure out why what he did worked. The herbal brew clearly wasn't the whole ballgame. As I hung out with him longer I began to realize that his mind was so centered and one-pointed that his being was stronger than their addiction. Somehow he conveyed to those addicts a sense of their nonaddiction that was stronger than their addiction. And I saw that his commitment was so total, that he wasn't just someone using a skill. He had died into his work. He was the cure.

This was the example I had been looking for. Just being with him I could feel the extraordinary quality of his mind. Meeting him reassured me that the ancient stories were probably true. I returned to meditation with renewed vigor.

⌒

Most of us are not really ready to become renunciates in order to develop the concentration and quality of awareness necessary to help others at such an extraordinary level. But if we are prepared to investigate our minds even a little bit, we start a process that can improve our effectiveness in life, and therefore in helping as well. If we are willing to examine the agitation of our own minds and look just beyond it, we quite readily find entry into rooms that hold surprising possibilities: a greater inner calm, sharper concentration, deeper intuitive understanding, and an enhanced ability to hear one another's hearts. Such an inquiry turns out to be critical in the work of helping others.

The phone rings. We turn from the checkbook we were balancing to answer. It's someone seeking counsel. Even as the person begins to speak, our minds are conflicted. We don't quite want to leave that column of figures unadded, and yet we know that we have to let go of our bookkeeping to listen carefully to the problem.

The voice on the other end tries to find words to describe suffering: "I'm just feeling so…it's like I…I really don't know, but…." Painstaking work. But sometimes even as it starts, our mind may begin to wander. "This is going to be a tough one…. Am I up to this?… What about dinner? I'd better circle that place where I think the bank screwed up." At a certain stage, personal judgments may start competing for attention. "He's really romanticizing it a lot…. He ought to be done with this one by now.

He's not hearing what I mean." We may get a little lost in evaluating—"Is it working? Am I helping?" Or we could as easily turn the evaluation on ourselves—"I don't care that much. I really don't like him."

Sometimes we catch ourselves in distraction and rejoin the person on the other end of the phone. Now it's better. Something's beginning to happen. Then we take an intentionally audible in-breath—we've got something helpful to say—but the signal goes by; he keeps right on talking. Off goes the mind to utterly unrelated topics: "Call Dad.... That picture on the wall is crooked.... I'm tired.... I have to feed the cat."

This mental chatter goes on and off. Sometimes we really get lost, and by the time we're back, we realize we've missed a key point, and it's too late to ask for it to be repeated. At other times we can take quick note of our reactions and still stay with it. Perhaps we just let it all run off; it's not something we even notice—it fades into the background like film-score music we're hardly aware is there.

Then the call is over. The voice on the other end says, "Thank you." We reply, "You're welcome." But how welcome was he? How much room did the mind give him? How much did we really hear? How much did he *feel* heard? Maybe we sit back in the chair and reflect on that for a moment. Or perhaps we get up, walk to the kitchen, and savor the "thank you" along with a sandwich. Perhaps we simply turn back to the checkbook.

Reckoning, judging, evaluating, leaping in, taking it personally, being bored—the helping act has any number of invitations to reactiveness and distraction. Partly we are agitated because we so intensely want to help. After all, someone's in pain. We care. So part of the time we are listening, but we may also be using our minds to try to solve the problem. There's a pull to be efficient, to look for some kind of resolution. We reach for certain familiar models or approaches. In order to be helpful, our analytic mind must stay on top of it all.

So we jump between listening and judging. But in our zeal to help, we may increase the distance between the person and our own consciousness.

We find ourselves primarily in our own thoughts, not *with* another person. Not only are we listening less, but the concepts our mind is coming up with start to act as a screen that preselects information. One thought rules out another.

One of the results of all this mental activity is that there's less room to meet, less room for a new truth to emerge, less room to let things simply be revealed in "their own good time." The mind tries to do too many things at once. It's difficult to know which mental vectors are useful and which are distractions, static on the line, bad connections.

This agitation and reactiveness should be no surprise to most of us. We have come to expect and accept this state except in rare situations. Yet it need not be that way.

A big, tough samurai once went to see a little monk. "Monk," he said, in a voice accustomed to instant obedience, "Teach me about heaven and hell!"

The monk looked up at this mighty warrior and replied with utter disdain, "Teach you about heaven and hell? I couldn't teach you about anything. You're dirty. You smell. Your blade is rusty. You're a disgrace, an embarrassment to the samurai class. Get out of my sight. I can't stand you."

The samurai was furious. He shook, got all red in the face, was speechless with rage. He pulled out his sword and raised it above him, preparing to slay the monk.

"That's hell," said the monk softly.

The samurai was overwhelmed. The compassion and surrender of this little man who had offered his life to give this teaching to show him hell! He slowly put down his sword, filled with gratitude, and suddenly peaceful.

"And that's heaven," said the monk softly.

If we continue to observe our mind over time, we notice that it's not always distracted and busy. For all of us, there are times when our minds become concentrated, sharp and clear. Perhaps we are doing a crossword puzzle, playing a video game, reading a mystery story, cleaning house, or cooking. For some, it's the simple tasks that engage us in ways that allow our mind to be composed and focused; for others, it's complex problem-solving.

Many times, however, the needs of others are what bring us to a state of sharp concentration. Whether it's because we feel very secure with those we're with or because we are functioning under conditions of extreme crisis, we find that in this state of intense concentration helpful insights arise on their own, as a function of our one-pointedness. In these experiences we meet a resource of remarkable potential. While we may be frustrated in not having access to it all the time, these experiences lead us to inquire whether there might be something we could do more regularly and formally to quiet the mind, strengthen its concentration, make available the deeper insights that often result, and bring them into closer attunement with the empathy and compassion of our heart. How immeasurably this might enhance our ability to help others.

Traditionally, one such way to begin this investigation is through meditation, systematically observing the mind itself and becoming more familiar with the ways in which we are denied the experience of full concentration. When we do this, with even a simple exercise like focusing our attention on our breath or on a candle flame, we begin to see that there is a continuous stream of thoughts going on all the time. Meditation may be frustrating if we think we can stop this process right away. We can't. But by penetrating and observing it, we can free ourselves from being carried away by our thoughts.

Our thoughts are always happening. Much like leaves floating down a stream or clouds crossing the sky, they just keep on coming. They arise in the form of sensations, feelings, memories, anticipations, and speculations. And they are all constantly calling for attention: "Think of me." "Notice me." "Attend to me." As each thought passes, either we attend to it or we don't. While we can't stop the thoughts themselves, we can stop our awareness from being snared by each one. If you are standing by a river and a leaf floats by, you have your choice of following the leaf with your eye or keeping your attention fixed in front of you. The leaf floats out of your line of vision. Another leaf enters…and floats by.

But as we stand on the bank of the river and the leaves float by, there is no confusion as to whether or not we are the leaves. Similarly, it turns out that there is a place in our minds from which we can watch our own mental images go by. We aren't our thoughts any more than we are the leaves.

If we imagine that our mind is like the blue sky, and that across it pass thoughts as clouds, we can get a feel for that part of it which is other than our thoughts. The sky is always present; it contains the clouds and yet is not contained by them. So with our awareness. It is present and encompasses all our thoughts, feelings, and sensations; yet it is not the same as them. To recognize and acknowledge this awareness, with its spacious, peaceful quality, is to find a very useful resource within. We see that we need not identify with each thought just because it happens to occur. We can remain quiet and choose which thought we wish to attend to. And we can remain aware *behind* all these thoughts, in a state that offers an entirely new level of openness and insight.

There are systematic exercises that can help to establish us in the sky-like awareness that encompasses thought. One of these meditation exercises is called "Letting Go." It very quickly can show us through direct personal experience that our awareness is separate from our thoughts.

For one who has not examined the mind and has always identified completely with passing thoughts, the possibility of being able to rest in awareness free of thought may be a bit disconcerting. It's a little like the caterpillar pointing up at the butterfly and saying, "You'll never get me up in one of those things." While we rarely are able to maintain this kind of awareness all the time, we have all experienced it at one time or another.

You're waiting tables, say, at a busy restaurant, setting one and clearing another, swinging through the kitchen door with an order and a funny remark for the cooks, then coming back out with a trayful and noticing what else needs to be done. The group of eight is eager to order, but they just sat down. The couple in the corner is stretching out their coffee while other folks are on line. It seems right to stop by and say, "Anything else?"

Or you're teaching in a nursery school. You've got your eye on the whole room. The boys are hogging the blocks from a couple of girls, as usual. Three kids over there are struggling a little over who's going to use the two easels. Janet hasn't played with anyone this morning, but she's better off working it out herself. Marc looks a little blue…you'd best spend time with him right now.

We're doing it all, attending to obvious needs, but we're also behind it. The consciousness we have access to is greater than the particular thoughts we're having or skills we've mastered. We have all these. But we have perspective as well—all within our spacious awareness. What's crucial is that this awareness allows us to hear, along with everything else, whatever it is that's going on inside us. *Our own mental reactions are equally objects to be observed as anything else in our field of awareness.* So you notice that perhaps you pushed the couple with the coffee just a little too much. You can see they're talking over something important. As you pass by, then, you say quietly, "Take a few more minutes; it's okay." Or you recognize, as you decide where to put your energies in the classroom, that you're really quite fascinated by Marc; that's why you want to work with him. And you're not all that crazy about Janet. You reconsider where to spend your time.

In skillful helping action, when our awareness remains quiet and clear, there's breadth to our perspective. It's aerial, wide-screen, panoramic, and yet able to focus quickly. With all of this, we are not only thinker-participants but observers of our thinking and participation as well. It's as if our mind is playing among various focal lengths. We're watching a TV show and we pull back; it becomes a show within a show, a picture of a picture, both on simultaneously. Of course, that's true of who we are too. We're not only a person, say, walking down a city street at night; we're also, as it were, already home in bed watching the TV show of us walking the street.

So the quiet mind makes possible an overall awareness of the total situation, including ourselves. It's sometimes called an awareness of the Gestalt—in which separate elements of consciousness are so integrated that they function as a unity.

There's a guy up on the roof, right at the edge, with his infant son in his arms; he's threatening to throw him off and then jump himself. Homicide-suicide—happens a lot with children. He's been having trouble with his wife—mother interfering, they lock him out, he's sleeping in the hallway, and it's gone to the edge. That's where he is, and I'm up there with him. I'm the final guy in the hostage recovery system we set up in New York City, which I've been working in for eight years and heading up for the last two. We haven't lost anybody in all that time.

Now, if you're not able to see the whole picture—how he's reacting, where and who your backup forces are, what's on the street, how long it's been going on, your own past experience, the chance that this is a new kind, and certainly what's going on inside you from moment to moment— if you can't hold on to all of that and still be there listening to this guy in a way he can feel…chances are he's gonna go over the edge. Someone is going to be killed. We've learned that.

And he's in this very intense, complex public situation. Several of us are up there—a net in the street below, a lot going on all around. To say nothing of what's going on in him: this lack of self-esteem and manliness, feeling pushed around by his family, no work. But I also can recognize this overriding love he has for his child, who he's convinced would be better off dead than with those two. Sounds crazy, but it was real to him. So there's a lot for all of us to take in.

So I'm helping him get a sense, an awareness of everything that's happening, just so he has the picture of it all. And the more he does, the more he is opening up to me. Turns out what concerns him most is that there be a hearing at family court to work out fair custody. He wants a hearing. But he won't accept a promise from me, or a signed note. He tells us we've got to get a lawyer and have it on legal paper—which we get for him by sending out a car and finding a local lawyer. When he feels he's got support from the system, he hands us the child. At that point we have to jump him, because we know that's the crucial moment to prevent the suicide. He gets pissed at me, because we were talking together and now this. And I have to give him this look of "That's how it all is, kid." Some part of him understands.

Other times, you're called into very tight situations which you have to loosen up. I was called into a classic family fight scene. A nine-by-twelve room with an eight-by-ten bed, on which is sitting a two-hundred-pound construction worker with a knife in one hand and the hair of his wife, who's half-naked on the floor, in the other. He's yelling about her infidelity, and he's already nicked her. Not much room to move around in. So in talking to him I'm trying to expand the situation. I try to get him to talk about how he got to this point, recognize he still has choices, and think about the future. It's like I'm making the room bigger, making more room for this guy. And I have to stay very steady to do that, because there is part of me which is saying, "Man, you got a lot of balls accusing your wife of something at a moment like this." But as soon as I could get him to pull back and look at it all, which is what I'm doing too, you understand, then there's a chance to see exactly what move will break through the pressure. That's how this one got resolved.

Funny thing is, I can't remember much of what I've been saying to people at the end of these episodes. I'm running very much on intuition from moment to moment. I've had special training, of course, but that becomes a part of you, and it's only a part of what you're calling on.

You have to be steady and quiet inside. You have to have a foundation of belief in the absolute value and beauty of life. You can't get too caught up in it all. You step back, get as much of the picture as possible, and you play it moment to moment. That's what I've learned from hundreds of these situations.

⌒

In the clarity of a quiet mind, there is room for all that is actually happening and whatever else might also be possible. Though we may be mindful of myriad details, our attention never wavers from the specific situation or person in need. The intimacy of our attention becomes a heart-to-heart life-line made firm and fast; no one need fall from the edge. The quiet appreciation of the total situation and its inherent possibilities steadily moves things toward resolution; we find ways to step back. In a spirit of compassion and reverence for life, these various skills flourish and combine appropriately.

Such feats might seem to be the result of crisis. Many of us have experienced rising to the occasion under such conditions. The intensity of the situation keeps the mind from wandering. For most of us, fortunately or unfortunately, our helping work doesn't entail the intensity that brings forth these heightened faculties. But whatever the circumstances, and however extensive the training and experience, it's important to recognize that the faculties of awareness being called into play are exactly those we have been cultivating and discovering in the practice of meditation and the investigation of awareness. General laws are operating under particular circumstances.

Why, for example, if one was tightly attentive to a single object—a man on the edge of a roof—wouldn't everything else disappear from awareness? Because, as we've discovered, it is possible to notice a single thought, sensation, or situation arise, but not get totally lost in identifying with it. We observe the cloud but remain focused on the sky, see the leaf but hold in vision the river. We are that which is aware of the totality. And our skills develop with practice. First, we have to appreciate the value of such qualities of mind and desire to develop them. Next, we have to have faith in the possibility that we can indeed make progress. Finally, we have to explore and practice appropriate techniques. Twenty minutes a day of such practice can lead to results and the incentive to go deeper still. Continuous practice brings about great transformation of mind and leads to a new quality of service.

When we function from this place of spacious awareness rather than from our analytic mind, we are often surprised to find solutions to problems without our having "figured them out." It's as if out of the reservoir of our minds which contains everything we know and everything we are sensing at the moment, all that could be useful rises to the surface and presents itself for appropriate action. Sudden flashes of memory, past experience, or understanding seem to get expressed: "I can't explain it." "It just came to me." "It all suddenly became clear." "I forgot I even knew that."

We often call this quality of mind "intuition" but often we don't trust or honor it. Unlike our thinking mind, which arrives at solutions through a linear process of analysis which we can follow, the intuitive mind seems to leap to a solution. Perhaps the process is going on outside the range of our consciousness; perhaps we are delving into regions of the mind where thinking, in the conventional sense, is not necessary. Whatever, it is still an important resource of our minds and worthy of more than incidental attention.

⌒

My father was dying, my mother was panicking. They were three thousand miles away from me. I had a family and a job. And all the familiar questions of these experiences: when to be with them, when to be at home and at work; when to call, when to wait to be called; medical decisions; hospital or home; and simply what to say, how to be.

I'd think and think about all this, but I would reach a point where I'd see I had to stop. My mind would go "tilt." So I would go out and take a walk, or watch the river change tides and empty into the Atlantic. I'd watch kids at the playground. I'd see how the tree line had changed shape at the top of a mountain meadow I'd known for years. Things like that.

And sometimes I'd hear—"Right. It's time to be out there. I'll leave in two weeks and stay ten days." Or, "Not so much advice-giving." Or "God is with them." The right thought. Something that would ring true. These seemed to come out of the blue, but I felt trust in them, and peaceful as a result.

It was very reliable and very inspiring, working that way. All through his illness and all the wild, anxious phone calls, I'd feel answers coming. It was very reassuring. I experienced it as grace. And at the end I was able to be with them at home and have his hand in mine as he died and my arm around my mother.

⌒

Ultimately, this kind of listening to the intuitive mind is a kind of surrender based on trust. It's playing it by ear, listening for the voice within. We trust that it's possible to hear into a greater totality which offers insight and guidance. But ultimately, we trust that when we are fully quiet, aware, and attentive, boundaries created by the mind simply blur and dissolve, and we begin to merge into All That Is. And All That Is, by definition, includes answers as well as questions, solutions as well as dilemmas.

When we have been used to knowing where we stand at every moment, the experience of resting in awareness without any specific thoughts to hold onto and trusting our intuition, turns out to be a refreshing and exciting adventure. In this choiceless spacious awareness, we don't necessarily know from moment to moment how everything is going to come out.

Nor do we have a clear idea of what is expected of us. Our stance is just one of listening...of fine tuning...trusting that all will become apparent at the proper time.

To rest in awareness also means to stand free of the prejudices of mind that come from identifying with cherished attitudes and opinions. We can listen without being busy planning, analyzing, theorizing...and especially judging. We can open into the moment fully in order to hear it all.

As we learn to listen with a quiet mind, there is so much we hear. Inside ourselves we can begin to hear that "still small voice within," as the Quakers call it, the voice of our intuitive heart which has so long been drowned out by the noisy thinking mind. We hear our skills and needs, our subtle intentionalities, our limits, our innate generosity.

In other people we hear what help they really require, what license they are actually giving us to help, what potential there is for change. We can hear their strengths and their pain. We hear what support is available, what obstacles must be reckoned with.

The more deeply we listen, the more we attune ourselves to the roots of suffering and the means to help alleviate it. It is through listening that wisdom, skill, and opportunity find form in an act that truly helps. But more than all these, the very act of listening can dissolve distance between us and others as well.

Heard...If they only understood how important it is that we be heard! I can take being in a nursing home. It's really all right, with a positive attitude. My daughter has her hands full, three kids and a job. She visits regularly. I understand.

But most people here...they just want to tell their story. That's what they have to give, don't you see? And it's a precious thing to them. It's their life they want to give. You'd think people would understand what it means to us...to give our lives in a story.

So we listen to each other. Most of what goes on here is people listening to each other's stories. People who work here consider that to be...filling time. If they only knew. If they'd just take a minute to listen!

⌒

There are so many ways in which we listen to one another. "I hear you," we say to one another. Such a message would be welcome indeed if, for example, it came in the words of a trapped coal miner or a deaf person who had just undergone corrective ear surgery. In most helping situations, however, "I hear you" reflects a much deeper message: "I understand. I'm with you." Such a message can be immensely reassuring for a person who has felt isolated or alone in their pain and suffering. The reassurance does not come from the words themselves, of course, but from what the words represent. It comes if the person indeed feels heard.

It may not be that a particular story from one's life is so important. But sharing it is a way of being together heart to heart. In those moments we are no longer alone with our fear; we are reminded that we are not forgotten.

⌒

When two people are at one
in their inmost hearts,
They shatter even the strength of
iron or of bronze.
And when two people understand each other in their inmost hearts,
Their words are sweet and strong, like the fragrance of orchids.

I Ching

⌒

To reach its full potential, however, this hearing from the heart requires that we remain alert to entrapments of the mind. Seeking to help others, we may start out open and receptive, but after a short time being with them seems to bring us down rather than lift them up. Somehow their suffering, self-pity, despair, fear, or neediness begins to get to us. It's a little like trying to pull someone out of quicksand and feeling ourself suddenly starting to sink. As reassuring as it may be for one depressed person to be heard by another depressed person, the relationship doesn't really open the door to escape from depression. Empathy is not enough.

Here, once again, our ability to remain alert to our own thoughts as they come and go serves us in our relations with others. We hear into their pain ...they feel heard...we meet together inside the confusion. And yet we ourselves are able to note, perhaps even to *anticipate,* that moment when another's entrapment of mind might be starting to suck us in. We are as alert to what is happening within us as we are to what is happening in them.

The ability to avoid being entrapped by one another's mind is one of the great gifts we can offer each other. With this compassionate and spacious awareness, and the listening it makes possible, we can offer those we are with a standing invitation to come out from wherever they are caught, if they are ready and wish to do so. It is as if we are in the room of experience with them, but also standing in the doorway, offering our hand, ready to walk out together.

⌒

A woman came to see me who was suffering greatly because of her daughter. She told me her daughter was real bad trouble. "She's run away to live with my other daughter down in Tennessee, and now she's forged a check with her sister's name on it, and she's gotten pregnant and she's only sixteen. I've been a seamstress all my life, supporting the kids and myself since my husband ran out when the youngest was still in the womb. Now she's run away, and you can't imagine what it's like...."

I'm shortening the story. It actually took about fifteen minutes to run it all down. I just listened as openly as I could. I could feel her pain and discouragement and felt my heart hurt at the hard life she had had. At the same moment I felt very quiet inside, figuring maybe all I had to offer was to be with her. A little bit I felt she was wearing the albatross of this story, like the Ancient Mariner, and I was just another in a long line of people who had heard it. So when she finished I said, "Right."

She sensed I wasn't getting caught, and her immediate reaction was "No, you don't understand." And she recited the whole thing one more time, fifteen more minutes. And when she'd finished the second time, I said again, "Right."

This time she stopped for a moment. She'd heard me. She paused, and then said with a kind of wry smile, "You know, I was kind of a hellion when I was a kid, too." She just let it go.

For someone deeply trapped in a prison of thought, how good it can feel to meet a mind that hears, a heart that reassures. It's as if a listening mind is, in and of itself, an invitation to another mind to listen too. How much it can mean when we accept the invitation and hear the world anew.

When she first came to see me, this woman hadn't been speaking for three months. But she was silent in many different ways. Resentful silence: "You do it for me." Agitated silence: "I'm scared." Bored silence: "I have nothing." A kind of interested silence too—but not knowing how to start. After several months she began to speak.

Now, after a number of years, she spends a great deal of time talking, and she's afraid of silence, scared of being quiet. There are things, she says, that she doesn't want to know. Any movement into silence, from outside or within, is really frightening.

One day there was a noise outside. She paused and said, "What's that?"

I said, "Let's listen." She listened for a moment and asked again, "What is it?" I said again, "Let's listen." And then she exclaimed, with total delight, "It's a bird! I haven't heard a bird in years. It's beautiful!" I saw it all go by: the noise; the not knowing (imagine the condition of one who doesn't know the sound of a bird!); her wish to hear; the listening; the sound recognized; the bird. There was another long silence. Then she said, "That's just so beautiful."

The sage helps the ten thousand things find their own nature.

Tao Te Ching

Much, then, can be accomplished in the work of compassion by exploring the activity of the mind. Through concentration, we are able to establish a more intimate contact with one another. Through spacious awareness we can sense the totality of situations and allow insight to come into play. More and more we are a vehicle for service. All of this may seem as if we are acquiring something new, but that is not so. Rather, we are clearing away obstacles that have prevented us from using our natural abilities. We regain what Suzuki Roshi, a Zen master, called "beginner's mind"—one that is open to the freshness of many possibilities.

To dissolve agitations and attachments of the mind is to remove the veils from our heart. It allows us to meet one another in the purity of love.

On the bulletin board in the front hall of the hospital where I work, there appeared an announcement. "Yeshi Dhonden," it read, "will make rounds at six o'clock on the morning of June 10." The particulars were then given, followed by a notation: "Yeshi Dhonden is Personal Physician to the Dalai Lama." I am not so leathery a skeptic that I would knowingly ignore an emissary from the gods. Not only might such sangfroid be inimical to one's earthly wellbeing, it could take care of eternity as well. Thus, on the morning of June 10, I join the clutch of whitecoats waiting in the small conference room adjacent to the ward selected for the rounds. The air in the room is heavy with ill-concealed dubiety and suspicion of bamboozlement. At precisely six o'clock he materializes, a short, golden, barrelly man dressed in a sleeveless robe of saffron and maroon. His scalp is shaven, and the only visible hair is a scanty black line above each hooded eye.

He bows in greeting while his young interpreter makes the introduction. Yeshi Dhonden, we are told, will examine a patient selected by a member of the staff. The diagnosis is unknown to Yeshi Dhonden as it is to us. The examination of the patient will take place in our presence, after which we will reconvene in the conference room, where Yeshi Dhonden will discuss the case. We are further informed that for the past two hours Yeshi Dhonden has purified himself by bathing, fasting, and prayer. I, having breakfasted well, performed only the most desultory of ablutions, and given no thought at all to my soul, glance furtively at my fellows. Suddenly we seem a soiled, uncouth lot.

The patient had been awakened early and told that she was to be examined by a foreign doctor, and had been asked to produce a fresh specimen of urine, so when we enter her room, the woman shows no surprise. She has long ago taken on that mixture of compliance and resignation that is the face of chronic illness. This was to be but another in an endless series of tests and examinations. Yeshi Dhonden steps to the bedside while the rest stand apart, watching. For a long time he gazes at the woman, favoring no part of her body with his eyes, but seeming to fix his glance at a place just above her supine form. I, too, study her. No physical sign or obvious symptom gives a clue to the nature of her disease.

At last he takes her hand, raising it in both of his own. Now he bends over the bed in a kind of crouching stance, his head drawn down into the collar of his robe. His eyes are closed as he feels for her pulse. In a moment he has found the spot, and for the next halfhour he remains thus, suspended above the patient like some exotic golden bird with folded wings, holding the pulse of the woman beneath his fingers, cradling her hand in his. All the power of the man seems to have been drawn down into this one purpose. It is palpation of the pulse raised to the state of ritual. From the foot of the bed, where I stand, it is as though he and the patient have entered a special place of isolation, of apartness, about which a vacancy hovers, and across which no violation is possible. After a moment the woman rests back upon her pillow. From time to time she raises her head to look at the strange figure above her, then sinks back once more. I cannot see their hands joined in a correspondence that is exclusive, intimate, his fingertips receiving the voice of her sick body through the rhythm and throb she offers at her wrist. All at once I am envious—not of him, not of Yeshi Dhonden for his gift of beauty and holiness, but of her. I want to be held like that, touched so, received. And I know that I, who have palpated a hundred thousand pulses, have not felt a single one.

At last Yeshi Dhonden straightens, gently places the woman's hand upon the bed, and steps back. The interpreter produces a small wooden bowl and two sticks. Yeshi Dhonden pours a portion of the urine specimen into the bowl and proceeds to whip the liquid with two sticks. This he does for several minutes until a foam is raised. Then, bowing above the bowl, he inhales the odor three times. He sets down the bowl and turns to leave. All this while, he has not uttered a single word.

As he nears the door, the woman raises her head and calls out to him in a voice at once urgent and serene. "Thank you, doctor," she says, and touches with her other hand the place he had held on her wrist, as though to recapture something that had visited there. Yeshi Dhonden turns back for a moment to gaze at her, then steps into the corridor. Rounds are at an end.

We are seated once more in the conference room. Yeshi Dhonden speaks now for the first time, in soft Tibetan sounds that I have never heard before. He has barely begun when the young interpreter begins to translate, the two voices continuing in tandem—a bilingual fugue, the one chasing the other. It is like the chanting of monks. He speaks of winds coursing through the body of the woman, currents that break against barriers, eddying. These vortices are in her blood, he says. The last spendings of an imperfect heart. Between the chambers of the heart, long, long before she was born, a wind had come and blown open a deep gate that must never be opened. Through it charge the full waters of her river, as the mountain stream cascades in the springtime, battering, knocking loose the land, and flooding her breath. Thus he speaks, and now he is silent.

"May we now have the diagnosis?" a professor asks.

The host of these rounds, the man who knows, answers.

"Congenital heart disease," he says. "Interventricular septal defect, with resultant heart failure." A gateway in the heart, I think. That must not be opened. Through it charge the full waters that flood her breath. So! Here then is the doctor listening to the sounds of the body to which the rest of us are deaf. He is more than doctor. He is priest.

I know…I know…the doctor to the gods is pure knowledge, pure healing. The doctor to man stumbles, must often wound; his patient must die, as must he.

Now and then it happens, as I make my own rounds, that I hear the sounds of his voice, like an ancient Buddhist prayer, its meaning long since forgotten, only the music remaining. Then a jubilation possesses me, and I feel myself touched by something divine.

*I*n the late 1990s, as members of the Zen Peacemaker Order, Joan Halifax and Bernie Glassman, together with a group of monks, students, and laypeople, journeyed to Auschwitz, the infamous camp where millions were put to death during World War II. With them they brought the desire to bear witness, to listen deeply within the walls of the camp which, for many of the world's peoples, calls up some of the most horrendous memories of degradation and human suffering. Already a practiced compassionate listener from years of working with prison inmates and people with life-threatening illnesses, Joan brought and shared the craft of Council with all in attendance. She is gracious enough to share it here in this collection.

The Craft of Council

Joan Halifax

REMEMBERING AUSCHWITZ, remembering those who died there, and remembering the perpetrators of suffering can teach us about the things in our own lives that we have rejected, hated, scorned, judged, and raged against. It can also teach us about the things in *others'* lives that we have loathed and judged intolerable.

All of us who participated in the Auschwitz Bearing Witness Retreat asked ourselves again and again: How could this have happened? Just as escape from the camp was impossible for the women and men who died there, we could not escape this question at Auschwitz.

The suffering that we touched upon during our retreat, at times led us into darkness and at times transformed into joy and healing as we sat and practiced together and listened to one another. Bearing witness is not only about bearing witness to one's own life but to all of life. And it was here at Auschwitz that we bore witness to the suffering of others, to the suffering of our ancestors, to our own suffering, and to the possibility of the transformation of suffering.

One of the ways that I practice bearing witness is in the experience of Council, a practice in which people sit in a circle with each other, speak clearly and listen deeply. Council at Auschwitz was a way for us to communicate about the deepest issues of our lives, including suffering, death and grief, as well as meaning, healing and joy. Indeed, Council was one of the deepest ways that we taught each other during the retreat.

Council is found in many cultures and traditions the world over. One finds reference to it in Homer's *Iliad* and finds it in the tribal world of earth-cherishing peoples. It is a key strategy of communion and communication in the tradition of the Quakers, who so influenced the Civil Rights Movement of the 1970's.

In the 1970's, I and others brought what we had learned in the Civil Rights and Anti-war Movement to our lives as teachers and people involved with social action and spiritual practice. Council, or the Circle of Truth, became a way for us to incorporate democratic and spiritual values into our collective and individual lives.

In the mid 1990's, I introduced the Council process to Bernie Glassman and his wife Jishu Holmes. It fit well with their work as peacemakers and they brought it to many places the world over. Council seemed to be a practice that was naturally based in the three tenets of the Zen Peacemaker Order: not knowing, bearing witness, and healing. And Council was to contribute as a profound firmament to our time at Auschwitz.

The practice of Council did not necessarily lead to us all seeing things the same way at Auschwitz—Council was not a consensus-making process. Rather it was a way for people to recognize that each individual in the circle had his or her own wisdom. When differing views and experiences were expressed in the Council circle, the depth of field seemed to be much greater and we began to discover the importance and richness of differences, a theme that related deeply to the Auschwitz where differences were annihilated.

The practice of Council allowed people to develop a natural appreciation for differences and to respect the different perspectives that were held by Germans and Jews, by men and women, by old and young, by rich and poor, by the joyful and the terrified among us. We saw clearly that it was the intolerance of differences that was a prime cause for Auschwitz.

This same intolerance continues to be found in many corners of the planet today, and we were to discover that this intolerance existed in our own hearts as well. Many of us saw that we are called to bear witness without shame to this Balkanization of the spirit; we needed to invite in the hungry ghosts and allow them to scour out our hearts so that our practice and resolve to make peace could deepen. Council is one way that this process happened. It was our medicine and our mirror.

When we sit in Council, it is usually important to sit in a circle. A circle has a feeling of democracy and equality. We can all see each other, and we are all in an equal position together. At Auschwitz in the morning councils, we sat in a circle. We found ourselves in hallways, in small rooms, in foyers, in restaurants, in a library, any place that could hold a dozen people in a circle. In the evening, when 100–150 of us were gathered, we sat in an auditorium, at the front of which was an open microphone. We tried to practice with four guidelines described below no matter how many or how few there were, no matter whether we were together in a circle or square.

The four guidelines have been articulated by my colleagues Jack Zimmerman and Gigi Coyle. The first is speaking from the heart; the second is listening from the heart; the third is being of lean expression; and the fourth is spontaneity. These four principles seem very simple, but they are skills that many of us have never been taught. At the Auschwitz Retreat we endeavored to learn them through the practice of Council. There we discovered that these skills made it possible for us to stay steady in the midst of profound complexity. They became like a meditation: a way for it to be possible to continually return our hearts and minds back to truth.

1. Speaking from the Heart

Many of us at the retreat were used to speaking from the head, speaking in terms of philosophical and political ideas. Council is about transparency, intimacy, and personal revelation. In speaking from the heart, we are called to speak from our personal experience, from the true stories of our lives.

Speaking from the heart means speaking honestly, speaking truths that are instructive and constructive. It does not mean complimenting people or trying to please someone. It means being in one's personal truth in this moment.

When introducing this notion of speaking from the heart, I invite people to consider that this is the speaker's last day on earth and to give the quality of attention that we would give to a dying person whom we know will pass on tomorrow, to receive unconditionally whatever the person is saying. That sense of listening with intense and loving devotion elicits a much deeper truth from us as we speak about our concerns, our fears, our feelings of shame and rejection, and as we explore issues related to racism, human cruelty, hopelessness, alienation, and redemption.

2. LISTENING FROM THE HEART

Listening from the heart is deep listening—listening in the true spirit of tolerance, with a vast and open heart. The Quakers call this "devout listening." The Council process removes the option to interrupt a speaker so that each speaker can speak in a very deep and true way without fear of being cut off and each listener can relax into a spacious quality of listening, without judgment or prejudice, listening not only to what is said, but also to what is left unsaid.

In Council, we are asked to listen from the point of view of beginner's mind, from not knowing, the first tenet that we practice in the Peacemaker Community. We also are asked to practice bearing witness, the second tenet. As you listen to another person, many responses can arise: memories, associations, insights, and so on. In Council we practice acknowledging that these things are there and we then practice being able to let them go.

At Auschwitz, many of us began to feel that each person who spoke was like a new world opening up to us. There was a sense of deep and surprising familiarity, and yet at the same time we often could not have articulated what was being said ourselves. We could hear ourselves in the words of another, and yet we felt we heard things that we could never have known, perhaps because they were held in the shadowland of our minds and hearts. Through the experience of Council and deep listening, some of us began to gain a kind of collective understanding that seemed to transcend language.

In the practice of Council, we did not respond or share our associations until it was our turn to speak. Thus, as we began to listen with a new quality of patience, Council practice seemed to help us shift from *reactive* listening to *attentive* listening.

I shared with others that when I listen to someone who is suffering, I do not listen with my ears—I am listening in my heart. I feel as if the sound is entering into my chest and shaping my heart. This practice of listening is very profound and subtle. From the Buddhist perspective, it is the practice of Avalokiteshvara, the bodhisattva of compassion, the one who hears the cries of the world and responds. Through deep and devout listening, we can open up the heart and mind to experience fundamental nonduality.

At this Bearing Witness Retreat, we were all shaped by what we did not consciously know. At times when we were in Council, I was in the most conflicted state. I struggled, as did others, with descriptions of experiences that seemed to go directly against the grain of human kindness, of good sense, of basic sanity. How could it have been otherwise? The only place in which I and others could find refuge was in the human heart. We tried to listen from this place with compassion, acceptance and directness.

3. BEING OF LEAN EXPRESSION

At Auschwitz, many of us wanted to go directly to the heart of the matter. We wanted to speak concisely and to recognize that every moment is precious. In that desolate November atmosphere, we wanted the opportunity to nourish and heal each other. We knew we could not heal and change the past, and we saw that we were doing this for the future. We found ourselves in the economy of a moment.

The practice of Council called for us to develop a way of clear and concise speaking from the very the bones and marrow of our being. One of the ways that I do this is to remember that we are all connected to each other. If we create a situation of deep consideration, we will recognize that we need to develop an efficiency of speech so that all those who wish to share their insights or confusion, their love or their fear can have the time to do so. Learning to be concise is a discipline; it is a practice that reminds us that all the voices want to be heard.

Engaging this practice, some of us began to experience time in terms of timelessness. Out of time, the past and future find their way into the present. And in turn we are called into a new of economy of time, aware that we have all the time in the world and that we are here for only an instant. We are called to make time and to transcend time.

Conciseness is difficult for many of us. We seek to sort out our thoughts and feelings, and for some of us this cannot be done instantly. And yet many of us struggle with the same issues. Seeing that we were in this place—Auschwitz—for only a few days, we could not talk at book-length about our feelings. We had to rely on the collective to hold the whole story. If we could surrender to the group, we were assured that someone would touch upon that piece that we could not address. When we focus the lens of our personal experience to create a multifaceted, nondominational eye of wisdom, we discover that our own experience is often that of others.

4. SPONTANEITY

At Auschwitz, some of us found ourselves rehearsing internally what we would say. We knew we were in a very sensitive situation and did not want to hurt others—trust is always a large consideration in Council. To foster spontaneity, participants are encouraged to ask: "What is the truth of what is happening to me at this very moment? What is the truth of what is happening to others?"

Sometimes it is a challenge to move beyond our own story, to step outside own perspective and listen to the stories and viewpoints of others but that is what we are asked to do in this practice—to move from the position of "I" and to listen to the wisdom of the circle. When it is our own turn to speak, we stop for a moment and release any feeling of anxiety, and come into the truth of the heart and mind in the moment.

The pain of the hell that is Auschwitz invites us to leave there as quickly as we can. How many forms of denial can we engage in? Trance and flight, good cheer and dance, "Hail fellow, well met!" or withdrawal. Our practice there however was about immediacy, intimacy, and transparency. These qualities are all based in the tenets of not knowing and bearing witness. To speak from the heart is to turn to the heart at the moment the heart is beating, not a second before or later. Don't look to outcome; fish with a straight hook; step off that hundred-foot pole.

Can we bear to listen to others and hear what we have not confessed to ourselves? Can we hear what we do not know? Can we stir the ocean with the broken stick of our aspirations? Can we free all creations?

No one answer can hold the truth of a good heart.

Human communication is complex and dynamic. Accurate communication that maximizes listening potential, that is succinct and responds to needs easily, is more often the exception than the rule. In this instructive selection, Michael Nichols, a longtime family therapist at the Philadelphia Child Guidance Clinic, presents his perspective on how we can be proactive listeners, responsible participants in communications that lead to accurate hearing and compassionate understanding. Learning to pay attention to setting, timing, and a message's explicit and implicit content, Nichols tells us, are but a few of the things that will aid us in becoming skillful listeners, even with people who are the most difficult for us to listen to.

The Rules of
the Listening Game

Michael P. Nichols

WE DON'T USUALLY stop to examine patterns of misunderstanding in our lives because we're stuck in our own point of view. Misunderstanding hurts, and when we're hurt we tend to look outside ourselves for explanations. But the problem isn't just that when something goes wrong we look for someone to blame. The problem is linear thinking. We reduce human interactions to a matter of personalities. "He doesn't listen because he's too preoccupied with himself." "She's hard to listen to because she goes on and on about everything." Some people blame themselves ("Maybe I'm not that interesting"), but it's almost always easier to appreciate the other person's contribution.

Attributing other people's lack of understanding to character is armor for our ignorance and passivity. That some people repeat their annoying ways with most others they come in contact with doesn't prove that lack of responsiveness is fixed in character; it only proves that these individuals trigger many people to play out the reciprocal role in their dramas of two-part disharmony.

The fixed-character position assumes that it's extremely difficult for people to change. But you don't change relationships by changing other people. You change patterns of relating by changing yourself in relation to them. Personality is dynamic, not fixed. The dynamic personality position posits that it is possible for people to change; all we have to do is change our response to each other. We are not victims—we are participants, in a real way, and the consequences of our participation are profound.

To participate effectively, we must know something about the rules of the game. I remember how confused I was the first time I saw a lacrosse game. From where I sat it looked as if some kids were just standing around while the rest raced up and down the field, using their sticks to pass the ball back and forth, club each other, or both. I got the gist of it—it was like soccer played by Road Warriors—but a lot of it was hard to follow. Why, for instance, did the team that lost the ball out of bounds sometimes get it back and sometimes not? And why, sometimes when one kid whacked another with his stick, did everybody cheer, while at other times the referee called a foul? The problem was, of course, that I couldn't see the whole field and didn't know the rules of the game. The same disadvantages—not seeing the whole field and not knowing the rules of the game—keep us from understanding our successes and failures at communicating with one another.

Earlier I said that listening is a two-person process, but even that is oversimplified. Actually, even an uncomplicated communication has several components: the listener, the speaker, the message, various implicit messages, the context, and, because the process doesn't flow one way from speaker to listener, the listener's response. Even a brief consideration of these elements in the listening process reveals more reasons for misunderstanding than simply bad faith on the part of the listener.

"What Are You Trying to Say?"

The message is the content of what a speaker says. But the message sent isn't always the one intended.

A family of four is invited to spend Sunday afternoon at the lake house of friends of the father. When the teenage daughter asks if she can bring along one of her friends, her father says, "I don't think we should bring extra guests when we're invited to dinner." The daughter looks hurt, and the man's wife says, "You're being silly; they never mind extra company." The man gets angry and withdraws, brooding over his feeling that his wife always takes the children's side and never listens to him.

The problem here is a common one—the message sent wasn't the one intended. One of the unfortunate things we learn along with being "polite" and not being "selfish" is not to say directly what we want. Instead of saying "I want..." we say "We should..." or "Do you want...?" When we're taking a trip in the car and we get hungry, we say "Isn't it getting late?" (When I was growing up I learned that guests weren't supposed to put people to any trouble. If you went to someone's house and wanted a glass of water, you didn't ask; you looked thirsty. If they did offer you something, you politely declined. Only if they insisted was it OK to accept. A really good boy waited until a glass of water was offered at least twice before accepting.)

Because this convention of indirectness is so universal, it doesn't usually cause problems. If the other person in the room says "Are you cold?" you usually know he means "I'm cold. Can we turn up the heat?" But indirection can cause problems when stronger feelings are involved. The father in our example didn't want his daughter to bring a friend. Perhaps his wife was right; the people who invited them wouldn't mind. But somehow he minded. Maybe he wanted his daughter to remain more a part of the family and less an independent person with friends of her own. Or maybe he wanted her to be part of the grown-ups' conversation, instead of off with her friend, because he found it easier to talk about the children's doings than his own. That's the trouble with indirection: there are always a lot of maybes.

When we're conflicted over certain of our own needs, we may infer (rightly or wrongly) that others would object even to hearing our wishes, much less acceding to them. Because indirection leads to so much misunderstanding and so many arguments that are beside the point, it does more harm than good. Two people can't have an honest disagreement about whether or not they want to move to another city as long as they engage in diversionary arguments about whether going or staying would be better for the children.

One reason others argue with us in a way that seems to negate our feelings is that we blur the distinction between our feelings and the facts. Instead of saying "I don't want her to bring a friend," the father tries to cloud his motives and bolster his argument by appealing to *shoulds*. When his wife argues with what he says instead of what he means, he feels rejected. Like every listener, he measured the intentions of other speakers by what they said-or what he heard-and asked that they measure him by what he intended to say.

As speakers we want to be heard-but not merely to be heard; we want to be understood, heard for what we think we're saying, for what we know we meant. Similar impasses occur when we insist we said one thing and our listener heard another. Instead of saying "What I meant to say was..." we go on insisting what we *did* say.

"WHY DON'T YOU SAY WHAT YOU MEAN?"

Implicit messages tell us more than what's being said; they tell us how we're meant to receive what's being said. Depending on the situation, inflection, and motives of the speaker, "Let's have lunch" could mean "I'm hungry," "I'd like to see you again," or "Please leave now; I'm busy." The statements "I love you" and "I'm sorry" are of course notorious for having multiple meanings. Knowing the other person makes it easier to decode implicit messages; suspecting his or her motives can make it harder.

According to Gregory Bateson, one of the founders of family therapy, all communications have two levels of meaning: report and command. The report (or message) is the information conveyed by the words. The second or command level (which Bateson also called meta-communication) conveys information on how the report is to be taken and a statement of the nature of the relationship.

If a wife scolds her husband for running the dishwasher when it's only half full and he says OK but turns around and does exactly the same thing two days later, she may be annoyed that he doesn't listen to her. She means the message. But maybe he didn't like the meta-message. Maybe he doesn't like her telling him what to do as though she were his mother.

In attempting to define the nature of our relationships we qualify our messages by posture, facial expression, and tone of voice. For example, a rising inflection on the last two words turns "You did that on purpose" from an accusation to a question. The whole impact of a statement may change depending on which words are emphasized. Consider the difference between "Are *you* telling me it isn't true?" and "Are you telling me it *isn't* true?" Pauses, gestures, and gaze also tell us how to interpret what is being said. Although we may not need the ponderous term meta-communication, misunderstandings about what is implied and how messages are to be taken are major reasons for problems in listening.

One winter when I was working hard and feeling sorry for myself, I wrote to a sympathetic friend, and in the letter I said jokingly that I was running away to spend two weeks on the white beaches of a deserted Caribbean island. The only trouble was that I didn't say it, I wrote it and she missed the irony I intended. The medium didn't carry my tone of voice or the facial expression that modified the message. Instead of getting the sympathy I was (indirectly) asking for, I got back a rather testy note to the effect that it's nice to know that some people have the time and money to indulge themselves.

We know what we mean; problems arise when we expect others to. How is our communication to be taken? Is it chat? A confession? An outpouring of emotion? When our listeners fail to grasp that we're upset and need to have our feelings listened to, who's to blame?

A woman told her husband that something her boss said made her afraid that she might be in for trouble at work. The husband responded by saying no, he didn't think so; it didn't sound that way. When she replied that he didn't listen to her, both of them got upset. She was annoyed because he didn't listen to her feelings. He was hurt because he was listening. He had responded sincerely. He just didn't realize how upset she was.

Perhaps to some people this woman's upset would have been apparent. Maybe a friend would have realized that she needed to have her feelings acknowledged, not disagreed with. But she wasn't married to that friend. She was married to a man who didn't automatically understand how she wanted to be listened to. (Some people try to make that clear: "I'm worried about something, and I need to talk about it." "I need your advice." "I just need you to listen.")

Occasionally, but not as often as most people think—the implicit message in a communication is a request for the speaker to do something. The teenage boy who says "I'm hungry" isn't just making small talk. (A teenage boy's appetite is not an idle thing.) Usually, however, *the most* important implicit message in what people say is the feeling behind the content.

When we're little, before we learn to act grown-up by masking our feelings, our communications are full of ill-disguised emotion. You don't have to be a neurolinguistics expert to figure out what children are feeling when they say "There's monsters under my bed" or "Nobody wants to play with me." The same emotions may be implicit, if less obviously implied, when an adult says "I've got that big meeting coming up tomorrow" or "I called to see if Fred and Teddy wanted to go to the movies, but they weren't home." One of the most effective ways to improve understanding is to listen for both content and implicit feelings in what people say.

Much of communication is implicit and—when people are on the same wavelength—decoded automatically. Often, however, what is implicit—what we take for granted—is not obvious to everyone. Much misunderstanding could be cleared up if we learned to do two things:

appreciate the other person's perspective and, at times, clarify what usually remains implicit.

"Is This a Good Time?"

The context of communication is the setting: the time, the place, who else is present, and, because communication cannot be reduced to the obvious, people's expectations. We ordinarily accommodate our talking and listening to the context of an exchange without even thinking about it. We don't spring bad news on people the minute they walk in the door, we don't talk loudly in public, and we don't argue in front of the kids. (As you can't see by the twinkle in my eye, I'm being ironic.)

No matter how much certain people care about us, there are times when they don't have the energy and patience to listen. If a husband calls his wife at work and starts to talk at length about something that doesn't seem terribly important, she may get impatient sooner than she would if the same conversation occurred at home. By contrast, even though her husband usually retreats behind the paper at the end of the day, a wife may succeed in getting his full attention by signaling her need for it. "Honey, I need to talk to you about something important."

Unfortunately, in many relationships spouses have different preferred times to talk. He likes to talk when he comes home at the end of the day. She's busy then and prefers to talk later, when they're watching TV or getting ready for bed. Fishing for understanding at the wrong time is like trying to catch a trout in the noonday sun.

When to Talk: Not When Your Partner Needs Some Space or Time to be Alone.

The idea that timing affects the listening we get may be painfully obvious; unfortunately, when needs collide, the resulting failures of understanding

---

are obviously painful. The end of the day can be especially difficult. Partners may be frazzled and frustrated. Worn out from running around all day, trying to make other people happy, attending mind-deadening meetings, fighting traffic, or chasing after children and answering endless questions, they have little energy left over for hearing each other.

The unhappy irony is that the domestic conversation people are too tired to engage in might provide emotional refueling: talking and listening reinvigorate us. If we take listening for granted, we may assume that the people we care about will listen to us whenever we feel like talking. But if we realize that good listening doesn't happen automatically, we'll learn to give a little more thought to finding the right time to approach people.

Setting has an obvious physical effect on listening—in terms of privacy and noise level, for example–and an equally powerful effect in terms of conditioned cues. Familiar settings, like a therapist's office or a friend's kitchen, can be reassuring places in which to open up. Other familiar settings, like your own kitchen or bedroom, can be anything but conducive to conversation. Memories of misunderstanding and distraction cling to some rooms like the smell of wet dog.

Conversation in many settings is governed by unwritten rules, some of which are obvious (to most people). At cocktail parties, for example, where conversational subgroups constantly shift in size and membership, conversations may be warm, candid, even intimate, but they are also generally brief (which may explain the warmth and candor). Anyone who tries to talk too long in a such a setting may strain a listener's sense of decorum.

Rules of decorum are based on a shared sense of what's appropriate and probably originally derive from practical considerations, like noninterference with others and respect for special places. Thus, talking loudly in a cathedral, on a train, or at the movies is frowned on. Because rules of decorum are implicit and widely shared, we tend to take them for granted, not realizing that we have done so until we or someone else breaks them.

In addition to general rules of propriety, most of us have personal preferences for settings in which we're comfortable talking. Some people like to talk on the telephone, for example. (Why, I have no idea.) Some people like to talk when they go for a ride in the car; others prefer to read or look out the window. And, of course, we may be in the mood for conversation in a particular setting at one time and not another. Often the best way to get someone's attention is to invite her away from familiar surroundings—by taking a walk, say, or going out to a restaurant. Many of these preferences are sufficiently obvious that we adjust to them automatically. We know not to call certain people at home in the evening, and we learn the most promising times and places to get the listening we need. When we don't, feelings get hurt. We blame others for not hearing us, and, alternately, we feel put upon by their lack of consideration in imposing on us at the wrong time.

Whenever conversation takes place in the presence of others, some aspects of listening are expressively accentuated while others are suppressed. If a couple goes out to dinner and the man talks about problems at work, the woman will probably listen more intently than she does at home because the setting suggests intimacy. If they bring along the children, however, she's liable to be less attentive to him and also less likely to talk about her own concerns. Sometimes that's why people bring the children. Togetherness is a hedge against intimacy as well as loneliness.

Most of us have had the disconcerting experience of talking to someone who seems to be interested until someone else appears. In some situations this is unavoidable. If two people are having lunch and a third person joins them, it's not reasonable to expect to continue a private conversation. But in other instances the person talking about something important might expect the listener not to accept and encourage an interruption, to say, for example, to a telephone caller, "Sorry, I can't talk now; I'm busy." Or if two people are having a confidential conversation in a public place, one might expect the other to greet a casual acquaintance who happens by, but not to break off the conversation or signal the third person that he or she is welcome to join in. Third parties are to intimate conversation what rain is to picnics.

Sometimes the effect of third parties works the other way. An adult may show more animated and sustained interest in a child's conversation when other adults are watching. Similarly a man who often interrupts his wife at home may show more respect and forbearance when they're out with another couple.

I remember once when I was being interviewed on a morning television show how the host, a dynamic and attractive woman in her early forties, was fascinated and intrigued by the book I'd written. She sat very close, kept her eyes on mine, and asked all the right questions. Here was this radiant woman, totally engrossed in what I had to say. It was very flattering. Then a commercial break came up, and the light in her face went out like the red light on the camera. I ceased to exist. After the break the interview resumed, and so did my interviewer's intense show of interest. Her pretense, in the face of a whole audience of third parties (and my susceptibility), was disconcerting, but after all, it was her job to show interest.

WHY SOME PEOPLE ARE SO HARD TO LISTEN TO

Even when you play by the rules, some people are hard to listen to. In some cases that's because their accounts run on to Homeric length. They're generous with details. You ask about their vacation and they tell you about packing the car, getting lost on the way, and all the various wrong turns. They tell you about the weather and who said what and where they ate lunch and what they had for dinner, and they keep telling you until something other than tact stops them. Others may not talk at all about what they did but instead go on at great windy length about what everyone else did, all those objectionable others who are such problems in their lives.

It's also hard to listen to people who talk incessantly about their preoccupations—a mother with a difficult child who talks of little else, a careerist who wants to talk only about his work, a man with allergies who's always complaining about his sinus trouble. One person's headache can become another's if she has to hear about it all the time. It isn't just the repetition that we tire of; it's being cast in the helpless role of one who is importuned about a problem with no solution, or at least no solution the complainer wants to consider. (If the complainer doesn't expect a solution, a simple acknowledgment of his feelings—"Gee, that's too bad"—may give a satisfactory punctuation to the exchange.)

Some people who talk too much are like that with everybody, but often, whether we appreciate it or not, some of them talk at such length with us because they talk so little with anyone else. Who other than his wife does the husband with no friends talk to? Who other than the friend who seems to have her life together and talks so little about herself does the over-burdened wife talk to? Some people need our attention, but if the conversation is consistently one-sided, maybe part of the reason is that we respond too passively.

Sometimes speakers are hard to listen to because they're unaware of what they've said—or of its infuriating implications. When the listener reacts to what wasn't said, the speaker responds with righteous indignation, wounded by the listener's "overreaction." If a mother says to her teenage daughter "Is that what you're wearing to school?" and the daughter bursts into tears and says "You're always criticizing me!" the mother might protest that the daughter is reacting unreasonably. "All I said was 'Is that what you're wearing to school?' How come you get so upset about a simple question?" Such questions are as simple as parents are free of judgmentalness and children are free of sensitivity to it.

My father has a way of packing what feels like a whole lot of disconfirmation into one little innocent statement that drives me crazy. If I tell him that something is so, even when it's not something particularly unusual or controversial, he'll often say "It could be." Arghh!! I think he does this because he can't tolerate overt conflict. So if somebody tells him something that he didn't know or isn't completely convinced is the case, he says "It could be." To me, this feels much worse than an argument. An argument, you can argue with. "It could be" makes you feel discounted. One consequence of these interchanges is that I become stubborn in my opinions. Having had my fill of being doubted, I can't stand not to be believed when I'm stating a fact. Like the fact that Lake Champlain is one of the five Great Lakes.

In case you think I've slid from talking about speakers to complaining about listeners, you're right. While it's possible to separate speakers and listeners conceptually, in practice they are inextricably intertwined. Listening is co-determined.

Some people are hard to listen to because they say so little, or at least little of a personal nature. If the urge to voice true feelings to sympathetic ears is such a driving desire, why are so many people numb and silent? Because life happens to them—slights, hurts, cruelty, mockery, and shame. These things are hard on the heart.

We come to relationships wounded. Longing for attention, we don't always get it. Expecting to be taken seriously, we get argued with or ignored or treated as cute but inconsequential. Needing to share our feelings, we run into disapproval or mockery. Opening up and getting no response or, worse, humiliation, is like walking into a wall in the dark. If this happens often enough, we shut down and erect our own walls.

Although a speaker's reticence may be seen as a fixed trait of personality, such traits are really nothing more than habits based on expectations formed from past relationships. People who don't talk to us are people who don't expect us to listen.

Therapists who encounter resistance to speaking freely engage in what is called *defense analysis*—pointing out to the patient *that* he is holding back, *how* he is holding back (perhaps by talking about trivia), and speculating about *what* might be on his mind and *why* he might hesitate to bring it up. Therapists have license that the average person lacks to ask such probing questions, but it's not against the law to inquire if a friend is finding it difficult to open up for some reason or to point out gently that she doesn't seem to talk much about herself. We shape our relationships by our response.

*W*hen we think of listening skillfully, for the most part we think of it as something we do only with our ears and the information available to them. In this contribution from Authentic Movement instructor, Nancy Mangano Rowe, we discover that there are many ways to listen and many places within us from which we can obtain critical information. From intuition as a felt sense within our stomach, chest, or throat, to the chronic back pain that perhaps lives with us on a daily basis, these bodily reports can speak volumes to us if we can truly learn to listen to them.

Listening Through the Body

Nancy Mangano Rowe

*The living body is thus the very possibility of contact,
not just with others but also with oneself, the very possibility
of reflection of thought, of knowledge. The common notion
of the experiencing self, or mind as an immaterial phantom
ultimately independent of the body can only be a mirage.*
~Maurice Merleau-Ponty

RECENTLY I attended an informal event where dancers performed short sketches in front of an audience of dancers and dance enthusiasts. Most of them sat or lay on the floor as they watched. One dancer was about to verbally share his thoughts around his work in process, but before he did, he said to the audience, "Any of you who don't want to hear about this put your hands over your ears. I won't be insulted. Really." He knew that for some of the more kinesthetically-inclined people, the voice of movement speaks equally, and often more loudly, than words. Words can actually dilute the experience of the dance.

Our bodies influence our ability to really listen to others. Consider how we sit when listening for information as compared to listening empathically or when just relaxing. For some people, like dancers, listening through the body is particularly important, as was evidenced recently during a contemplative dance training program. During the day, workshop activities centered around dance, movement, activity with limited amount of talk;

in the evening we would discuss the papers that we had read. On the first night, the oversized chairs were moved into a carpeted area of the building and all the participants tried to listen and discuss the papers. Midway through the evening, we all noticed that we were exhausted and felt somehow disconnected from ourselves. Finally, we left the chairs, went into the dance studio and huddled around a corner by one of the walls. Our arms and legs were going in all directions and sometimes legs rested upward against the wall; some of us sat cross-legged, some of us lay on our backs, others on our sides or stomachs. We were happy in these postures and we could really hear. Our bodies felt like part of the discussion.

Honoring myself as a fully embodied person has been important in my life. It is through the rich language of my body that I make a connection to my personal truth, my creativity, and my Spirit. When I listen to the *felt sense* and to my intuitive voice, I feel more centered. It informs me about my path and where I need to heal. It has been my ally and a tremendous source of intuition and guidance. The body carries a wisdom of its own that can guide each of us through our lives if we listen. Developing a special quality of attention to this inner voice can also serve our psychospiritual processes. This paper is about the rich language of our bodies and how the body can guide us toward a more alive and connected life.

LISTENING TO THE BODY

I remember the first time that I noticed my intuition. I was very young, perhaps five or seven years old. I had deep in my being a physical sensation that made me think that an event would happen. It was like a premonition—nothing extreme, just an inner knowing. I decided that it was only my imagination. A few days later, the event did happen. Shortly after this occurrence, I experienced the same sensation. I recognized the feeling, and this time, I decided to wait and see if it would happen again. Sure enough, it did. When the same thing happened a third time, I understood it as part of my inner voice. I had learned to listen to my body.

This was the first time that I consciously remember becoming aware of my body's voice. It was also the first time that I remember thinking about my inner process, listening to my "inner witness" and perhaps, opening to consciousness. Since that time, I have paid great attention to my intuition. It has since been my ally and has guided my life.

Think of a time when your *felt sense* was too strong to ignore. When have you felt *something in your bones* or had a *gut feeling*? When has being in someone's presence made you uncomfortable for no rational reason? These experiences are physical sensations that are often associated with intuition and instincts that help us on life's journey. On a psychospiritual level, they guide us by informing us when we are in our integrity and when we are not. They are also there, in a more basic way, to ensure our survival and our self-preservation.

Understanding and awareness that originates from body perceptions are available to all of us when we pay attention. We can cultivate the quality of sensitivity and self-awareness that is required to listen to these internal cues and discover the unique ways that our body sends messages. Physical sensations might provide information about the body's needs and functioning. We might detect an illness before it is diagnosed or these sensations might help us to be aware of what our body needs to sustain itself at this time. It is not unusual for vegetarian women to begin incorporating fish or other forms of protein into their diets as their hormones begin to change at midlife.

In a more basic way, physical sensations can ensure our survival and our self-preservation. Listening to this inner voice assisted my recovery from a seven-year journey through environmental illness. I learned to listen for what to eat and was often surprised. As an example, I went through a period when my body cried out for lamb on a daily basis, a food I rarely ate before this time. I listened, thanked the lamb, and found the strength

I needed to sustain me through the day. Then one day, I heard my body say, "no more lamb" and I stopped. The message was clear. During this time, I learned to rest when I was tired, eat when I was hungry, and spend time nurturing myself by checking in with my felt sense. I truly believe that listening to this inner voice was at the core of my healing; it often trumped my doctor's recommendations. My body knew what was required to develop strength and perseverance during this time.

Our felt sense can also serve as a barometer for noting danger. Some people speak of hair rising on the back of their necks during times of peril. To me, it feels like anxiety that emerges for no apparent reason. On one occasion, I recall seeing a man walking toward me. He was alone and gazing straight ahead. When I was in his energy field, I felt uncomfortable and sensed that there was something "amiss," so I moved out of his path into a parking lot. Within a few minutes he entered a store, then came running down the street with a woman's purse. I had learned what this physical sensation meant to me, and this time, unlike previous times, I listened.

These sensations don't always reflect danger; sometimes they are more neutral and relatively insignificant or reflect a more positive experience. Recently I was leading a labyrinth walk. At 7:30 A.M., when the walk was to begin, I felt my body saying not to move… just wait… someone would arrive. The physical sensation felt like *stuckness,* for lack of a better word. I could have pushed forward and moved my body but I felt resis-tance, so I waited. Several minutes later, two participants arrived for the walk. It felt right that these participants begin with me.

Bodily sensations also give us feedback related to making decisions or coming to a solution. In her book *Alive and Well,* Rita Justice describes Louise, who when she would meet a man would physically get very cold or very hot. Over time, she learned that when she felt cold it indicated fear and when she felt hot it meant lust in her body symbology. John Coan, a psychosynthesis colleague, described a client who after being encouraged to dialogue with this sensation realized that his chronic sore throat was a message for him to speak up more in his life. He believes that: "The purpose of learning and listening to the language of the body is to help us find the truth that is trying to emerge from within. This process empowers each individual to listen to the voice of the deep self, the place where true healing is possible."

Each of us embodies our own symbology. What is yours? Ask yourself: What does it feel like when speaking from a place of personal truth? What does it feel like when couching language to please another? Where do I feel this in my body? What does it do to my body? What does it feel like when with people who honor my perspective or people who judge me? Notice how your felt sense shifts in each of these situations.

This *checking in* process can be experienced by consciously asking for information but first we must stop, breathe, pay attention, and then ask. Sue came to me to help her make a decision between moving to a new home or staying put. When she checked into her body as she thought about staying in the home that she lived in, she experienced a quality that spoke to her of being "fine, okay, this is an option." When she checked into her felt sense while considering moving she began to feel grief. As she entered the grief she discovered that it was not about the new house but about how leaving the home that she had lived in would mean leaving the place where her youngest child was born. The new house represented a new stage of life for her. Once she received that information, she was able to more clearly decide what to do. She eventually moved to her new home but only after embracing the loss that moving represented for her.

In all of the scenarios, each person learned what was uniquely true for his or her own body. Each person tested the waters and learned which clues revealed fear, intuition, lust, health, danger, and the like. They learned how to listen to and read their bodies. This sensitivity allowed them to eventually trust their felt sense. They knew that their bodies would reveal the truth which can lead to clearer judgment, wiser decisions, self-esteem, and confidence, all of which can produce better quality relationships with others.

Authentic Movement:
the Practice of Listening to Our Body

There are many spiritual practices that incorporate awareness as a way of accessing the body's wisdom. These practices help us to shift from thinking and conceptualizing into cultivating a life of fully experiencing the physical truths of the body. I know of nothing that more fully helps me to practice listening to my body's voice and to befriend my true self and others, than the practice of authentic movement. Authentic moving is nothing less than my spiritual practice.

Authentic movement is a practice where one or more people move in silence and with eyes closed, in the presence of one or more witnesses, for a predetermined period of time. The mover follows her bodily felt sensation and allows her being to be moved from inner impulse. She surrenders to the movement rather than controlling it, while in a deepened state of consciousness, a state where she only observes rather than engages with her mind and body. In this state, she may experience personal narrative, connect with the collective unconscious, or experience transpersonal information. She may uncover personal pain or trauma, access healing energy, or experience deep prayerfulness.

The mover doesn't know what will happen until the movement, until she listens to her body. She just lets it happen and sees where her impulses lead as she listens and responds to "deeper levels of kinesthetic realities."

The witness, the person who observes, simply brings a "specific quality of attention or presence to the experience of the mover." This quality of attention is nonjudgmental and compassionate and allows the mover to feel safe, both physically and emotionally, and to deepen her process. The witness also becomes aware of what the mover awakens in her own psyche. In other words, while compassionately witnessing the mover, she becomes her own inner witness. In a sense, it is a dance where body listens to body, suspending thinking and judgment. In this space, the witness cultivates presence in its fullest sense, and in this spiritual practice, such presence feels like a privilege.

Another level of witnessing happens within the mover herself. As she moves she also notices what is emerging from a place of meta-awareness. She moves, is moved, and notices this with the same quality of self-acceptance, nonjudgment, and compassion. There is no concern for performance, only a deep listening to her body's movement, while noticing and fully accepting what arises. The practice of unconditional positive regard for self is part of the dance.

After the allocated time, the mover(s) and the witness either move their dance into another creative form of expression such as pastels, clay, poetry, or journal writing, or they might choose to speak briefly about their experience. In a typical peer authentic movement circle, this is not a deep psychological processing time, rather, the mover selects particular parts of the experience that she wishes to share, or chooses to remain silent. The witness might share her experience as well and it is always about her *own* response to the mover. The mover or witness might share using movements, sounds, or visuals, without words. Interpretations or judgments during this time are not appropriate.

Authentic Movement as Spiritual Practice

Not everyone considers authentic movement to be a spiritual discipline. The casual mover can join groups periodically and benefit greatly from it, without thinking of it as a spiritual practice. But for me it is, not only because of the regularity of my commitment to it, but also because of the profound influence it has had on my life and spiritual unfolding.

In the decade that I have been involved in the practice of authentic movement, I have been so grateful for what it has taught me. Since authentic movement is a practice concerned with being seen and genuinely seeing others, it has helped me to cultivate nonjudgment and deeper levels of unconditional regard. As I witness the movement of others as well as myself, I have been in awe of the beauty of our interior lives and how profoundly it can inform. I have felt deep compassion in the witness role, and when I remember to move this awareness into life, I can be kinder to others. I can witness rather than judge. When I remember the witness role, I more easily flow with life's rhythms, with all its ups and downs. Authentic movement has helped me to grow, to mature, and to uncover my authentic self.

Authentic movement has also helped me to connect with Spirit in a more embodied way. For me, it is akin to prayer, not a prayer where I necessarily ask a question (although that is one of the ways it can be used) but rather a means for inviting Spirit to speak to me and through me without an agenda and especially without thinking. As in any spiritual practice, the material is sometimes difficult, but always received as sacred text. It is my informant, a guide to becoming more conscious. Through this form, I have also grown to understand what it means to think of the *body as temple*. I feel honored as I experience the movement of Spirit and grace within my personal being and the being of others. It is what I think of when I say, "Namaste." And all this can be applied to my daily life and my relationship with others.

I experienced the richness of this practice toward the end of my grandmother's life as she began to lose her ability to speak. Her language was expressed through her failing body. I would visit her from time to time, and my desire was to really be present in a way that made sense to her. Authentic movement had taught me about the strength of nonverbal communication and had taught me to witness. When I visited her in her later days, I began to realize how the act of touch or merely being present to her seemed more like an expression of caring than attempting to talk. Her frame of reference had grown so small; so had her cognitive, listening ability. Touch or just being near seemed more relevant to our personal connection.

On one visit, I noticed how speech was becoming more difficult, almost impossible for her, so we began to relate through dance. I moved my hands and upper body and she would follow; then she would move and I would follow. We danced like this for a long time and we laughed, which didn't happen much for her in the home where she was now placed. It was through this nonverbal dialogue that we were able to communicate in a loving way. There was little to speak about at that time in her life but we could enjoy each other's company through movement and listening.

Then she became bedridden and basically nonverbal, although she tried. There was nothing left to do but touch and witness. In my last visits with her I told her that I was there, and she didn't have to say or do anything. I heard a sigh of relief and saw a smile that lasted for a brief moment. Then she relaxed as I stroked her head and merely witnessed as I had done time and again in my authentic movement groups. All judgment from the past melted away as I entered into the witness stance, and from that place it was easy to just be present and open my heart. I was there at the moment that life left her body. I was privileged to be a witness to her final authentic movement.

A Few Last Words

Our bodies are such vital sources of information and truth. The wisdom that lies within each of us is so vast and helpful to our developing psyche and spiritual growth. As such I say, celebrate the body and listen to what it has to offer, whether it is on a day-to-day, checking-in basis or as a spiritual practice. As I end this paper, I want to share a sure fast way to begin the listening process. Check in with your body as you make a decision, no matter how big or small. Stop, breathe, and draw your awareness to the felt sense within then ask yourself: Does my body respond with a thud or a ping? See what your body reveals!

References

Abrams, D. (1996). *The Spell of the Sensuous: Perception and Language in a More-than-human world.* New York: Vintage Books.

Adler, J. (1999). Body and soul. In P. Pallaro (Ed.), *Authentic Movement: Essays by Mary Starks Whitehouse, Janet Adler, and Joan Chodorow* (pp. 166–189). London & Philadelphia: Jessica Kingsley Publishing Co.

Adler, J. (1999). Who is the witness. In P. Pallaro (Ed.), *Authentic movement: Essays by Mary Starks Whitehouse, Janet Adler, and Joan Chodorow* (pp. 141–59). London & Philadelphia: Jessica Kinsgsley Publishing Co.

Coan, J. III. (Fall 2002). Listening to the Body. *Synthesis Newsletter.* Amherst, MA.

Goldberg, P. (1983). *The Intuitive Edge: Understanding Intuition and Applying it in everyday life.* Los Angeles: Jeremy P. Tarcher.

Justice, R. (1996). *Alive and well: A Workbook for Recovering Your Body.* Houston, TX: Peak Press.

Knaster, M. (1996). *Discovering the Body's Wisdom.* New York: Bantam Press.

How many of us have ever been taught skillful ways of asking difficult, courageous questions to which the answers were not already known? Honed on her activism all over the world, this contribution from Fran Peavey provides instruction in this delicate art. She shows us how to skillfully ask the "unaskable" questions and demonstrates practical ways in which the empowering questions of dynamic listening can work to dissolve individual and collective denial and help reveal the "profound uncertainty that is embedded in all reality." Frequently, it is only by deploying this "communication of the second kind" that we uncover, with great relief, the deepest desires of the human heart.

Strategic Questions
Are Tools for Rebellion

Fran Peavey

I N THESE DAYS of constant change, and the need for even more change if we are to live peacefully in a healthy environment, we ask ourselves: "How can our organization weather the tides of constant reorganization and restructuring and still maintain a clear vision of its mission?" "How can I make decisions about my future that will draw from the most interesting alternatives?" "How can we participate in the creation of social change?" "How can a new vision arise in our organizations and societies?" I have been working on the concept of strategic questioning for some time as a way of facilitating "dynamic" listening. I also call this experiment in the developing field of communication theory "communication of the second kind," since it is a special kind of communication. It creates new information and uncovers deep desires of the heart rather than communicating information already known. Communication of the first kind involves transmission of information in a static and passive voice. It is focused on how reality is now. What is, is. Communication of the second kind, according to Mark Burch, who coined the term, refers to the "immersion of the person in a vibrating, tingling, undulating ocean of 'transactions.'" Communication of the second kind is focused on what could be, and upon the creation of active participation in present and future transactions. In a social, as well as a personal sense, we are involved in innate, spontaneous imagery, which organically draws us forward to appropriate realities of the future.

The key elements of communication of the second kind which relate to strategic questioning are:

New information is synthesized from that which is already known.

Ownership of the new information is with the person who is answering the question.

Energy for change is generated in the communication process.

The answer to a powerful question is not always immediately known but will emerge over time.

Emotion sometimes accompanies the answering of a powerful question and this is part of releasing the blocks to new ideas.

Communication between members of a society in a dynamic and visionary sense releases forces into the human organism as a whole that are complex, consensual, and cocreative.

A STRATEGIC QUESTION IS A SPECIAL TYPE OF QUESTION

Questioning is a basic tool for rebellion. It breaks open the stagnant hardened shells of the present, revealing ambiguity and opening up fresh options to be explored.

Questioning reveals the profound uncertainty that is imbedded in all reality beyond the facades of confidence and sureness. It takes this uncertainty towards growth and new possibilities.

Questioning can change your entire life. It can uncover hidden power and stifled dreams inside of you, things you may have denied for many years.

Questioning can change institutions and entire cultures. It can empower people to create strategies for change.

Asking questions that lead to a strategy for action is a powerful contribution to resolving any problem.

Asking questions that open up more options can lead to many unexpected solutions.

Asking questions that help adversaries shift from stuck positions on an issue can lead to acts of healing and reconciliation.

Asking questions that are unaskable in our culture at the moment can lead to the transformation of our culture and its institutions.

Asking questions and listening for the strategies and ideas embedded in people's own answers can be the greatest service a social change worker can give to a particular issue.

Strategic questioning is the skill of asking the questions that will make a difference. It is a powerful and exciting tool for social and personal change. It is a significant service to any issue because it helps local strategies for change emerge.

Strategic questioning involves a special type of question and a special type of listening. Anyone can use strategic questions in their work or in their personal lives to liberate friends, coworkers, political allies and adversaries, and to create a path for change.

Strategic questioning is a process that may change the listener as well as the person being questioned. When we open ourselves to another point of view, our own ideas will have to shift to take into account new information, new possibilities, and new strategies for resolving problems.

What would our world be like if every time we were listening to a gripe session, someone would ask, "I wonder what we can do to change this situation?" and then listened carefully for the answers to emerge and helped that group begin to work for change? What would it be like for you to do that in your work, family, or social context? Your attention and context might shift from a passive to an active one. You could become a creator, rather than a receiver, of solutions. This shift in perspective is one of the key things that people need in our world just now. And the skill of asking strategic questions is a powerful contribution to making such a shift.

Were you ever taught how to ask questions? Were you ever encouraged to ask questions where the answers are not already known? Have you ever been taught about asking questions that will really make a difference? Most of us who were brought up in traditional families or in a traditional education system were not. Traditional schooling was based on asking questions to which the answers were already known: How many wives did Henry the Eighth have? What color is that car? What is four times five? We learned that questions have finite and "correct" answers, and that there is usually one answer for each question. The wrong answer is punished with a bad grade. The landscape of learning was divided into "right" and "wrong" answers to questions. Questions can be divided into those which made the "authority" comfortable (the ones where he knew the answer) and those not-okay questions (those which exposed the authority's ignorance or culpability).

This may be a convenient way of running schools and testing people's capacity for memory in examinations, but it has not been a very empowering learning process for students, or a good preparation for the questions that will be coming up in life.

In some families, children are taught that asking a question where there is no known answer is to be avoided, because it makes people uncomfortable. Adults or parents who are supposed to be in charge of things seem to hate saying, "I don't know." It may even be true that asking embarrassing questions, or in any way threatening the power of adults, is a punishable offense. The child learns to stop questioning before the unknowns are revealed.

All this is unfortunate in our times, because in our personal, professional, and public lives, we are surrounded with questions that have no simple answers. We find that we must look at complex situations and create fresh responses. And if you haven't been taught how to work with such situations and ask questions, then this can be intimidating and provoke fear. Learning how to ask strategic questions is a path of transforming passive and fearful inquiry into the world into a dynamic exploration of the information around us and the solutions we need. We can create answers to almost any problem.

Take the traditional school. What would it have been like if, when the teacher asked "What is four times five?" and we had said "twenty-nine," the teacher had not said "Wrong!" and left it at that, but she asked us to explain our thought process and how we got twenty-nine. We would have learned about ourselves and our thinking process, and we might have discovered mathematics in an active way. The teacher might have learned something about increasing the effectiveness of her teaching methods.

In families that don't encourage questioning, an adult would rarely follow up an "I don't know" with a "How can we find out?" They are often so absorbed by their embarrassment that they do not show the child how to find out. It is important for children to grow up knowing that doubt, uncertainty, and unknowing exist in the adult world—a world that they will inherit and where they will need to play their part in creating solutions.

THERE ARE EIGHT KEY FEATURES
OF SHAPING A STRATEGIC QUESTION

A strategic question creates motion

Most of the traditional questions that we've been taught to ask are static. Strategic questions ask, "How can we move?" They create movement. They are dynamic rather than allowing a situation to stay stuck. Often the way a conversation is structured creates resistance to movement. The martial art Tai Chi teaches a lot of wisdom about meeting resistance. It says that when you meet an obstacle, you only make it more firm by pushing directly on it. If you meet an object coming at you with resistance, it is not very useful at all. Tai Chi says that if you meet and move with the energy of the obstacle coming at you, taking the energy from the other, then motion in a new direction emerges. Both parties end up in a different place than when they started, and the relationship between them is changed.

It is the same with asking a strategic question. As an example, suppose Sally is working on where she will live, and perhaps she has heard of some good real estate bargains in Sydney, and she's a bit stuck on what she should do next.

I could say to her, "Why don't you just move to Sydney?" This question might be provocative, but not very helpful. It is really a suggestion that is pretending to be a question. For my own reasons I think she should move to Sydney. Perhaps I am projecting into the question my own wish to move to Sydney. Whatever my reasons, I'm leading her because I am asking a manipulative question, and it is likely that the more I pressure Sally, the less likely she is to consider the Sydney option.

A more powerful strategic question would be to ask Sally, "What type of place would you like to move to?" or "What places come to mind when you think of living happily?" or "What is the meaning of this move in your life?" Sally is then encouraged to talk about the qualities she wants from her new home, to set new goals. You can then work with her to achieve these goals.

Asking questions that are dynamic can help people explore how they can move on an issue. On my first working trip to India with the Friends of the Ganges project, I asked the local people, "What would you like to do to help clean up the river?" Now, you might ask, "How did I know they wanted to clean up the river?" Well, I wanted to ask a question that assumed motion on this issue. I assumed that people always want to act more appropriately. I further assumed that they wanted to move out of their state of powerlessness regarding what to do about the pollution in the Ganges. Many interesting ideas emerged when I used that question, some of which we have implemented.

When we are stuck on a problem, what keeps us from acting for change is either a lack of information, the fact that we have been wounded in our sense of personal power on an issue, or that there is no system in place that enables us to move the issue forward. In our stuckness, we don't see how to make the motion.

When I ask a question like, "What would you like to do to help clean up the river?" I open up a door for the local people to move beyond their grief, guilt, and powerlessness to active dreaming and creativity. This is one of the gifts visitors can offer when they travel. Coming from outside may sometimes give the visitor a fresh perspective from which curiosity and questions can be drawn. But strategic questions may be used by anyone who wishes to bring fresh thinking into a situation.

A strategic question creates options

If I asked Sally, "Why don't you move to Jerome?" I have asked a question that is dynamic only in one direction (Jerome) and it very much limits the options she is challenged to think about. A more powerful strategic question opens the options up. "Where would you like to live?" or "What are the three or four places that you feel connected to?" These are much more helpful questions to ask her at this time. Sally might have been so busy thinking about the real estate bargains in Jerome, that she has lost a sense of all the other possibilities and her real goals.

A strategic questioner would help Sally look at the many options equally. Supposing Sally says she could move to x or y. It's not up to me to say to myself, "I think z is the best, and I should encourage her down that path." If you're being ethical about it, then you could best help Sally sort out her own direction by questioning all the options even-handedly, with the same enthusiasm and interest in discussing both a and b. Not only that, but you could help by asking if there are any more options that occur to her during the questioning time. Out of these questions, new options may emerge.

It is particularly important for a strategic questioner not to focus on only two options. We are so accustomed to binary thinking, either Jerome or Buhl, that Brisbane cannot emerge as a viable alternative. Usually when someone is only considering two options, they simply have not done the creative thinking to look at all the possibilities.

People are usually comfortable when they have two options and think they can make a choice at that level. This is part of the delusion of control. And since two alternatives is already more complex than one, people stop thinking. The world is far more varied and exciting than any two options would indicate, but having two options creates the idea that a choice, however limited, is being made.

Community consultation is enjoying popularity even though most organizations do not want real community input into their functioning. For instance, under the guise of consultation, a district roads group in New South Wales asked community members to choose between two alternative routes for a new road. In this case there were too few choices for the community to give real input. This was a bogus consultation process; probably there were some members of the community who wanted no new roads or wanted the money to go to public transportation.

A strategic question avoids "Why"

When I ask Sally, "Why don't you move to Sydney?" it is a question that focuses on why she doesn't do it, rather than creating a more active and forward motion on the issue. Most "Why" questions are like that. They force you to defend an existing decision in terms of the past or rationalize the present. "Why" questions also may have the effect of creating resistance to change. The openness of a particular question is obvious at the gross extremes, but becomes far more subtle and subjective as you deepen your understanding of the skills of strategic questioning. For example, can you feel the difference between asking, "Why don't you work on poverty?" and, "What keeps you from working on poverty?" Sometimes a "Why" question is very powerful as you focus on values and meaning. But in general it is a question which does not open up many possibilities.

A strategic question avoids "Yes" or "No" answers

Again, these types of questions ("Have you considered...?") don't really encourage people to dig deeper into their issues. A question that is answered with a "Yes" or "No" reply almost always leaves the person being asked in an uncreative and passive state. A strategic questioner rephrases their queries to avoid the dead end of a "Yes" or "No" reply. It can make a huge difference to the communication taking place.

A young man decided to experiment with the ideas behind strategic questioning. He realized that he hardly ever spoke a question to his wife without getting simply a "Yes" or "No" reply. A week after the class on strategic questioning, he reported that the technique had completely changed his home life! He had gone home and told his wife about these special types of questions, and they agreed to avoid asking a question that had a "Yes" or "No" answer for a week. He reported they had never talked so much in their lives!

A strategic question is empowering

A strategic question creates the confidence that motion can actually happen, and this is certainly empowering. When I asked people in India, "What would you like to do to clean your river?" I assumed that they have a part in that picture of healing. The question expresses a confidence that the person being questioned has a contribution to make in designing the cleanup process.

One of my favorite questions is "What would it take for you to change on this issue?" This question lets the other person create the path for change. Imagine an environmental protester going to a lumber mill owner and asking, "What would it take for you to stop cutting down the old-growth trees?" This question is an invitation to the mill owner to cocreate options for the future of his business with the community. The owner might tell the questioner the obstacles he faces in making changes to his business, and maybe they can work together to satisfy some of their mutual needs so that the old-growth trees can be preserved.

The planning that comes out of asking such a strategic question may not exactly resemble what either party wanted in the beginning, but a new reality is born out of the dialogue, and could well work to achieve both the protester's and the mill owner's goals. Empowerment is the opposite of manipulation. When you use strategic questioning, rather than putting ideas into a person's head, you are actually allowing that person to take what's already in their head and develop it further.

I had a student who worked in the command structure of a large police force. Like many government departments, his department had been restructured and this led to stress and disgruntlement between colleagues. They were not working together as a team. For weeks in their staff meetings, members of the department had been asking themselves, "What is wrong with the way we are working?"

My student took the strategic questioning method back to his unit and his department started to approach their difficulties with different, more empowering, questions. They asked, "What will it take for us to function as a team?" "How do we want to work together?" "What does each of us want to do?" "What support do we each need?" They reported that after the strategic questioning session, the low morale started to improve, meetings became creative, and a sense of teamwork returned to the unit.

A strategic question asks the unaskable question

For every individual, group, or society, there are questions which are taboo. And because those questions are taboo there is tremendous power in them. A strategic question is often one of these "unaskable" questions. And it usually is unaskable because it challenges the values and assumptions that the whole issue rests upon.

I like the fairytale about the emperor who went on a parade without any clothes because he had been tricked by some unscrupulous weavers into thinking he was wearing a magnificent costume. It was a child that asked the unaskable question, "Why doesn't the emperor have any clothes on?" If that child had been a political activist, she might have asked other unaskable questions, like, "Why do we need an emperor?" or "How can we get a wiser government?"

After the child asked that question, what are the strategic questions that could have followed which could have made major changes in that society? "What was it about us that did not allow us to tell the truth about what we saw—and didn't see?" "What was it that allowed the child to ask the question?" "What kept us from telling the emperor that he had no clothes on before he went out like that?" "What kind of an information system does he have?" "Why does it take a child to see the emperor's naked-ness?" "How come he's the only one to wear fancy clothes like this? Can we all wear nothing?" "Why did he spend all the treasury funds on.... The press will go wild." "Do we need an emperor who can't tell if he's got clothes on or not?" "How could we organize ourselves to take care of our community business without a king that bankrupts the treasury with his clothing addiction?" "What are the values of this society?"

Most of these questions have a dynamic quality to them. In them are the seeds of revolution, of inner change inside the individual, inside the various groups, and inside the society. In the interconnectedness of a sys-tem, all relationships are questioned. Each group in the society is going to have to ask, "What part did we play in this delusion, in this fraud? We each had a role. What was our role?; how can we stop colluding with the emperor, because we can't afford many more fraudulent clothes schemes." So those are strategic questions that came from the unaskable question.

In the early 1980s, one of the unaskable questions for me was, "What shall we do if a nuclear bomb is dropped?" You couldn't answer that with-out facing our overwhelming capacity for destruction, and the sense-lessness of it. That question allowed many of us to move beyond terror and denial, and work politically to keep it from happening. Some other unaskable questions might be: for the seriously ill person, "Do you want to die?" For those involved in sexual politics: "Is gender a myth?" For the workaholic: "What do you do for joy?" For the tree activist: "Where should we get building materials?" Or for the politician: "What do you like about the other party's platform?" or "How could both parties work closer together?"

Questioning values is a strategic task of our times. This is because it is the values behind highly politicized issues that have usually gotten us into the trouble in the first place. We need to look at a value, a habit, an institutional pattern and ask, "Is this value working or not?" "Are these values working for the common good?" "Are these values prosurvival (prolife) or antilife?" If you can ask the unaskable in a nonpartisan way, not to embarrass someone but to probe for more suitable answers for the future, then it can be a tremendous service to anyone with a "stuck" issue.

A strategic question is a simple sentence

The question enters a mind like a diver slips into water. It should not need a lot of analysis, so answers can be easily formed. The sentence should not be complex. For instance: "What are the tasks that would need to be done in moving and getting a new job?" is really focusing on two things: 1) moving and 2) getting a job. Better to ask the questions separately: "What would need to be done to move?" Wait for an answer, then ask "What would need to be done to get a new job?"

What would you be willing to do to clean the river Ganges?" I would ask assuming that naturally, a person would want to help clean it. This question is always controversial because people feel that it is possibly inaccurate to assume that people want to do something to clean the river. If people indicated that they did not care about the river I would not ask the question. In strategic questioning it is important to have an assumption of health and the desire to find health. The opening questions, in which you have checked your assumptions carefully, are the key to strategic questioning in a social situation just like in an interpersonal situation.

We must always check our cynicism and arrogance in asking a question. The questioner must always come to each question session confident that this person or group possesses the answers needed and is more powerful to affect the situation than we (or probably they) know. When I hear what sounds like uncaring or apathy in questioning periods, I interpret this as fear of caring too much, and dig deeper. I have never been disappointed with this approach in the long run, though some people stick with their apathetic position in the short run. The question can then be changed to, "If you cared about the river what actions do you think would be likely to have positive results?"

It is my observation that most people wish there were leadership or an organization that would assist them in changing those aspects of their society which cry out for change. With no structural way to participate in changing the system, they are left with only their ideas and passive desire. Often in order to maintain stability, people bury their ideas and a desire to work for change in a self-protective mechanism. What looks like apathy is actually fear of caring too much, and denial of anger at helplessness. Questions are a good way to penetrate such apathy.

A strategic question respects the person

A strategic question respects the person who is being questioned. If you don't respect a person you won't ask them strategic questions because you won't have confidence that anything useful can come from them. So strategic questioning assumes that there is something that everybody can do. And it assumes equality. More and more I'm thinking about communication of the second kind (of which strategic questioning is one important technique) as a part of the new democracy. It assumes that we have the answers right here at the grassroots. Our basic problem is that our institutions are not organized to move us, to get us involved for things to happen. We do not even know how to talk to each other in order to create new ways.

WHEN TO USE STRATEGIC QUESTIONING

- When your organization is undergoing major change.
- When you are thinking about organizing around resistance or acceptance of a proposal.
- When you as an individual are trying to make a life-changing decision.
- When a city council, administration, or board of directors is interested in what the membership or citizenry is thinking about a specific policy, or needs to know what latent ideas are bubbling around.
- When your organization or work unit is being restructured. Strategic Questioning will help the group work through the stages of resistance/acceptance and response to the situation.
- When you are writing a leaflet or creating an ad and you need to know what the logic of the resistance or acceptance is, and what language will be useful.
- When a group or organizer is contemplating a shift in strategy and needs to consider new alternative ideas.
- When you have been working on something for a long time and have run out of ideas.
- When you need to know how your clientele views your agency or what ideas they would like to suggest. Feedback is important for any group.
- When your membership is feeling isolated from the populace, or is cynical that anybody cares about the things they care about.
- When your staff, board, or administration is feeling they are somehow very elite and superior to others.
- When you need to understand the life experience, rationale, or degree of commitment of the people or organizations comprising the resistance to your campaign.
- When your group is fragmented and conflicted, strategic questioning will help clarify positions and look for new alternatives.

•When a group only sees one or two alternatives and needs to do some creative thinking together.

CHANGE IS ACCOMPANIED BY ...

•Shock

> *This can not be happening ...*

•Denial

> *This is not happening ...*

•Grief

> *"I feel so sad about what I have lost..."*

•Fear

> *This **is** happening ... What will happen to me?*

•Resistance

> *I don't want this ... I want that.*

•Struggle

> *There is something important about what I want ...*

•Possibility

> *Integration, adaptation, or new ideas are born ...*

The process of working through these levels of response with careful questioning and listening may take hours or years depending upon how substantial the change, how much opportunity one has for communication at a deep level, and the support one has in the process. Strategic questioning can be of great assistance in the process of creating a response to a changing situation.

Building Bridges to Other Points of View

In these times of tremendous diversity and conflict we are challenged to find ways of building bridges and cocreating new ways of working together to meet common goals. An important feature of strategic questioning is to put one's own opinions to the side and strive to find new ideas and ways. When Barbara Walters asked Anwar Sadat what kept him from going to Jerusalem to meet with Menachim Begin, suddenly Sadat was examining the obstacles to this goal in a fresh way. In the way she phrased the question, Walters enabled Sadat to think freshly about the political realities and envision a different reality of his own making. She was identified as a neutral. I believe she was just honestly asking about the obstacles in Sadat's way of change. He found his own way through those obstacles under good questioning.

Check Your Assumptions

Strategic questioning is a way of talking with people with whom you have differences without abandoning your own beliefs and yet looking for common ground which may enable both parties to cocreate a new path from the present situation. In every heart there is ambiguity; in every ideology there are parts which don't fit. Strategic questioning by someone who is perceived as neutral may help the questionee think beyond old answers. New policies may be envisioned, whistle blowers encouraged. This is one of the most important features of strategic questioning.

A couple of weeks after attending a strategic questioning workshop in Auckland, New Zealand, a woman (I will call her Joan) saw a television show about violence against women. The show did not adequately condemn such violence and it carried a commercial that was also antiwomen. The women's community was upset about this show and the commercial. They put out the message that women should call the manager of the station and give him a piece of their minds. Joan decided to see what would happen if she tried strategic questioning. She called the manager but instead of lecturing him about what she thought, she started off with some questions: "How does a show get on the air?" "What review policies do you have about combining commercials and the content of your shows?" "How could the women's community work with the television station to create better programming around this issue?" (Notice here the "How could..." nature of the question. If she had phrased the question "Is there a way we could work together?" she might have received the answer, "No, there is no way." Avoid yes/no questions if you want to generate a fresh response.) Finally the manager said, "Say, you seem to be quite knowledgeable about this matter. Would you like to be on the advisory board that screens each show and commercial and decides what should go on the air?" No one else who had called with an opinion was invited on to this powerful board.

Using Strategic Questioning for Individual Growth

An important task of strategic questioning is to create the environment where people can see the solutions that are within themselves. You listen deep into the heart of the person opposite you and this creates an atmosphere conducive to generative searching for "new" truth. We all know of many people who are perfectly content to tell you what you should do. They are people who love to dispense "solutions." And we all know of experts who go from one country to another or from one community within a country to another, telling people what to do. I call it the "consultancy disease."

Change that happens as a result of the "this is what I think you should do" school of consultancy is often too shallow and too fast to have long-lasting effects. It is not empowering for the people who are trapped within the issues at stake. The people involved might look as if they have changed but, because the change strategy has not come from them, they don't own it, they have not invested themselves in the change.

A strategic questioner listens for the latent solutions that are hidden within every problem. And this involves a special type of listening. You are not merely passively listening. You are creating an action path with your attention. An attitude of expectancy helps fresh ideas emerge. This dynamic listening is in itself a special type of communication. It involves immersing yourself within the sea of "transactions" that surround an issue. You are not just listening to this information in a static or passive way. Your attention is focused on the reality of now and also paying attention to the clues of what could be.

It is this dynamic listening that opens doorways within the issues being discussed. Your attention creates space around the speaker—space within which they can explore their own options.

For me, dynamic listening is more like looking than listening. Usually when you listen, you hear everything around you in one total "hearing." But the kind of listening I am talking about is listening in only one direction—your ears are turned only toward the deepest part of the person opposite you. You are listening to their thinking, to their feeling, to their dreams, and to their essence. Your ears wander in between their words, their sighs and their questions, searching out meaning, resolve, and need.

You look for the obstacles to caring, the blocks to action.

You look for what is pushing the person, and why they feel compelled to do—or not do—something about the issue.

You look for the person's ideas of how they want things to be—how they see that things could or should change.

You look for how the person thinks about change and how change happens in their lives.

You look for the path to change that the person sees—however dimly and timidly they see it. Sometimes you explore the path together, asking questions that allow you both to think freshly and creatively.

You look for how to remove the resistance that is found on the path of change.

You look for what the person feels as they anticipate each possible choice or option in front of them.

You look for what support the person would need to move on any path of change.

Our minds are often not paying full attention. While we hear another person speaking, our thoughts are full of reactions, distractions, fantasies and judgments. We are concentrating on what we are going to say and so we do not listen.

My friend Karen Hagberg is a musician, and has written eloquently about the importance of dynamic listening. She notes:

Without careful listening, a pianist cannot understand the various ways a single note can be played. It seems impossible that we do not listen to ourselves. What else is there to do while we are practicing? What else are we doing? There are many things, actually, that I am able to do instead of listening. I can hear an imaginary pianist, Horowitz for example, and imagine his sound as mine. I can feel the music instead of listening to it and move around a lot as I play, imagining that my feelings must becoming out as sound. Possibly I am daydreaming, half-asleep, not concentrating. Usually, though, I am merely thinking about something. Thinking is not listening, nor is judging the performance as it evolves. Listening is listening.

There are times when we truly listen—usually when we sense ourselves to be in danger. We stop in our tracks, our ears prick up, and we listen as if our lives depend on it. The listening required for strategic questioning is like that; we need to listen as if someone's life depends on it, because it may.

Through this dynamic listening to ourselves, to the earth, and to our fellow citizens—even those we might consider our adversaries—we may create the space where people can discover themselves expressing great ideas, or finding the energy and will to make changes happen in their lives.

LONG-AND SHORT-LEVER QUESTIONS

Questions differ in their power. There are what I call long-lever questions and short-lever questions. A long-lever question opens up more possibility for motion than a short-lever question.

Suppose we have just a short-lever question. The question comes straight into our head and, metaphorically speaking, we can only open a crack. But if we have a more dynamic question, or a longer lever, we can open the mind wider, can't we? If we think of a powerful question, we can let a lot of the inert stuff out that's trapped inside a person's head. There is new possibility for creating synthesis, and increased motion and zest. Whereas before the person might have not known how to move, now that person has their own ideas of where to go and what to do.

It's not a matter of a question being a strategic question or not. Each question we ask falls along a continuum, say of one to ten. There are ones and tens but most questions are somewhere in the middle. And in one situation a question might act as a three in its ability to unlock motion, while in another situation it might act as a seven. It's not a rigid system. There are questions that differ in their power to elicit dynamic responses and energy.

Strategic questioning is the opposite of manipulation. Rather than putting ideas into a person's head, you are actually allowing the person to take what's already in that head and work with it. When you say "Jennifer, you should recycle," you communicate 1) Jennifer probably doesn't know about recycling; 2) all she needs is someone telling her what to do and she will do it; and 3) Jennifer must have been sleeping these past twenty years.

Telling people what they should do, personally or politically, rests on an authoritarian model of humanity—a model I reject. When you ask Jennifer what is her next step in helping the earth survive, Jennifer has a chance to set her own goals. It is a far superior strategy to get all the minds working on what needs to change rather than to convince each person to do what we think is best. I would reiterate that "why" questions are not usually very dynamic questions because they ask the questions to rationalize the present rather than explore her own options.

A question can be more or less dynamic, more or less strategic, inspire more or less action. To adapt creativity expert Edward de Bono's terms, there are "rock" questions, those that assume a hard truth, which focus on hard-edged, permanent, unchanging reality; and there are "water" questions, those which flow, which work to find a way through, a reality that moves, a focus on "how can" rather than "is."

*C*aregiving serves as a deeply spiritual practice for many people around the world. From hospital and hospice workers and licensed professionals, to mothers, fathers, and assorted relatives, the work of caring for others offers untold opportunities to practice patience, forgiveness, compassion, and learning to let go. Some people consider caregiving to be the ultimate ego-dissolver. In this contribution longtime hospice psychologist Kathleen Dowling Singh, author of The Grace in Dying, relates her personal experience of the spiritual nature of caregiving. From the often painful struggle to find a workable balance between one's own needs and those of another, to the power inherent in the cultivated capacity to lend our full attention as a healing gift to another, Kathleen offers us the benefit of years of hard-won wisdom.

The Gift of Attention

Kathleen Dowling Singh

I N THE YEARS of being a mother, a single mother at that, I would often watch wistfully as one friend after another, unfettered and free, took off for this ashram, that monastery, the annual thirty-day retreat. There were, for me, many moments of self-pity, of frustration, even depression. At one point, I began to contemplate the possibility, at least on an intellectual level, that my spiritual practice was right in front of me. There they were: four little ones, lined up and waiting for dinner, needing baths, wanting me to wipe a nose or settle the latest squabble. They were waiting, in short, for my attention.

It has been a long sadhana—and fruitful, far beyond what I could possibly have imagined when I so hopefully mouthed the words, "caring for the children is my practice." The last child is grown and gone now; grandchildren are growing in number and shoe size. The lessons that I was given as a parent, simply caring for my children, continue to grow in me. They grow as I allow—indeed, implore—them to touch and open my heart and as I deepen them through more formal, deliberate practice.

Like many others, I entered into caregiving with a self-centered mind, without preparation, with virtually no insight, and with no guidance whatsoever in caregiving as a spiritual path. It was a rocky road that I traveled, often gracelessly, before I came to a point where the truths of this particular path finally began to resonate in me. Even so, I consider myself blessed to have had even the slightest awareness that caregiving can be a spiritual practice. So many caregivers, especially those in the helping professions, share stories of struggling to find a balance between their recognition of the great need for their work and the burnout they feel. I cannot imagine how hard, how lonely, how depleting it must be for all of those engaged in caregiving who have no spiritual practice at all.

Nearly 75 million people in the United States are involved in the care of a loved one. Hundreds of thousands of us have chosen to be members of the helping professions. In many ways, especially as medical advances extend life, we are increasingly becoming a nation of caregivers. Most of us have engaged or will engage in this role, in one way or another—either professionally or for family—at some time in the course of our lives. Certainly, when we begin to grow in compassion, our natural tendency will move us toward being a caregiver, in the most basic sense of the word, for all those around us. With this awareness, it seems wise to examine some of the deeper levels of this role so many of us will choose or will have chosen for us.

Caregiving, in and of itself, obviously, does not necessarily lead to enlightenment. If so, all parents and therapists and health professionals, for example, would already be buddhas. But, with the slightest openness to the daily lessons, and a mind predisposed to recognize those lessons, those who walk on the solitary path of caring for others can begin to discern some wisdom. With deeper recognition and commitment to growth, what begins to light the way are the increasingly obvious signs of the benefits of cherishing others. These signs and indications illuminate a way out of the painful struggle, experienced by so many caregivers, between the needs of self and others.

In any kind of caregiving, we discover—actually, we are forced to discover—that there is little room for the self-centeredness with which we ordinarily enter the situation. This self-centeredness is the mind in which we habitually operate, no matter how good our intentions. Our self-centeredness, it quickly becomes obvious, does not lead to beneficial results for the person for whom we are "caring"—nor, ultimately, does our self-centeredness benefit us.

To speak of self-centeredness in this way is not to imply that martyrdom is the path to take. It is to isolate and illuminate self-centeredness as the cause of our stresses as we seek to balance the needs of self and other. Of course, we must always exercise adequate and loving self-respect. Of course, we need to keep ourselves healthily nourished. An empty cup doesn't "runneth over." Honest, self-honoring care for ourselves, however, can be easily distinguished from self-centeredness. Self-centeredness is self-cherishing, a mind that values my own desire for happiness and freedom from any suffering no matter how slight, far above the desire of anyone else for that same happiness and freedom. Although we were certainly not taught in our culture to recognize this to be true, the mind of self-cherishing is always a problem, and is a particularly big problem in caregiving.

Keeping our attention primarily on ourselves, on our own self-cherishing desires and aversions, in a time of being with another who needs care, simply doesn't work. All hell breaks loose. The things that need to be done go unattended and the "to do" list just gets longer and more overwhelming. The person not receiving the needed care suffers, requiring even more care. We ourselves endure the hellish emotions of frustration, unhappiness, guilt, burnout, and resentment—all the fiery waves of an unpeaceful mind. Again and again, we are forced to recognize the truth, as the Jesuits put it, "long hidden in plain view." Keeping our attention fixed in the small world of our own self-centeredness causes problems on every level.

When we truly need nourishing, release, or respite, it is beneficial to keep our wise and compassionate attention on our own essential needs for healthy maintenance. The point is that the control and appropriate placement of the attention is one of the keys to maintaining equanimity in caregiving. When we are with another, engaged in caregiving, we take our attention off our self. Doing this, we find that, placing our attention on another, everything else falls into place. The switch of the object of cherishing, from self to other, is the cause of greater happiness all around.

Lessons such as this, the lessons of caregiving, are straightforward and plainspoken. They are starkly simple. They may even be deceptively simple, just as Jesus of Nazareth's advice to "love one another" is often thought to be understood just by being heard. The lessons of caregiving have just that same quality of easily-overlooked obviousness. The baby calms when we hold her, cuddle and warm her, look into her eyes. The teenager actually shares the confusion with which he's struggling when we simply sit with him, side by side, on the couch. The crankiness of the elderly man diminishes when we stop and listen to a story or two. The work of therapy progresses when the therapist is fully present. The person who is seriously ill, even too weak to talk, shows how meaningful our even momentary presence is in a glance or a relaxation of breathing. These lessons stare us in the face, wide-eyed and direct, waiting only for our recognition.

There is, for each of us, as we grow into being caregivers, a first shocking moment when we turn our view outward. The population of the world is, indeed, more than one. From that moment forward, we can begin to recognize what is being revealed around us—in circumstances, in other people. We are forced to acknowledge that each and every "other" has the same desire for happiness and the same desire to avoid suffering, in equal measure to our own. When we respond to that fact appropriately, when we are offering another human being the precious gift of our attention—actually being with him or her—we begin to see that the signs of meaningful appreciation, the evidence of the power of nurturing, and the sweet and quiet joy of connection are everywhere apparent.

We have all been conditioned in the West, so impoverished in our abundance, with the fearful thought that giving might diminish or take away from "I" and "me" and "mine." With the gift of attention, we find that what appears to be a gift from us to another is, in fact, a gift to both the apparent receiver and to the apparent giver. What really creates true happiness in the other also really creates true happiness in us—a simple, natural, lovely symmetry. The beauty of a virtuous action, as Buddha taught 2500 years ago, is that its benefit is universal. This profound truth is revealed, always—if we look—in the simplicity of caregiving.

The Importance of Being Understood

Every form of caregiving is a treasury of teaching. The treasure is offered whether the caregiving occurs in the form of caring for babies and children, the lonely, the elderly, the frail and infirm, the disturbed, or the dying. It is also offered simply caring for the person who next walks in through the front door or sits by our desk at the office. Each act of care brings us into the realm of the private, the intimacy of the interpersonal. Although often unacknowledged and rarely honored in our public culture, we do come to know that these private and hidden acts of caring do much to sustain everyday life. They allow us to recognize and respond to the precious fragility of the individual in a world of often brutal indifference. Each act of caring holds the key to understanding, quite simply, how we may live together well. Each act of caring illuminates how we may live together at a deep and meaningful level of mutual benefit.

Caregivers access deep and direct insight into what's valuable, virtuous, and effective, in terms of fostering human growth. What's valuable, virtuous, and effective is the gift of our attention. Our simple attention, offered to another person, is the most underused of human resources, one of the least costly, one of the most freely available, and—without doubt—one of the most powerfully beneficial.

The gift of our complete and focused attention is one of the kindest gifts we can give each other. It confers on both parties, apparent giver and apparent receiver, a sense of meaning, of value, of mattering. Why? Because, in the moment of the gift of attention, we are actually *present;* our attention is deliberately and single-pointedly placed, our very life in that moment is meaningful. Whenever we ingather or re-collect our attention, the vividness, the depth and breadth, and the subtlety of our awareness automatically increases. So accustomed to our own self-centeredness, we find that when we focus our attention on another, that "other" becomes more real for us, more meaningful, and we become naturally more compassionate. The sense of the solidity of our "I," obscuring our heart of compassion, begins to thin.

If we take a moment to think about it, among the most precious moments in our life are those moments when we have felt ourselves to be most deeply understood by another human being. If we recall just one of those moments, we can see that, in it, our feeling of being understood occurred when another person kindly and deliberately bestowed upon us the gift of his or her attention.

With attention, we feel heard, seen, understood; the power of that experience cannot be underestimated. So often, we are held back in an inner way by perceived obstacles, "stuck" until a felt need can find expression. When we are given the space to express ourselves, knowing that what we express will be received, there is a new freedom of movement from the ultimately inessential to the ultimately essential.

I have come to think that "being understood" is sometimes even more of a fundamental human need than "being loved." We are nurtured in the gift of another's attention. It provides the safest of places in which to share our vulnerabilities, fears, doubts, and triumphs. We are known in our utterly unique, endearing, earnest, and creative attempts toward peace, both inner and outer. To feel understood in any and all of these private facets of human experience—sadly, so rarely shared—is to feel validated in our own being. We feel reconnected to our common humanity in the moment of being present with each other.

Deepening the Lessons of Caregiving

We can, if we choose and if we are fortunate, learn a bit about each of these lessons through caregiving. Caregiving provides homespun Dharma. This is the gradually developing insight arising from living everyday life with and in caring. Slow learners that we are, fumbling often (I remember, with regret, the many times my children called to me: "Earth to Mom"), we still do eventually catch a glimpse of wisdom out of the corner of our eye. In each and every moment of caregiving, we have the opportunity to prolong our glimpses of insight into genuine understanding: our healthy attention, voluntarily offered, nourishes others—and nourishes us, too, in the process.

This practice, this caregiving, both applies and elicits teachings. There is a jewel shining through our experience of the pressures and strains of caregiving's demands, a quintessentially pivotal and transforming Dharma teaching. It is this: in learning to cherish others, we diminish our own self-cherishing—the cause of all of our own suffering and of all our unskillful, unhelpful, or insensitive actions relating to others, with which we so often bruise them in our wake.

The lessons we begin to learn in the chaos of caregiving, where we are often tossed about and toss ourselves about, unprepared and unguided, are haphazard. Our grasp on them is not always so sure. The lessons are glimpsed amidst the messiness of laughter, diapers, medicine, paperwork, tears, fears, other pressing commitments, and crisis.

How to deepen these lessons we glimpse in caregiving? That becomes the question. How do we directly apprehend these insights with crystalline clarity? How do we make them our own? Human suffering in six billion individual aspects calls for compassion and wisdom and skill. How do we develop these qualities in ourselves? And how do we express or offer them in ways that do not leave us depleted?

The sophisticated, deliberate teachings of Mahayana Buddhism hold authentic answers to such fundamental questions. They offer a veritable treasure house of insights and practices for all of us who are engaged in caregiving, occupied with the struggle to balance what we so often perceive as conflict between the needs of self and others.

Buddha taught that our very thinking about this perceived conflict is mistaken. Self-cherishing will never bring happiness. Our own happiness and the happiness of others are not in conflict. Happiness is not, all worldly thought to the contrary, a commodity that decreases for us as it increases for others, nor does it reside in the manipulation of external circumstances. Happiness is, rather, a state of mind. Even if such an inner peace seems unattainable in many of the chaotic moments of caregiving, even if we feel at our lowest ebb, countless thousands who have followed the path of Dharma bear testimony to the truth that inner peace is most assuredly within the capacity of all of us to cultivate. It is, after all, a facet of our essential Buddha nature—our birthright as living beings.

Unlike the glimpses and brief tastes of insight afforded to us in the chaos of caregiving, the Mahayana teachings are dazzling in their clarity. Deepening the lessons of caregiving, these teachings are even more piercing in their insistence on the absolute necessity of developing a mind of compassion. The teachings offer deliberate methods: a precise, ordered, progressive, and brilliantly insightful path. Well-followed, the path of Dharma ripens the insights of caregiving to their realized perfection. The teachings of Buddha lead us, in short, with great wisdom and efficiency, to a mind that has exchanged its object of cherishing from self to others[1] and, then, to the precious mind of universal compassion.[2]

The practice of Dharma allows us, simply, to transform our minds into pure minds, our hearts into loving hearts, our very being into benefit for all beings—our self and others. It leads us to exactly what we've been struggling to find: genuine and growing happiness, all around.

Buddhist wisdom suggests that, if we are in the midst of the chaos and stresses of caregiving, we actually stop for a moment. Neither martyrdom nor resentment are viable paths to the happiness we seek. Instead, we set aside any time we can manage to set aside—an hour, twenty minutes, even five minutes—to meditate, to simply and single-pointedly mix our mind with the virtuous qualities of enlightened mind, qualities such as love and wisdom and compassion.[3] Our meditations, repeatedly practiced with sincerity and faith, familiarize our mind increasingly with virtue, leaving it far more peaceful as a consequence. Our meditations begin to transform us. Our practice more beneficially and more joyfully reorganizes our mind and being at very subtle levels.

We grow steadily and gradually—as Buddha suggests, "drip" by "drip," one drop at a time filling a bucket. So, rejoicing with each drop of progress, we extend great patience and compassion to all beings, including our self. Judgment does not help here, just continuously renewed commitment. At first, as we try this new way, this deliberate attempt to reduce self-cherishing and to exchange the object of our cherishing from self to other, it may feel difficult, unnatural, forced. Whenever discouragement raises its head—in whatever form—it helps to think not so much how hard this new practice is but how hard it is *not to* have this new practice. This is a path out of burnout and into happiness. It is helpful to remember that we are doing the practice precisely because we have a larger goal. We are not just trying to make it until the end of our workday or last until respite help comes or the kids grow up. We are working toward a mind that is indestructibly peaceful, a being that is a genuine benefit both for our self and for others.

Sometimes slowly, sometimes dramatically, the transformations effected by our practice begin to illuminate even our most ordinary mind and actions. Meditation practice allows the breathtakingly beautiful and blissful qualities of our own Buddha nature to gradually emerge in our hearts and in our lives. This is where life is meaningful. This is where it is more than worth the effort.

Buddhist wisdom also suggests that we continue our practice during our "meditation breaks"—i.e., the rest of our lives, the millions upon millions of moments, ordinarily so squandered. The practice of giving—one of the six perfections: giving, patience, moral discipline, effort, concentration, and wisdom[4]—is an easy practice to undertake as we live our daily lives, as we engage in caregiving. It is a sustained and deliberate effort to gradually live more and more of the precious moments of each day in such a way that the insights, transformations, and growing happiness of our meditation permeate and are applied in all that we do, all that we say, all that we think. So many caregivers are concerned with decreasing stress. Dharma *is* a path that will decrease stress; more significantly, Dharma is a path that will increase joy.

THE PRACTICE OF GIVING ATTENTION

The practice of giving attention, included within the practice of giving, can be done anywhere, anytime, with anyone. It is an easy way—and, quite soon, a gratifying way—to start on the path of Dharma.

Not so long ago, I had run down to our local pharmacy. In the small parking lot, I pulled in next to a shiny, immaculate, older white Cadillac—the certain sign in Florida of a senior citizen. At the counter, I stood behind a very elderly lady requesting her prescriptions, clearly the owner of the big white car. Waiting in line, I couldn't help but notice that she was impeccably dressed: a violet-print dress, leather heels with appliqued sections of lilac and purple, a lilac overcoat, even pale lilac gloves. Every silvery hair was perfectly in place. It dawned on me suddenly that this was her big outing for the week—this visit to the pharmacy—and that she had put much time and attention into her appearance for the outing. Noticing someone behind her, she turned to glance at me. And so I simply said to her, "What lovely colors you have on." She beamed. She turned back two or three times to beam even more. The last look, filled with such sweetness and happiness, was if I were her long-lost lover, home finally from the war. Once she got her medications and made ready to leave the pharmacy, she said goodbye twice, each time with a lovely, loving smile. The warmth and joy that filled me carried me through the day.

Once we begin to open our eyes and minds and hearts, to enter deeply into the present, one of our first awarenesses is of our relatedness. I and others—*we*—do not exist quite as separately as we have been accustomed to believing. We begin to appreciate at a very deep level that "we are all interconnected in a web of kindness from which it is impossible to separate ourselves."[5] When we think deeply about it, absolutely everything we have and are and can be comes not from ourselves. Everything from which we benefit, including our own bodies, we receive from the kindness of others. This understanding greatly motivates us, helps us genuinely cherish others, and leaves us with the experienced recognition of our deep connection. Recognizing the reality of interbeing, it becomes very clear that the gift of attention is one of the most appropriate of responses.

The practice of giving attention is hardly a passive process. It is interesting that, although so much of caregiving involves an active, thoughtful, responsive mode of being, it is often thought of as passive. The practice of giving attention is an action; it is participatory. Arising from a full heart, the practice demands all we have to offer of compassion, presence, and whatever wisdom and skill we have managed to acquire. In the demand for all of the virtuous qualities we have to offer, the practice also further develops each of these qualities in us. This is meditation with open eyes, Buddhism in action. It is the recognition that compassion is a necessary and an appropriate response simply because all living beings caught in *samsara*—the uncontrolled cycle of ordinary existence—suffer. The gift of attention expresses that compassion.

The gift of our attention to another human being allows us to enter a state of communion, of deep listening. Deep listening is 180 degrees from our normal, mindless, ordinary way of listening. Our ordinary way of listening is ego's posture. The gift of attention and the consequent deep listening that it allows arise from a strong and deliberate inner stance, at a deep remove from our usual superficiality and frivolity. It arises from choosing to actually be here, with another, in the present moment.

When we deliberately and consciously practice the gift of attention, it is not with the ordinary mind of self-cherishing that we listen to another or simply be with another. It is with a much more open and inclusive mindfulness, motivated by compassion. In such deep listening, we listen far more with our hearts than with our ears. It is helpful to think of this experience as "listening with the third ear." The third ear, of course, is the heart.

It is also helpful to remember that this "listening" can occur without a word being said. Once I sat by the side of an elderly man who was in a hospital, very close to the moment of death. I sat with him for many hours, although he neither knew me nor seemed to know that I was there. For many hours, I simply matched my breathing with his and offered him my full attention. To my surprise, when he spoke several hours later, he thanked me for "not knitting, not reading, not talking on the phone." He thanked me for just sitting with him.

Deep listening, simply being with another, is subtle and involves much more of our being than we ordinarily invest in listening, in being together. We allow the sounds and the silences and the words and the meaning behind the words to touch our heart, such an act enabled by our intention, mindfulness, and full presence. The practice of the gift of attention is an act of commitment, of engaged loving. Recognizing the profundity of the very act of interpersonal communication, we let our whole being resonate with the other person, just as our whole being might resonate with a mantra or the radiant lights of an inner mandala.

TECHNIQUES OF THE PRACTICE

Practicing the gift of attention is simple. Through breathing meditation, mantra recitation, or any other preparatory practice, we keep ourselves at the threshold of meditation as we go through our daily lives. Centered, peaceful, with a mind as clear as possible in that moment and a heart as full, we remain prepared for the next human being to arrive, grateful that his or her presence allows us to practice once again.

With each interpersonal encounter, we simply remember to begin the practice. The face, the voice, the presence of another human being becomes the signal to us. We simply place our attention single-pointedly on the other as the object of our meditation, our entire being open to the other in a never-to-be-repeated moment.

If it is obvious that the other person has no real desire at that moment to connect, we bestow our full attention while we are together, wish him or her well, and move on to the next moment and the next person. At the least, we have created the space and the opportunity for communion. We quickly become more skillful in distinguishing who wishes to enter that space with us and how he or she wishes to "dance" in it. And we certainly become more adept at "dancing" with each new partner.

Invariably, as we listen to another living being, many responses arise in our mind. Just as when we are sitting to abide in regular meditation, our ordinary mind continues with its deep, pervasive, habitual inner dialogue. It mindlessly follows its own generation of memories, associations, insights, criticisms, judgments, agreements, thoughts of what we want to say or do, thoughts relating to anything in the past prior to this precious moment of communion, thoughts relating to anything we imagine in the future after this precious moment of communion.

The point in the practice of the gift of attention and the deep listening it allows, as in the practice of meditation per se, is not to engage in these inner conversations, not to become wrapped up in them. When we notice them arise, we simply let them float on by. We can trust that they will return to dissolve back into the clear awareness from which they arose, as have the millions of thoughts before them. When we notice them arise, we simply note their floating and return our spacious attention to the speaker.

As we practice the gift of attention, we gain great clarity in our awareness.

We begin to recognize the "posture of listening" anytime our attention returns to our own self-centeredness, self-importance, and self-interest. We may notice ourselves spending our time, ostensibly listening, thinking our own thoughts and chafing at the bit to give voice to them. We may notice ourselves, for our own self-cherishing needs and reasons, listening only to certain parts of what another is sharing. We miss not only the nuances but the essence of all that is integral to the interaction. We can recognize this "posture of listening," a clear reflection of our own "I" and its greed for itself, anytime we act interested when we are not. When we search for openings so that we can sneak in our own viewpoint, we begin to quickly recognize our own self-cherishing mind. It is far better to sit with the silence or to let ourselves be moved to speak by our heart alone. And when we do speak, we should always ask ourselves the three questions advised by those in the Sufi tradition. Is what I am about to say truthful? Is it necessary? Is it kind?

We may notice, as we begin to perfect this practice, that we often place greater value on our own preconceptions, so dearly held in our self-cherishing mind, than on being receptive to the expression of another's human experience. Or we may notice that we feel a need to have "the right thing to say," the solution to the problem, the fix. When we do any of these things, motivated by self-centeredness, we do not see or hear the other. We see or hear only ourselves. And we leave the precious, never to be repeated interaction not only *not* having grown, but actually diminished. We are diminished in the missed opportunity to be present with and grow with another living being. We are diminished in the drain it takes on the self-cherishing mind to adopt the "posture of listening," to feign compassion.

Feigning compassion, we "tolerate" or offer pity or fancy ourselves as "helpers/rescuers." We may find ourselves robotically acting in ways that accord with the unexamined shoulds and oughts and musts in our mind's images of goodness and caring or of professionalism. Feigning compassion, we try either to protect ourselves or to feel good about ourselves. It is self-cherishing that is the source of burnout, of "compassion fatigue," in caregiving. Genuine compassion *doesn't* fatigue. Genuine compassion is simply an inner stance, wishing that suffering and its causes cease and standing committed to their cessation. Genuine compassion naturally enhances both beings.

Our practice of the gift of attention is a perfect mirror for our self-cherishing mind. It reveals every intrusion of "I" with great clarity. We can watch ourselves, catching this mind of self-cherishing whenever it arises. And we transform ourselves, moving toward greater bliss, genuine inner peace, each time we let go of a little more of that attachment to "I."

The gift of attention can be seen as the practice of simple mindfulness meditation with our eyes open—and our ears and our heartminds. With the "other" as our object of meditation, we can begin to pierce through the illusory veils of self and other. In regular meditation practice, we move from a feeling of separation between ourselves and our object of meditation to the experience of being absorbed in the object of meditation itself, with no gap between observer and observed. In the same way, with attention completely focused on the "other," we can begin to enter a state of communion with each other—a subtle and sacred moment, indeed.

We can, if we wish, maintain the perspective of "pure view" throughout this practice. That is to say, we can view each person that we meet, with whom we practice the gift of attention, as a Buddha. This pure view, as with any virtuous action, benefits both people. The other is given cause to realize his or her own enlightened nature. And pure view allows us to study and practice Dharma in every second of our lives. We receive enormous blessings, the blessings of a Buddha, and these blessings help increase our capacity to be of benefit to all other living beings.

During times of silence with another person, still maintaining the gift of our attention, we can also practice "taking and giving." Taking and giving—in Tibetan, *tonglen*—is a deep practice, working at a breathtaking level of profundity. In taking and giving, we can maintain our attention on the other person, even deepening it, and magnify its benefit beyond measure, in this most beautiful of meditations.

We "take" first, imagining that we are freeing the other person from suffering. This opens the space for him or her to receive the inner peace we are "giving." With practice, we can combine this meditation, its thoughts and intentions, with our breathing. Very simply, with each inbreath, we imagine our compassion growing, like a glowing ember being blown upon so that its brightness and intensity increase. We think, "May you be free from suffering. May I take all of your suffering and negativity upon myself right now. May you be free from suffering." With our compassion, our deep wish that no other living being suffer, we imagine all the suffering and negativity of the other being entering us, because we *will* it, in the form of dense, thick smoke. We imagine, very strongly, that we do take his or her suffering and negativity upon our self and, in so doing, our own self-cherishing is destroyed. We feel great joy about that. The object of our meditation is joy.

With each outbreath, we imagine our love growing, again like a glowing ember growing in brightness and intensity. We think, "May you be happy. May you find true and lasting happiness. May you find inner peace." With our love, our deep wish that all other living beings experience true and lasting happiness, we imagine that we send out in the form of radiant, white light everything, absolutely everything, of our own goodness and merit to the other person. We imagine that they now have whatever they want, and it gives them pure happiness, whatever it is. And, again, the actual object of meditation is joy.

We continue with each round of breath—inhalation and exhalation—to focus single-pointedly on the visualization and the intention, with a very strong faith that, on a subtle level, we are creating the causes for these wishes to be accomplished.

All of these instructions in the practice are for our intellect. In order to approach this living meditation, our intellect needs to understand clear methods to practice correctly. The instructions for the heart are far more direct. Simply be the way a wise and caring parent would be with his or her dearest child, the way a grateful and concerned son or daughter would be with a frail, beloved parent; or the way a loving spouse would be with a precious, lifelong companion, now in need. These are the usual jumping-off places for so many of us to expand the inclusiveness of our caring and to extend that spontaneous love eventually to all beings.

The practice of giving attention is, at one and the same time, a rare and precious jewel and as everyday as holding a little one, sitting by a bedside, being with another's sorrow. Deceptive in its simplicity, it is a powerful practice. With it, we bring, with greater ease and greater spontaneity, the care our heart of hearts so wishes to offer others. We also create the conditions for our own being to enter into deeper levels of love, wisdom, and genuine happiness.

How many times have we wished that the next step on our spiritual path would be revealed to us with great clarity? Practicing Dharma in this way, moment by moment, our next step is revealed with each next person who comes along, the next person who can benefit, along with us, from the gift of our attention.

NOTES AND REFERENCES

1. The Lojong teachings, *Eight Verses of Training the Mind*, written in twelfth century Tibet by the Bodhisattva, Langri Tangpa, are particularly applicable for those caregivers who see the ultimate unworkability of viewing the needs of self and other in opposition and who seek to find a way to give care and benefit to both self and other simultaneously. These Dharma teachings bridge the gap from ordinary mind to enlightened mind, illuminating the process whereby, with effort, we are able to exchange the object of our cherishing from self to other. Step by step, the Lojong practices, when practiced with sincere effort, strong faith, and deep intention, move us through the stages of the Mahayana path. We develop "equalizing self and others," the capacity and willingness to cherish all living beings to the same degree that we cherish our self. We work

to develop the capacity for wishing love, that is to say, the wish that all living beings be happy, that all living beings never be separated from their happiness. The Lojong practices then offer skillful means to develop our compassion, the wish that all living beings without exception be free from suffering and its causes. We make the precious practice of taking and giving second nature. This practice enhances and completes our exchanging the object of our cherishing from self to other. From this attainment, we can develop the mind of enlightenment—*bodhichitta*—and from then on we work toward the even more profound attainment of developing the mind of spontaneous, indestructible, and blissful universal compassion and wisdom—the mind of a Buddha.

2. Gyatso, Geshe Kelsang. *Eight Steps to Happiness*. London: Tharpa, 2000.

3. ———. *The Meditation Handbook*. London: Tharpa, 1990.

4. ———. *The Bodhisattva Vow*. London: Tharpa, 1991.

5. ———. *Transform Your Life*. London: Tharpa, 2001, p. 108.

PART THREE

The Power of Listening

Be quite still and solitary.
The world will freely offer itself to you
to be unmasked.
It has no choice.
It will roll in ecstasy at your feet.
~ Franz Kafka

*M*any of us in the helping professions are already familiar with the fundamentals of basic listening skills. In this selection from Karen Wegela's book, How to Be a Help Instead of a Nuisance, *to many of these skills are presented anew with uncommon awareness. As the former director of the Contemplative Therapy graduate program at the Naropa Institute, Karen elucidates the importance of discerning and deciding what parts of a message we decide to respond to, as well as the value of silence as part of a listening practice. And like Fran Peavey, she also gives extensive attention to the process of selecting and framing strategic questions. Karen stresses the importance of creating contexts—the fields within which the questions we ask can be answered—that produce the optimum good of brilliant sanity.*

Being a Good Listener

Karen Kissel Wegela

O NE OF THE WAYS WE SHOW PEOPLE that we are present with them is by how we listen. Being a good listener seems to come naturally for some people, but most of us benefit from learning some basic listening skills. These are the same techniques taught to students training to be counselors and psychotherapists, and they can be useful to all kinds of helpers.

We often find that instead of listening, we are just waiting to speak. We might be busy planning what we are going to say next. We might even interrupt and jump in with our own ideas. The person who is speaking will quickly understand that we're not really paying attention. Sometimes people shut down when this happens. They stop talking about what matters to them. They stop telling us, and often they stop letting themselves know too. We are sending the message that their experience is not interesting or worthy of attention. Children especially take to heart these unspoken messages.

BASIC LISTENING SKILLS

The first basic listening skill to practice is really paying attention. From our meditation practice we know that our minds tend to jump around. First we're present and then we're not. The same thing happens when we are with others. We might begin by listening carefully; then suddenly we're lost in our own thoughts about something else. When we notice this, we can gently bring ourselves back. If we've been absent so long that we've lost track of what is being said, we can say so. This lets others know that we really do want to know what they're saying.

We can show that we are following, listening, by nodding and looking at the person who is talking. We can interject brief comments like, "I see," or "Umm hmmm." I have been told that in some cultures the expectation is that when one person talks the other people present listen. In those cultures one is not expected to show that one is listening. It is taken for granted. But most of us in the West don't feel heard unless listeners show us, by their body language or their words, that they are really attending.

Along with paying attention, we can work with allowing silence. We don't have to respond immediately. We can take our time and see what our reaction is and formulate what we want to say. This also helps us drop the pressure to come up with a reply before the other person is done speaking. Some people are not comfortable with silence and tend to fill it up right away. We can feel our way with this. For many, allowing there to be some silence provides an opportunity to slow down a bit. That can be quite a relief in itself. So the first skill of listening is learning to come back, to drop our own distractions, and to allow some space into the conversation.

The second skill is paraphrasing. We let the other person know that we are hearing them by letting them know what we have heard. We put what we have heard into our own words rather than simply repeating the same words as though we were parrots. Obviously, we can't say everything we've heard, but we make a statement that shows that we've heard what's been said.

When I work with couples in counseling, we often spend a lot of time practicing just this skill. We call it stop, say, go. After one partner speaks, the other one says, "This is what I heard you say. Is that right?" If the first speaker agrees that the paraphrase is correct, then the other partner speaks. The first speaker then does the same paraphrasing exercise. Obviously, the conversation gets very slowed down, but each person begins to feel heard. After all, most couples come for help when communication has become problematic, so learning to listen is extremely important.

I remember one couple I worked with: I'll call them Gina and Frank. Gina said something like, "I would like to have some time to do some of the things I used to do before we got married. I would like time to paint and take walks alone."

Frank's first paraphrase was, "You don't want to be with me."

"No, I want some time to do some things alone."

He tried again. "You want to be alone. You're tired of me."

Clearly, Frank was hearing more than Gina was saying. With another try, he got much closer. "You haven't been doing the things you used to do before we got together. You'd like to have some time alone to do things like paint and go for walks." Gina agreed that this was what she had meant. Next it was Frank's turn to speak.

"When you talk about wanting to be alone, I get afraid that you want to leave me and end the marriage."

Gina's first attempts at feeding back what she heard from Frank were not any more accurate than his had been.

"You want me to always be right there where you can see me. You don't trust me at all."

You can imagine the kinds of communication that were going on with both partners mind reading the way they were! Neither one felt heard, and both were quite fed up. Beginning to listen—or even trying to listen—was a powerful message of caring for these two people.

As helpers, we don't usually need to slow things down this much, but the skill involved is the same. We simply let the other person know that we have heard the substance of what they have said.

The next skill builds on this one. This one is listening for the feelings. Instead of just feeding back the content of what is said, in this skill we let the person know what feeling we are hearing in the words. The person may have referred to feelings directly or not.

For example, when Janie was complaining about her landlord and the burdens of looking for a new place to live, Carol could have paraphrased by saying, "Sounds like your landlord is causing you a lot of problems and you'll have a lot to do if you move." A response based on listening for the feelings might go deeper: "It sounds like you're pretty angry at your landlord and scared about finding another place to live."

This kind of listening is more active and invites the speaker to look more closely at what they are experiencing on the spot. Notice that when we reply with either a paraphrase or from listening for the feelings, we do not add anything of our own. All we are doing with these skills is helping others become more clear and present with their full experience.

As a listener we can also help others to focus. A skill we might use here is summarizing what we've heard. We've been listening to Glenn. "You've been talking about the problems you've been having with your boss and also about what's going on with your girlfriend. Now you're starting to talk about your plans for next summer. Would it be helpful to focus on one of those or is talking about a number of different things helpful right now?" Once again, we're not adding our own opinion about what Glenn should choose—or even that he should focus only on one thing. By summarizing we show him what we've heard and give him a chance to decide what he wants to do next.

A very simple technique that we teach to counselors in training is to repeat a word or phrase to show that we are listening. For example, let's look one more time at Gina's first statement about wanting time for herself. "I would like to have some time to do some of the things I used to do before we got married. I would like time to paint and take walks alone."

If I were responding by using this repeating skill, I might say, "Alone?" That seems like the most potent word in what she said. Someone else might pick a different word or phrase to repeat. For example, "Used to do?" or "Paint and take walks?" Each of these would invite a somewhat different response from Gina.

With all of these skills it is important to be really interested, not just to go through the motions that show we are interested and listening. I hear many jokes and see cartoons that make fun of therapists who might, for example, be shown listening to a suicidal client and then saying, "Oh, you're depressed and now you're planning to commit suicide."

Whenever we present the simple repeating skill to counseling students we are likely to get teased by them. I might ask, "Are there any questions?" And students will reply, "Questions?" or "Any?" or even "Are there?"

In my own training, I used to worry about when I should say, "um hmm" and when I should be quiet—as though my timing were so crucial! The most important thing is really be there with the intention to hear what we are being told. We can trust our basic sanity to decide when to speak up and when to be quiet, when to merely listen and when to get more actively involved. First, though, we need to be able to hear.

Hearing includes not just what we're told in words. We also need to pay attention to tone of voice, body language, and all the clues that are part of communication. I once heard a speaker demonstrate the difference between listening only to the words and listening to the whole message. "I love you!" she shouted in an angry voice. "What would you believe?" she asked us, "My tone or my words?" Most of us believe the nonverbal message first and the words only if they match. When parents' nonverbal and verbal messages are in conflict too often, children grow up very confused and, some people say, are likely to become psychologically disturbed.

DEALING WITH OUR OWN REACTIONS

I've said that when we are listening we don't add anything of our own. Strictly speaking that's not really true. Whenever we listen we pick up on some things and don't pick up on others. This will affect what we respond to, which, in turn, may direct the conversation in one direction and not in another. I don't think we are ever completely neutral, but we can do our best to try to stay with the concerns and priorities of the person we are listening to and not to interject our own agendas. Again, the more we know about our own intentions, the less likely we are mindlessly to impose our own needs on others.

Sometimes we need to let other people know if we cannot put aside our own concerns. If I am trying to help a friend who is agonizing about whether to have an abortion or whether to go ahead with an unplanned pregnancy, it is probably important for me to let her know if I have a strong opinion of my own. If I do, I may or may not be able to listen and help her clarify her own mind. If because of my own mindfulness practice I am aware of the solidity of my views, I need to let her know that I might not be the right person to help with this problem right now and why.

On the other hand, if I tell her where I stand and she still wants to talk with me about her dilemma, maybe that's a clue for her about her own preferences. I find that often people choose to discuss things with someone who will reflect back to them what they really want to hear. That's fine. It's their intelligence at work, and we can make the process more visible by commenting on it.

For example, once a new student came to talk to me about a drug problem with which she was working. She had just stopped smoking marijuana for the first time in a number of years. By telling me—the head of her training program—she was making sure that she could not mindlessly go back to her old habits. She was blowing her cover. If I knew her to be indulging her old habit again, I would not be able to ignore it; it would most likely mean that she would be asked to leave the program. We were able to talk about how risky and intelligent it was for her to choose to discuss her situation with me.

I am often impressed by how important these simple listening skills are. Many times just being heard is comforting in itself. Sometimes all that people need to become more clear about what to do is to have the chance to air their thoughts and contact their feelings. These basic skills can provide the space and support that help people to see for themselves what to do next.

GOOD QUESTIONS

We probably all know what it is like to be asked questions that are not helpful. It can be irritating, confusing, and distracting when our well-intentioned friends and family rally around and bombard us with a thousand questions or suggestions just when we are trying to sort things out for ourselves.

"Well, why did you invest in that company anyway?" "Who is she going out with now? What did you do to drive her away?" "Isn't this exactly the same thing your father used to do?"

These questions tend to take the person away from their experience in the present moment. They may imply a sense of blame. Or they suggest that the answer is already known before the question is asked.

Probably the worst kind of question is like the old joke: "Answer yes or no, did you stop beating your wife?" Of course, if you never beat your wife, you can't answer with either yes or no. This is an example of asking the wrong question altogether.

How can we ask good and useful questions that lead others to become more clear about how they are feeling, what their concerns are, and what actions they want to take? How can we do this in a way that supports both their intelligence and the development of maitri?

There are some basic skills that we can learn and practice. The first steps in asking good questions are what we have already looked at: being present and listening. The more open we are to really hearing how things are for the other person, the less likely we are to impose our own biases on the situation. So the first step, as always, is to show up with an open mind and heart.

We can then ask questions that are based on the present situation. In general, it is rarely useful to get caught up in how things came to be this way. That might be an interesting pursuit some other time, but when people are in pain and need assistance, tracking history is not usually a helpful approach. It tends to take people away from their present experience, and it gives them the message that we are not as interested in helping as we are in trying to satisfy our own curiosity.

Questions that help people focus on the present moment tend to begin with what and how, and not with why. Let's look first at why questions.

"Why did you do that?" "Why do you want to hurt me like this?" "Why aren't you more like your brother?"

Why questions invite people to explain and defend themselves. Usually this leads to their feeling attacked or blamed. It may not be our intention to attack or blame, yet it is the response most people feel. When they feel this way, they also feel pushed away by us. They tend to pull back and feel more guarded and wary. This may be just the opposite of what we intended when we asked our question. Another unwanted result of our asking why questions can be that the others receive the message that we think they are stupid or incompetent. "Why did you do that?" is easily heard as, "You nitwit! Why would anybody in their right mind do that?"

Another problem with why questions, but not limited to them, is that they often veil our own agendas. When we ask, "Why?" we may really be saying, "I think…" It looks as if we're asking, but we're really telling. For example, "Why did you accept that position?" may sound like "I never would have taken that position." "Begging the question" means to assume we know the answer and then to ask a question that nearly forces the other person to frame the situation as we have done.

"How come you came to dinner tonight dressed so inappropriately?" Notice that the options available to a teenager addressed in this way are pretty limited. He can defend his choice of attire; he can deny its inappropriateness; he can storm out of the room. What he probably hears is, "You've dressed inappropriately for dinner, and I think you are a bad person." Notice too that how come is just another way of saying why.

Finally, why questions invite others into the past; they don't help them become more present now. "Why" suggests that we look at what has already happened—that is not necessarily a bad idea for another occasion. But when help is needed, it is only by coming into the present moment that we can discover where we are and what needs to happen next.

We can try to explore for ourselves by noticing how we feel when others ask us questions that begin with why. Notice the difference in how you respond as you imagine someone asking you, "Why do you feel that?" and "What do you feel?"

Instead of asking why, we can ask how or what. "How does that make you feel?" "How does losing your job affect your plans?" "What do you think about that?" "What options are you considering?"

Questions that begin with how or what tend to open things up. They invite exploration and curiosity. When we feel distressed we are likely to close down. We may feel as if the world is quite small and options are very limited. We may feel trapped and hopeless. It is as if we are walking around in a dense fog. Things suddenly loom up out of the murkiness, but we can't get a sense of how things go together or what else is there, just out of sight. Our emotions may be in a swirl: we don't know how we feel. Or we feel numb. Anything that helps us to open up a bit, that disperses the fog, can be quite valuable.

Questions that begin with how or what can be good ways to help us focus on what is happening right now. Questions that invite us to be more present with our bodily experiences, with our emotions, and with our thoughts can be very useful.

Tracy just heard the lab results of her annual physical. She has a suspicious-looking cyst on one of her ovaries. Like most of us, it is very easy for her to think of the others she knows who have had ovarian cancer. Her own mother died of it. She can fall into remembering the past and quickly turn that into a dire fantasy about her own future. She can become lost in a tumult of thinking and fear about what might happen. Inviting her back to the present moment and to the reality of uncertainty can help her cut the painful buildup of past- and future-centered thinking. It might even let her touch the appreciation she feels for those who are in her life right now.

Another dimension we can pay attention to when we ask questions is whether our questions are open-ended or closed-ended. We'll call these open or closed questions.

Closed questions call for a one-word or very brief answer. They are often questions that ask for yes or no as the answer. These questions can be helpful when someone is feeling very confused. They can be used to help the person focus and become more grounded in body and environment.

"Can you see me sitting here?" "Do you know where you are?" "How many fingers am I holding up?" Closed questions can also be used to gather factual information. "Was there anybody else in the car with you when you went into the ditch?" "What's your name?"

The drawback to closed questions is that they may keep the focus narrow when it is more helpful to open things up more.

On the other hand, open questions are good for helping us to explore things and to open up our minds. They are a way of inviting others to relax and let go of any fixed views that may be getting in their way.

"What would happen if you didn't go back to school?" "When you see your girlfriend talking to another guy, what do you imagine is going on?" Compare this question to a why question like, "Why do you get so jealous when you see your girlfriend talking to another guy?" The second one seems more blaming and also assumes that jealousy is the person's response.

Open questions invite the person to tap into their creativity and can also suggest that there is more than one way to look at things. Sometimes this provides welcome relief.

A mistake helpers often make is to ask more than one question at a time. "What are you feeling right now? Do you want to stop talking? Is it okay if I ask you about your mother?" Most people will find a series of questions confusing. More often than not, people answer only the last question asked.

One last thing to keep in mind when we begin to ask questions is whether we have been invited to do so. Any time we present ourselves as helpers it is good to be sensitive when we begin to go deeper. Whenever we ask questions, we are going more deeply into the other person's feelings and thoughts. When people are distressed it is harder for them to tell us that they wish we would go away. It is up to us to try to be sensitive to what is wanted and needed.

I have a friend who is also a therapist. Often our conversations are chatty and humorous. Sometimes one of us will want some help. We have developed a kind of password with each other. "Do you want to really talk about this?" one of us will ask the other. This is a way of asking permission before going further. There are no sure ways to know when we are being a help instead of a nuisance, but when we are in doubt we can check it out by asking what kind of help would be useful.

Soon after I began dating my husband Fred, I received some unwelcome news from a doctor. When Fred heard the news from me by phone, he asked if it would be helpful to me if he came over. He didn't assume that he knew what I needed. I felt respected and cared for by his thoughtfulness.

Here are some other possible questions. "Would it help if I asked you some questions?" "Is it okay to ask you more about that now?" "Would you rather be alone now?" "Do you know what you'd like me to do?"

If we're told that someone would rather be left alone, we should respect that. We can let the person know how to reach us, or we can stay nearby— for example, in another room—if that seems appropriate. This can be a very important message: we are saying that we respect the person; that we will not aggressively intrude; and that we are really listening.

No discussion of skillful listening would be complete without including some aspects of Marshall Rosenberg's Nonviolent Communication. In this selection, Marshall instructs us on how to learn to listen with vigilant awareness to the words that regularly course through the mindstream, and to specifically note how they separate and disconnect us from others. Such watchful awareness is a critical component of any kind of personal or spiritual practice. Because we have all had to be cared for, protected, and necessarily restricted during our childhood years, much of the early language we learned has often had the unfortunate side effect of limiting possibilities for our lives. In this selection Marshall offers us effective tools for removing the shackles of delimiting language, and frees us to be more fully awake and present as our lives unfold in each moment.

Liberating Ourselves
Through Nonviolent Communication

Marshall Rosenberg

While Nonviolent Communication is a means to effectively communicate and connect with others, it also enhances our inner communication. We can translate into feelings and needs the many condemning and demeaning voices inside ourselves where, in fact, we often exercise our harshest judgment.

We have all learned things that limit us as human beings, whether from well-intentioned parents, teachers, clergy, or others. Passed down through generations, even centuries, much of this destructive cultural learning is so ingrained in our lives that we are no longer conscious of it. In one of his routines, comedian Buddy Hackett, raised on his mother's rich cooking, claimed that he never realized it was possible to leave the table without feeling heartburn until he was in the army. In the same way, pain engendered by damaging cultural conditions is such an integral part of our daily lives that we can no longer distinguish its presence. It takes tremendous energy and awareness to recognize this destructive learning and to transform it into thoughts and behaviors which are of value and of service to life.

Resolving Internal Conflicts

We can all apply Nonviolent Communication to resolve the internal conflicts which often result in depression. In his book, *Revolution in Psychiatry*, Ernest

Becker attributes depression to "cognitively arrested alternatives." This means that when we have a judgmental dialogue going on within, we become alienated from what we need and cannot then act to meet those needs. Depression is indicative of a state of alienation from our own needs.

A woman studying Nonviolent Communication was suffering a profound bout of depression. She was asked to identify the voices within her when she felt the most depressed and to write them down in dialogue form as though they were speaking to each other. The first two lines of her dialogue were:

Voice One ("career woman"): I should do something more with my life. I'm wasting my education and talents.

Voice Two ("responsible mother"): You're being unrealistic. You're a mother of two children and can't handle *that* responsibility, so how can you handle anything else?

Notice how these inner messages are infested with judgmental terms and phrases such as "should," "wasting my education and talents," and "can't handle." Variations of this dialogue had been running for months in the woman's head. She was then asked to imagine the "career woman" voice taking a "Nonviolent Communication pill" in order to restate its message in the following form: "When *A,* I feel *B,* because I am needing *C.* Therefore, I now would like *D.*"

She subsequently translated, "I should do something with my life. I'm wasting my education and talents" into: "When I spend as much time at home with the children as I do without practicing my profession, I feel depressed and discouraged because I am needing the fulfillment I once had in my profession. Therefore, I now would like to find part-time work in my profession."

Then it was the turn of her "responsible mother" voice to undergo the same process. The lines, "You're being unrealistic. You're a mother of two children and can't handle *that* responsibility, so how can you handle anything else?" were transformed into: "When I imagine going to work, I feel scared because I need reassurance that the children will be well taken care of. Therefore, I now would like to plan how to provide high-quality child care while I work and then to find sufficient time to be with the children when I am not tired."

This woman felt great relief as soon as she translated her inner messages into Nonviolent Communication. She was able to get beneath the alienating messages she was repeating to herself and offer herself empathy. Although she still faced practical challenges such as securing quality child care and her husband's support, she was no longer subject to the judgmental internal dialogue that kept her from being aware of her own needs.

Dream-Killing Language

My own career was profoundly affected by another exercise that demonstrates how Nonviolent Communication can help liberate us from self-created mental prisons. In this exercise we explore whether we are closing out possibilities in our lives by using "dream-killing language" that obscures our options.

We start by listing the things we see ourselves having to do, even though we don't like doing them. When I was a practicing clinical psychologist, the first item on my list was, "I have to write clinical reports." I hated doing these reports, yet I was spending at least an hour every day on them. My second item was, "I have to drive the children's carpool to school." The next step is to translate each "I have to do X…" statement into: "I choose to do X because I want…" This process allows us to realize that we always have options, even if in some situations, we may not like any of them. We also become more aware of the reasons why we choose to do the things we don't like doing.

When I first tried to translate my "have to" into a "want to," I found myself stumbling over, "I have to write clinical reports, because I'm a clinical psychologist, and all clinical psychologists write reports." Recognizing the futility of this line of thinking, I questioned my motives more closely. Several months earlier, I had already determined that the reports did not serve my clients enough to justify the time they were taking, so why was I continuing to invest so much energy into their preparation? Finally, I realized that I was choosing to write the reports solely because I wanted the income they provided. From that day, I never wrote another clinical report. Having clarified to myself that money was my primary motivation, I chose then to generate income from activities that had deeper purpose for me.

When I pursued the reason behind my choosing to drive the carpool, however, I realized I wanted my children to enjoy the benefits of the particular school they were attending. They could easily walk to the neighborhood school, but their current school was far more in harmony with my educational values. With this purpose more clearly in focus, I continued to take my turn with the carpool. However the simple shift in thinking from "have to" to "I choose to because I want…" had affected my attitude. Each morning, having reminded myself of the purpose of the task, I found the drive to be much more agreeable than before.

Caring for Our Inner Environment

When we are entangled in critical, blaming, or angry thoughts, it is difficult to establish a healthy internal environment for ourselves. Nonviolent Communication helps us create a more peaceful state of mind by encouraging us to focus on what we are truly wanting rather than on what is wrong with ourselves or others.

A participant once reported a profound personal breakthrough during a three-day training. One of her goals for the workshop was to take better care of herself, but she woke at dawn the second morning with the worst headache in recent memory. "Normally, the first thing I'd do would be to analyze what I had done wrong. Did I eat the wrong food? Did I let myself get stressed out? Did I do this; did I not do that? But since I had been working on using Nonviolent Communication to take better care of myself, I asked instead, 'What do I need to do for myself right now with this headache?'

"I sat up and did a lot of really slow neck rolls, then got up and walked around, and did other things to take care of myself right then instead of beating up on myself. My headache relaxed to the point where I was able to go through the day's workshop. This was a major, major breakthrough for me. What I understood, when I empathized with the headache, was that I hadn't given myself enough attention the day before, and the headache was a way to say to myself, 'I need more attention.' I ended up giving myself the attention I needed and was then able to make it through the workshop. I've had headaches all my life, and this was a very remarkable turning point for me."

At another workshop a participant asked how Nonviolent Communication might be used to free us from anger-provoking messages when we are driving on the freeway. This was a familiar topic for me! For years my work involved traveling by car across the country, and I was worn and frazzled by the violence-provoking messages racing through my brain. Everybody who wasn't driving by my standards was an arch-enemy, a villain. Thoughts spewed through my head: "What the hell is the matter with that guy!? Doesn't he even watch where he's driving?" In this state of mind, all I wanted was to punish the other driver, and since I couldn't do that, the anger lodged in my body and exacted its toll. Eventually I learned to translate my judgments into feelings and needs and to give myself empathy, "Boy, I am petrified when people drive like that; I really wish they would see the danger in what they are doing!" Whew! I was amazed how much less stressful a situation I could create for myself by simply becoming aware of what I was feeling and needing rather than blaming others.

Later I decided to practice empathy toward other drivers and was rewarded with a gratifying first experience. I was stuck behind a car going far below the speed limit that was slowing down at every intersection. Fuming and grumbling, "That's no way to drive," I noticed the stress I was causing myself and shifted my thinking instead to what the driver might be feeling and needing. I sensed that the person was lost, feeling confused, and wishing for some patience from those of us following. When the road widened enough for me to pass, I saw that the driver was a woman who looked to be in her 80s who wore an expression of terror on her face. I was pleased that my attempt at empathy had kept me from honking the horn or engaging in my customary tactics of displaying displeasure toward people whose driving bothered me.

REPLACING DIAGNOSIS WITH NONVIOLENT COMMUNICATION

Many years ago, after having just invested nine years of my life in the training and diplomas necessary to qualify as a psychotherapist, I came across a dialogue between the Israeli philosopher Martin Buber and the American psychologist Carl Rogers in which Buber questioned whether anyone could do psychotherapy in the role of a psychotherapist. Buber was visiting the United States at the time, and had been invited, along with Carl Rogers, to a discussion at a mental hospital in front of a group of mental-health professionals.

In this dialogue Buber posited that human growth occurs through a meeting between two individuals who express themselves vulnerably and authentically in what he termed an "I-Thou" relationship. He did not believe that this type of authenticity was likely to exist when people met in the roles of psychotherapist and client. Rogers agreed that authenticity was a prerequisite to growth. He maintained, however, that enlightened psychotherapists could choose to transcend their own role and encounter their clients authentically.

Buber was skeptical. He was of the opinion that even if psychotherapists were committed and able to relate to their clients in an authentic fashion, such encounters would be impossible as long as clients continued to view themselves as clients and their psychotherapists as psychotherapists. He observed how the very process of making appointments to see someone at their office, and paying fees to be "fixed," dimmed the likelihood of an authentic relationship developing between two persons.

This dialogue clarified my own longstanding ambivalence toward clinical detachment—a sacrosanct rule in the psychoanalytic psychotherapy I was taught. To bring one's own feelings and needs into the psychotherapy was typically viewed as a sign of pathology on the part of the therapist. Competent psychotherapists were to stay out of the therapy process and to function as a mirror onto which clients projected their transferences, which were then worked through with the psychotherapist's help. I understood the theory behind keeping the psychotherapist's inner process out of psychotherapy and guarding against the danger of addressing internal conflicts at the client's expense. However, I had always been uncomfortable maintaining the requisite emotional distance, and furthermore believed in the advantages of bringing myself into the process.

I thus began to experiment by replacing clinical language with the language of Nonviolent Communication. Instead of interpreting what my clients were saying in line with personality theories I had studied, I made myself present to their words and listened empathically. Instead of diagnosing them, I revealed what was going on within myself. At first, this was frightening. I worried about how colleagues would react to the authenticity with which I was entering into dialogue with clients. However, the results were so gratifying to both the clients and myself that I soon overcame any hesitation. Today, thirty-five years later, the concept of bringing oneself fully into the client-therapist relationship is no longer heretical, but when I began practicing this way, I was often invited to speak by groups of psychotherapists who would challenge me to demonstrate this new role.

Once I was asked by a large gathering of mental health professionals at a state mental hospital to show how Nonviolent Communication might serve in counseling distressed people. After my one-hour presentation, I was requested to interview a patient in order to produce an evaluation and recommendation for treatment. I talked with the twenty-nine-year-old mother of three children for about half an hour. After she left the room, the staff responsible for her care posed their questions. "Dr. Rosenberg," her psychiatrist began, "please make a differential diagnosis. In your opinion, is this woman manifesting a schizophrenic reaction or is this a case of drug-induced psychosis?"

I said that I was uncomfortable with such questions. Even when I worked in a mental hospital during my training, I was never sure how to fit people into the diagnostic classifications. Since then I had read research indicating a lack of agreement among psychiatrists and psychologists regarding these terms. The reports concluded that diagnoses of patients in mental hospitals depended more upon the school the psychiatrist had attended than the characteristics of the patients themselves.

I would be reluctant, I continued, to apply these terms even if consistent usage did exist, because I failed to see how they benefited patients. In physical medicine, pinpointing the disease process that has created the illness often gives clear direction to its treatment, but I did not perceive this relationship in the field we call mental illness. In my experience, during case conferences at hospitals, the staff would spend most of its time deliberating over a diagnosis. As the allotted hour threatened to run out, the psychiatrist in charge of the case might appeal to the others for help in setting up a treatment plan. Often this request would be ignored in favor of continued wrangling over the diagnosis.

I explained to the psychiatrist that Nonviolent Communication urges me to ask myself the following questions rather than think in terms of what is wrong with a patient: "What is this person feeling? What is she or he needing? How am I feeling in response to this person, and what needs of mine are behind my feelings? What action or decision would I request this person to take in the belief that it would enable them to live more happily?" Because responses to these questions would reveal a lot about ourselves and our values, we would be feeling far more vulnerable than if we were to simply diagnose the other person.

On another occasion, I was called to demonstrate how Nonviolent Communication can be taught to people diagnosed as chronic schizophrenics. With about eighty psychologists, psychiatrists, social workers, and nurses watching, fifteen patients who had been thus diagnosed were assembled on the stage for me. As I introduced myself and explained the purpose of Nonviolent Communication, one of the patients expressed a reaction that seemed irrelevant to what I was saying. Aware that he'd been diagnosed as a chronic schizophrenic, I succumbed to clinical thinking by assuming that my failure to understand him was due to his confusion. "You seem to be having trouble following what I'm saying," I remarked.

At this, another patient interjected, "I understand what he's saying," and proceeded to explain the relevance of his words in the context of my introduction. Recognizing that the man was not confused, but that I had simply not grasped the connection between our thoughts, I was dismayed by the ease with which I had attributed responsibility for the breakdown in communication to him. I would have liked to have owned my own feelings by saying, for example, "I'm confused. I'd like to see the connection between what I said and your response, but I don't. Would you be willing to explain how your words relate to what I said?"

With the exception of this brief departure into clinical thinking, the session with the patients went successfully. The staff, impressed with the patients' responses, wondered whether I considered them to be an unusually cooperative group of patients. I answered that when I avoided diagnosing people and instead stayed connected to the life going on in them and in myself, people usually responded positively.

A staff member then requested a similar session to be conducted as a learning experience with some of the psychologists and psychiatrists as participants. At this, the patients who had been on stage exchanged seats with several volunteers from the audience. In working with the staff, I had a difficult time clarifying to one psychiatrist the difference between intellectual understanding and the empathy of Nonviolent Communication. Whenever someone in the group expressed feelings, he would offer his understanding of the psychological dynamics behind their feelings rather than empathize with the feelings. When this happened for the third time, one of the patients in the audience burst out, "Can't you see you're doing it again? You're interpreting what she's saying rather than empathizing with her feelings!"

By adopting the skills and consciousness of Nonviolent Communication, we can counsel others in encounters that are genuine, open, and mutual, rather than resorting to professional relationships characterized by emotional distancing, diagnosis, and hierarchy.

Nonviolent Communication enhances inner communication by helping us translate negative internal messages into feelings and needs. Our ability to distinguish our own feelings and needs and to empathize with them can free us from depression. We can replace "dream-killing language" with Nonviolent Communication and recognize the existence of choice in all our actions. By showing us how to focus on what we are truly wanting rather than on what is wrong with ourselves or others, Nonviolent Communication gives us the tools and understanding to create a more peaceful state of mind. Nonviolent Communication may also be used by professionals in counseling and psychotherapy to engender relationships with clients that are mutual and authentic.

*S*killful listening takes place only in the present moment. The amount of ourselves that we can consistently bring to that moment necessarily dictates how skillfully we are able to attend to the sounds that fill our lives. In this selection from Toni Packer, founder of the Springwater Center in New York, she artfully describes what it's like to bring a full listening presence with us wherever we may be. It is through the meditative practice of loosening identification with what most of us have identified for much of our lives as "me," that we begin to be able to listen directly to the world. Paradoxically, it is also by learning to attend closely to our own internal experiences, by paying attention to those things inside us that yearn to be heard, that we can begin to build a multipronged, skillful practice.

Finding a New Way to Listen

Toni Packer

BEFORE INQUIRING into a new way of listening, let me just share the joy of walking through the fields and woods on this extraordinary land. Just stepping out of the reception area, closing the door behind me, walking away from the overhang that is shielding the building from sun and rain, there isn't any enclosure left—not even a body! All I am is the birds singing and fluttering, bare branches swaying in the breeze, the ground partly frozen, partly melting, the pond covered with a thin layer of ice and the blue hills, sky, and wandering clouds within close reach. Also there is my throbbing heart and the people walking on the path. Even those who are not physically here—aren't we all together in this one moment— beholding everything out of stillness?

It is the stillness born of not being identified with "me"—the endless stories of the past and the various images that have represented "me" to myself and others. Identification with "me" is a living prison. In it we constantly want to be accepted, feel important, be listened to, be encouraged, supported, and comforted in this separate life of ours. But now, here, in the fresh air under the open sky, there is the freedom of not needing to be anything, not needing anything—just being this open listening space where people walk, crows caw, and ice cracks underfoot.

Why do I feel that listening is so immensely important in living alone and together? It is because listening quietly, passionately, now, without expectation or effort, is the gateway to living in wholeness without the separation of you and me.

This is our main question: can we listen in a deep way at a moment of silence and stillness? Or is the mind preoccupied with the ten thousand worries of this world, of our life, our family? Can we realize right now that a mind that is occupied with itself cannot listen freely? This is not said in judgment—it is a fact. It's impossible to hear someone else while worrying about myself. Bird calls and the songs of the breeze do not exist when the mind is full of itself. A full mind is within the experience of all of us. So, can the mind put its problems aside for one moment and listen freshly? This moment! Are we listening together? The caw-caw-caw of the crows, the quiet hum of a plane, a dog barking, or whatever sounds are alive where you are listening right now.

It is relatively easy to listen happily in nature—the leaves and grasses, flowers, trees, lakes, and hills do not think and worry like we do and therefore do not provoke thinking. Maybe for deer and birds there is some rudimentary thinking going on but that need not engage us in thought (unless we are avid birdwatchers or worry about the plight of too many deer and too many hunters next season). Thought can make a problem out of everything, but most of us find the beauty of unselfconscious listening much easier to come upon in nature than among people.

Why is it so inordinately difficult to listen to each other? Is that a question we would like to explore? When we are present with the abundant energy of listening, I do not find it difficult to hear what you are saying. Instead of being busy with self-concern, the space is open to hear, see, and understand the meaning of your words. If it's not understood, then there is the freedom to ask you for clarification.

Without this open space of presence-energy, the inner tapes of human conditioning press hard to reel off and be heard—they do not want to make way for listening to others. How can I possibly hear you when I am dying to say something myself? How can I take the time and care to understand you when I think that I am right and you are wrong? When I'm sure that I know better? When I sorely need to be given attention and resent anyone else getting it?

Can I hear you when I have fixed images about how you have been in the past, how you have criticized or flattered me?

Can I listen freely when I would like you to be different from the way you are?

Is there the patience to listen to you when I think I already know what you are going to say?

Am I open to listen to you when I'm judging you? Judgments and prejudices lie deeply hidden in the recesses of the mind and require curiosity and inner transparency in order to be discovered. Only what is discovered can end.

Do I really hear what you are saying when I imagine you to be holy, to be worshiped, adored, and surrendered to?

Will I expect every word you say to be infallible wisdom? Or the opposite—can I hear what you are saying when I'm convinced that you are stupid?

Am I listening to you the same way that I listen to someone else?

We can add more and more to this list but the important thing is to start questioning our listening fundamentally. Not asking, "How can I achieve pure listening?" but rather, "Where is my listening coming from this moment, in the light of all these questions?" Is it hampered by different ideas and attitudes or does it arise from a moment of being truly present—at one with you and your whole situation?

Many of us sincerely desire to become better listeners and may think that will only happen once we are free of the "me" sometime in the future. This is an erroneous assumption. Even though the "me-circuit" is deeply ingrained within brain and body, a genuine desire and interest to understand you allows energy to gather in listening attentively to what you are saying. This attentive listening may empty out the preoccupation with myself. Just listening to your words and truly wishing to understand what you mean to convey, I enter you—your question, your condition, the whole *you*.

When I'm not really interested in what you are saying, can I pause and listen within? Take a glance at what is going on inside—resistance? Boredom? The passing by of words that are not really heard. When there is clear seeing, that in itself is a shift. Listening purifies itself. Not that there is necessarily a new interest in what you are saying. I may prefer to dialogue deeply while you want to relate your story (to get my attention, to be of interest to me?). When listening comes out of wholeness, an appropriate response happens. That is the wisdom of listening.

Sometimes, while talking in a meeting, a flock of crows is flying by— *caw, caw, caw, caw, caw*. I raise the hand a bit and ask: "Do you hear that?" The person may shake her head for a moment—the listening space was filled up with other things. Are we here right now?

When you hear that question, what happens? Is it simply *caw caw caw*, or are you thinking, "Am I doing it right?" or, "What does she want me to say?" Hear those thoughts like you hear the wind in the trees! It's the same listening. It's different things—the sound of wind and trees and birds is different from the sound of thoughts—but it's the same listening. One whole listening!

So for unknown marvelous reasons, once in a while we are completely here. For a moment we hear, see, and feel all one. Then the mind comes in to explain it, to know it, compare it, and store it. This is not an intentional process—it's habit. No one is doing it. The naming, the liking and disliking, wanting to keep something and fearing to loose it—these are all ingrained mind processes rolling off on their own. If we get a glimpse of that, get a feel for what is purely habitual, then we will be much more tolerant and patient with the so-called "others" and ourselves.

When I talk about listening I don't mean just listening with the ear. "Listening" here includes the totality of perception—all senses open and alive, and still much more than that. The eyes, ears, nose, tongue, body, mind—receptive, open, not controlled. A Zen saying describes it as "hearing with one's eyes and seeing with one's ears." It refers to the wholeness of perception, the wholeness of being!

Another Zen saying demands: "Hear the bell before it rings!" Ah—it doesn't make any sense rationally, does it? But a moment can happen when that bell is ringing before you know it! You may never know it! Your entire being is ringing! There's no division in that—everything is ringing.

So, can we learn more and more about ourselves—not studying in order to increase our store of information? I mean awaring in wonderment what keeps us from hearing the bell before it rings.

*T*hroughout history, the land itself has been the literal ground of being that much of spiritual authority grew out of. As consciousness begins the journey of growth and expansion and extends beyond the needs of daily survival and other ego-centered concerns, the plight of the land and the larger world inevitably begins to filter into awareness. In addition to the deprivation—physical and material and spiritual—that touches people in virtually every corner of the earth, the larger plight of the planet itself must arise into consciousness at some point along the path. In this contribution from ecopsychologist Michael S. Hutton, we are encouraged to push through our denial and attend and minister to planet Earth as a sentient being.

Listening to the Land

Michael S. Hutton

L ISTENING TO THE LAND is the practice of listening to what the Earth
is saying to us, both for our own health and healing, and the health
and healing of the entire planet. It means facing the ecological crisis before
us, finding places where we can listen to nature, tuning into our hearts and
bodies, and truly listening.

In discussing our listening practices, we often are speaking of the practice of listening to each other, that is, to other humans, and learning to listen in such a way that we really hear and understand one another. In this
way, as humans we become connected and in relationship with one
another. This is a vital practice in interpersonal relationships, such as
between partners or in families, and also within and between communities and nations. Learning to listen is one step in understanding one
another, in being heard by the "other," and then reaching some sense of
connection and resolution. Of course, one of the difficulties in teaching
listening "skills" or "principles" is that because there are so many different
human cultures, the rules or suggestions for listening are often culture-
based.Furthermore the person who is suggesting the "appropriate" listening practice may not realize his or her own cultural bias. In reality, what
one person might consider to be "good listening" might be anathema to a
person from another culture.

For example, my friend, who is Jewish, listens closely to me, an Anglo-
American, by often interjecting her thoughts and ideas. In her view, it is

her animation and the regular interjection of her thoughts and feelings, not to mention occasionally bumping my arm with her hand, which demonstrates that she is really listening to me. But sometimes her listening style doesn't work well for me at all; it does not make me feel heard. Likewise, my listening politely and quietly while she talks, does not communicate to her that I am really "listening." She fears I have drifted off, and often comes back with, "Do you understand?" This is obviously a microcosm of the huge challenges we are facing in communicating across cultures.

What considerations are relevant when we consider listening to the culture called the land? When we speak of developing listening abilities, we usually are referring to listening to people, but despite our ever-increasing numbers (over 6 billion currently on the planet and counting), humans are only one aspect of the land to which we need to listen. Here, I want to present some thoughts on listening to the land as a way to get to know this planet on which we live, and also, perhaps, to get to know ourselves a little bit better.

ECOLOGICAL CRISIS: WHAT WE ARE FACING

Listening to the land is a process of tuning in to what the land is saying to us at this time of ecological and social crisis. Listening to the land is paying attention to this lifesource for each of us. It is an ecological practice and so it is concerned with systems of relationships and interrelationships, and fundamentally about our home (the word *ecology* comes from the Greek word *oikos*, which means "home"). In acknowledging our deep relationship with this Earth, we must acknowledge the ecological crisis we all face here in our home.

Because we live in a human culture which is in such denial about the ecological crisis, we have to continue to remind ourselves that this crisis is happening *now*, it is affecting us *now*, and that it will continue to get worse before it gets better. We are going to have to change our lifestyles, we are going to have to alter our behaviors, we are going to have to go *without* (at least in the more advanced countries; those in the less economically developed countries are already going *without*: food, clean water, clean air, a healthy environment, safety, etc.). The land is screaming out to us, but we are not listening. We are intentionally or unintentionally ignoring the cries of our suffering planet. The biosphere of the planet *as we know it* is dying.

The planetary ecological crisis includes: the pollution of our waters, our air, and our land through various mining, logging, agricultural, and manufacturing practices; overpopulation by humans beyond the carrying capacity of the planet; the warming of the atmosphere through the burning of fossil fuels and other polluting gases; eradicating the wilderness on which we survive through human encroachment, clearcutting forests, overgrazing by livestock, mineral extraction, as well as allowing oil and gas exploration and mining in wilderness areas; encroaching on the habitat for most other plant and animal species; the insidious destruction of natural plant and animal diversity through such practices as the introduction of non-native and genetically modified crops and animals; the devastation being wrought on wild species through unregulated fishing, hunting, and poaching, which is leading to mass species extinctions; and the consequent loss of connection to nature which is brought about by urban sprawl. In short, people are being separated from the natural world, the more-than-just-humans world, through modern industrial living, increasing reliance on technology, and the burgeoning human population, which is forcing more and more people to live in urban settings. We are fouling the air we need to breathe, we are fouling and endangering the water we need to drink, we are endangering ourselves through the food we eat, through chemicals and pesticides we spray. This is called eco-suicide. To make matters worse, we don't even know it, or we don't even realize it. Or we don't think it will matter, or we think that someone else will solve the problem, or we feel powerless to stop, etc.

Part of what makes this listening to the land practice challenging is that not only do we have to hear some painful information, but we also then have to face our own denial, and feelings of guilt, anger, fear, and grief. The challenge as we will see, is not to get overwhelmed by these feelings and thus overcome with inertia.

I believe that listening to the land could quite simply save us in this mad rush toward eco-death, which we seem so determined to ignore and deny. Listening to the land is akin to having to sit down and listen to your partner who has years of complaints about what hasn't been working in the relationship. It is going to be painful and difficult, but it may be the only way we can wake up and begin to turn the tide of what needs to be done.

We can listen to the land through listening to our hearts. I feel such a deep sadness in reading that soon the songbirds in the United States will be gone, or their numbers significantly diminished, due to global warming and the habitat changes that result from this. Soon there may be no birdsong in our forests. Sometimes information like this allows us to open to the voices inside which whisper to us of the grief or sadness we might feel.

Try this: next time you are outdoors, in a natural setting, stop what you are doing for a moment, and just listen. What do you hear? This is the sound of the world speaking and even singing to you.

This practice of opening up to this beautiful planet is one way to overcome the inertia or the overwhelming feelings we may experience when we contemplate what is to be done for the planet. Open up to the experience of intense beauty, the beauty of the sounds of this amazing planet. Through this opening process, we will enliven ourselves and reconnect to the Earth.Listening to the land means engaging the various sense modalities. It is not only hearing, but seeing, tasting, touching, and smelling this wonderful world.

Interestingly, there are indigenous peoples who claim they can hear the voice of the tree spirits, or animal spirits, which are in agreement with their sacrifice when it is right for the balance of the needs of the tribe. So if these people can hear the trees (animals, plants, rocks, streams, etc.), why can't the rest of us?

The Western psychological framework would say that these people are merely projecting their own voices, thoughts, or ideas onto nature. Another explanation from this psychological paradigm would be that these people are merely making this up, that it's just fantasy. Or perhaps if they have really heard these voices, then they are hallucinating, and have a psychopathological condition. Whatever the explanation from this Western, Eurocentric psychological paradigm, the answer neatly dismisses the reality of the hearing of these voices, and leaves the listener discredited. The reality from the indigenous viewpoint is that people have always had the ability to talk with these other spirits, and that modern people have lost that ability. It is listening in nonordinary reality, an ability modern people have lost.

Beginning the initial practice of listening to the land requires slowing down so that we can really hear what is being said. Listening is an act of connecting. Listening involves actively opening our ears and hearts to hear the world.

Noise Pollution

We are constantly bombarded with noise at almost all hours of the day and night. This originates with human-generated sources, some of which we are choosing to engage, such as the television, radio, music, movies, etc., but more often we are subtly and not-so-subtly being subjected to noise from engines, machines, computers, and other human-created objects. We can call this *noise pollution,* and just like air pollution, it invades our environment and is unhealthy for us—even if we fail to notice it.

The problem is that there is still some cost to our sense of wellbeing and health when we are in this state. When we need to shut down our sensory input, what is lost in that process?

There is a sociocultural aspect of this level of noise pollution as well. It is as if we have a constant soundtrack to our lives. There is continuous piped-in music in the grocery store. There are televisions blaring in our airports, and in most bars. There is music in the corridors of hospitals. There is music, and now even television, in elevators and on airplanes. This constant barrage of sound is something to which we become adjusted. In fact, it is something to which we become addicted, in that we begin to feel uncomfortable when there is silence. We turn to noise to quiet our inner anxieties; it seems soothing.

Furthermore, when we try to listen as we select the food for dinner at the grocery store, or pick our children up from school while talking with friends, colleagues, or spouses on the cell phone, or when we listen with "half an ear" to what someone has to say.

We are not only subjecting *ourselves* to this kind of noise pollution, but the rest of the world as well. The wolves, bison, and elk in Yellowstone National Park have been noticeably impacted by the reintroduction of snowmobiles to the park. What kind of listening are the whales, dolphins, and other marine mammals doing when the U.S. Navy is blasting them with subsonic noise louder than an atomic blast, bursting their eardrums and causing them to beach themselves in record numbers? What does this tell us about our own connection to deep listening that we can allow this to happen? Clearing out human noise is one of the key elements in listening to the land. We must get to noise-free places in nature.

LISTENING PRACTICES

So how do I listen to the land? What does that look like? How would I know if it is really happening? How does the land speak to me?

To listen to the land we do need to give it our full attention. The ways that the Earth speaks to us are subtle. We can listen with our ears, but in another way, we must listen with our hearts as well; we must listen with our whole bodies. When we listen in this way, we are immediately rewarded.

Listening with just our ears, we hear many things. There is the song of birds, which is so amazing in variety, pitch, intonation, and meaning; or the sound of wings beating against the breeze; there is the sound of the wind soughing through trees, and grasses, sometimes in a whisper and sometimes like a giant roar; there is the crashing of the surf on a beach, or rocky headland, announcing the arrival of another wave of seawater at our feet; there is the gurgle or splash of a river as it tumbles over rocks and boulders in the riverbed; there is the patter or drumming of rain coming forth from the heavens, or thunder crashing; there are the varied animal calls, roars, bugles, chirps, squawks, barks, hisses, and rattles, far and near, which announce the inhabitants of our neighborhood.

A listening practice could include learning to differentiate the various bird or animal calls we hear in our location. I remember two wonderful volunteers from Trees for Life, located in Findhorn, Scotland, who were escorting me around their planting site near Glen Affric in the Western Highlands. As we walked along the misty boglands on a drizzly, gray April morning, they quickly identified a variety of bird calls both nearby and far off, differentiating between this trill which ended on an up note from that one which ended on a down note. This kind of noticing speaks to a deep listening practice with the land and its inhabitants. And I could see the joy of familiarity they shared together in this ability to know their neighbors.

One could also practice noticing the silence of newly falling snow, or that on a mountaintop, or in a deep forest, or in the depths of the sea. There is the sound of silence of the late night, or predawn hours, before the world awakens to a new day. When we are truly in the silence, we open not only our hearing, but our curiosity as well: what is there?

We may become aware of the subtle sound current which is often there, a very quiet vibration which may be background vibration of the Earth. Listening to silence is truly one of the great spiritual practices, in which we tune into a deeper level of being and of experience. Silence in nature can facilitate that deeper connection to ourselves through allowing us to listen more deeply to our hearts and bodies. Nature or wilderness can provide a holding environment so that we can relax the ways we chronically constrict ourselves.

The Earth speaks to us in so many ways which are interesting, soothing, curious, and sometimes frightening. Hearing the sound of a large animal passing through the brush near a wilderness trail can be disconcerting until you can identify it as a deer, and not a bear. The Earth speaks when you hear, but cannot see the cause of, a large tree limb snapping in a forest; it awakens you to your surroundings. The sudden outbreak of barking from a neighbor's dog can be startling, even alarming, until you see the cat leaping high onto a fence to escape the danger.

All these stimuli which come to our ears speak to us; they have a communication that our ears have known, not only for our own personal lifetime, but for 4 million years as these bodies have been evolving as humans—and which we have only recently lost the ability to hear.

James Hillman, the noted depth psychologist and author, brings in another element of listening to the land: the land listening back. In his article, *Anima Mundi: The Return of the Soul to the World,* he says: "To speak, to ask to have audience today, in the world, requires that we speak to the world, for the world is in the audience; it too is listening to what we say. So these words are addressed to the world, its problems, its suffering in soul. For I speak as a psychologist, a son of soul, speaking to psyche."

This is the other side of our listening to the land: recognizing that the planet is also listening to us—and listening very carefully because her future is dependent on what we are saying. Another element of this practice involves having conversations with the Earth, speaking directly to it, and relating to it as an ensouled entity, as Hillman suggests. I would invite you to adopt a stance of being in relationship, so that the Earth experiences you as relating to it. This is a stance of respect and compassion, and an interdependent relationship of care.

This practice has quite practical implications. Now some architects, educators, builders, and even developers are adopting this kind of respectful stance toward the Earth. Listen to this description of how this practice works in the case of the Ozark Regional Land Trust:

> Every piece of land in the Ozarks has been altered by the human hand. Only small fragments of the whole area are still pristine. Yet even the condition in which we find land today represents an opportunity to preserve natural values into the future for the benefit of the wildlife and future generations. By protecting the land from further harm we provide opportunities for regeneration and restoration. So we "listen" to the land first. Try to understand what it once was as an undisturbed ecosystem and what pieces of that remain. We also consider the natural resource value of land at present. Is it offering forests, recreation, open space, agricultural, educational, historical or other uses? Could the land revert to its former natural state if managed or left alone? Will protecting its current use provide natural values which would be lost by further development? What kind of human use would be compatible with sustaining certain natural values or the ecosystems? So the "package" must answer these and other questions about the land by "listening" to the land.

INWARD JOURNEY

Listening to the land is a practice of healing and balance for us as humans. It is listening to the whole body which is none other than the whole world. This practice involves taking time to be with ourselves, and to listen to what our bodies are saying. We all know the major signs with which our bodies speak to us, such as hunger, thirst, fatigue, stress, and pleasure. But there are also more subtle messages from our bodies: discomfort, unease, peacefulness, and relaxation. An integral aspect of this practice is turning inward to ourselves, quieting down the outer and inner chatter, and attending to our inner experience.

As we learn to listen inwardly, we learn how we can respond, and in the process develop intuitive abilities as well, since we are working with that aspect of the mind that connects with the world in a holistic way. This practice involves a suspension of judgment, not blocking what we may be hearing but accepting it. This is a kind of inward journey, and we find that this connecting more and more deeply with ourselves also connects us with something greater than ourselves as well.

This practice is transformative. We begin to expand as we take in more and more of the world. The world outside of me slowly transforms to become the world inside of me. Soon, there becomes no difference, only complete interconnectedness.

The Council of All Beings

Listening to the land also means listening for the possible responses which are available for the difficulties we are facing. One way to do this is in concert with the Council of All Beings.

John Seed, the noted Australian ecologist and ecological activist, together with Joanna Macy, Mary Fleming, and Arne Naess, has devised the Council of All Beings as a way of attempting to listen to the land through an active imagination exercise. In this group exercise, outlined in the book *Thinking Like a Mountain,* the participants each take on the voice of one aspect of the Earth, perhaps an endangered species, perhaps a tree, rock, or some other aspect of nature, and speak together in the group to bring out what these elements of nature might say to us humans if they could. This listening practice is done in a ritual format, with a sacred opening to set a tone for this work. Participants are often guided through a visualization process, to ask for the energy or spirit of a particular aspect of nature to come to them. Alternately, the participants may go out onto the land, in a silent and meditative way, to open to the land around them and listen to what is being said, and attempt to make contact with nature.

One important element of this practice is the idea that the participant is being chosen by that other being, "In this process, we imagine that other beings, other life-forms apart from humans, seek to be heard at our Council" (Macy & Young, p. 161). Participants are encouraged to stay with the first impulse of being chosen, which is often surprising, and is not by a species with which the person is familiar. This is a way of allowing the intuitive ability to be acknowledged in creating this experience.

After this introduction, participants may be encouraged to actually make a mask, or in some other way symbolize the taking on of the other lifeform perhaps through movement or sound. The idea is to actually embody that spirit. They sit in a circle council-style, coming together to discuss their common concern—life on the planet. People may speak, they may cry, or wail, or dance, or rage. Generally there is very thoughtful discussion; often there is grieving, confusion, and a sense of loss. Discussions, and even arguments may ensue between antagonists; strange alliances are built between "Redwood Tree," "Water," and "the Desert Floor." "Crow" may help "Real Estate Developer" to see how his rampant building projects are destroying habitat for other species.

Every time I have conducted or participated in such sessions I have seen a transformation in consciousness take place among the participants. Their minds are opened, often the grieving is a way of releasing feelings, and a new sense of energy and relief is present. Participants often feel they have contacted the spirits, or essences, of these various aspects of the more-than-human world. There is an opening mentally, emotionally, and spiritually to these other beings which inhabit this world with us. It is often a healing experience for the group. This practice allows us to use our active imagination to engage with the world and listen to what it has to say.

Listening in Wild Nature

Another listening practice is actually being out in wild nature. I admit to a bias here, in that I believe that undisturbed wild nature exhibits the elements of nature which unfold in an organic process according to that environment. There is a kind of "voice" that is developed in a wilderness area, where the species have been able to co-evolve over hundreds of years. It is the voice of evolution, of co-evolving species, and the undisturbed voice of Life, as it continues to develop. One can sense a different tone in the air, a different quality of the music, as it were, which vibrates in this kind of environment. It is a kind of intelligence of nature, and I think of it as connecting to our own greater intelligence. People who have been in the wilderness will swear that it is absolutely necessary to spend time in these environments in order to fully know who we are as humans. This is why so many of us are so passionate about preserving these few remaining places in nature; it feels like preserving ourselves, our heritage, and our ancestors.

Recently I was hiking in the Adirondack Park of upstate New York, and although this land had been logged at some point in the past, the way the forest had been permitted recently to develop relatively undisturbed, allowed me to hear what this land had to say. It spoke to me eloquently of the way that trees grow in one another's shadow and light, of how they support one another; how the wind soughs through different trees in different ways; how the rain, which was pouring down in a Nor'easter, was dripping just so from the leaves and needles of the trees, more and more to the forest floor as the canopy became drenched and saturated. The dry and pungent smells of the forest began to give way to a musty dampness as the rain continued through the day. The steady dripping rain over the course of the day combined with the changing light patterns as the gray clouds became thicker, and then dropped lower down the sides of the ridges, becoming fog, and drifted across the surface of the lake. The steady dripping became slowly building streams, gurgling at first, and then rivers as the accumulated water found its way downhill. I became aware of water rushing along beside me as I began to descend Tongue Mountain.

The sounds of the Earth and the sky became one with the light, the trees, the mud at my feet. Nature was fully alive and interrelated through this day, and the health and vitality of the forest was singing a bright song as I hiked deeper and deeper into the forest. This song, this symphony, was healing for me, as the normal chatter of my mind became quieter and quieter. I noticed patterns of light and patterns of sounds, and recognized that nature has a self-organizing ability, when left to its own devices.

Listening to the land also has an element of allowing ourselves to be open to what is said, and allowing lessons and symbols to enter into our awareness. I realized that I don't need to push in my own life so much; I can relax a bit, and trust that there is a self-organizing principle in the world of which I am a part as well.

DAILY INTERACTIONS

We can also listen to the land through our daily interactions.

The other day, while sitting comfortably with my friend Lana, sipping tea and talking on a cloudy, drizzly afternoon, I became aware of the ongoing buzzing of a tree-mulcher in the neighborhood. The sound was a steady droning in the background of our conversation, and we occasionally commented on it—it was annoying, it was loud, it went on for hours! One reason the sound was remarkable was that we seldom hear noises at her house except the occasional traffic going by in the street. However, the wall of Douglas fir, arbutus, and mountain ash trees that cover her property, which act as an auditory as well as visual barrier to the road, did not prevent this loud, insistent noise from reaching us.

The sound represented many different things to us. There was the fact that it was so loud that it could be heard in the house, and also what that work entailed—mulching trees. Poplars which had grown "too tall" and "too overgrown" in the neighbor's yard were being trimmed. Once again, the anthropocentric view—that humans have the right to shape and mold the environment in any way they choose—was triumphing over "wild" nature.

On a daily basis, I work to find moments of listening to the land. It may be a small moment: Standing on my deck early in the morning—tuning into the sky brightening with the approaching sun, and listening to the sounds of the birds awakening—may be my moment for the day. Or maybe taking a walk in a local park, and tuning into the sounds of the wind in the trees, or pausing in my afternoon run to listen to the creek flowing beneath the bridge, allows me to have that sense of communion.

When we engage in daily acts like this we allow ourselves to expand, or open to these sounds of the world speaking to us. And we will often find ourselves refreshed, more relaxed, perhaps a bit more open.

CONCLUSION

Listening to the land connects us to our roots as people, to the Earth which supports us with all that we need to survive. Listening to the land will assist us in surviving on this planet, and assist us in making sure that all the other living species on this planet survive with us. Listening to the land provides us with healing for our body, mind, and spirit, and thus it is beneficial for us and for all those around us. It is a practice in which contemporary tribal peoples still engage, and which all our ancestors once engaged, and which many of us have lost through the advancement of modern culture, and our focus on only the human world. It is a practice which we need to relearn, and which will reconnect us to the greater source of life on this planet. It will change our lives, and our future.

An interesting tale about listening to the land also points out one potential outcome of this practice, which may be unexpected, and perhaps unintended, but which may help us to rethink our place here on the Earth:

One day a man who owned a field left it in the care of another man. He took good care of the land, ploughing, weeding, planting, and harvesting it. When the owner came back he said to the man who had been taking care of it, "Give it back now. The land belongs to me."

"No," said the other man, "I won't. The land belongs to me. You are the owner, but I am the one who has taken care of the land all this time. The land is mine."

They began to fight, until the neighbors brought them to a judge to settle the dispute. The judge happened to be Hodja Nasrudin. Each man said, "The land is mine! The land belongs to me!"

Hodja walked to the field, lay down in the dirt, and put his ear to the ground. "What are you doing, Nasrudin?" they asked.

"I'm listening."

"What are you listening to?"

"The land."

Both men laughed at him. "Listening to the land? Listening to the land? What does the land have to say?"

Hodja looked up and said, "The land says that both of you belong to the land."

References

Anonymous 2002. *Who Owns the Land? An Oral Tale*. Author unknown; retrieved from the Internet on Dec. 7, 2002 from *http://www.unicef.ca/eng/unicef/story/who.html*

Hillman, J. 1982. Anima mundi: The return of the soul to the world. *Spring,* 71–93.

Keller, C. 2001. *The Greening of Apocalypse*. Retrieved from the Internet on Dec. 7, 2002 from *http://www.thewitness.org/archive/april2001/williamsinterview.html*

Line, L. Dec/Jan 2003. Silent spring: A sequel? *National Wildlife* 41(1), 20–29.

Macy, J. & Brown, M.Y. 1998. *Coming Back to Life: Practices to Reconnect our Lives, our World*. Gabriola Island, BC, Canada: New Society Publishers.

Ozark Regional Land Trust 2002. Land preservation. Retrieved from the Internet on Dec. 7, 2002 from *http://www.orlt.org/protection_options.htm*

Seed, J., Macy, J., Fleming, M. & Naess, A. 1988. *Thinking Like a Mountain*. Gabriola Island, BC: New Society Publishers.

Sewall, L. 1999. *Sight and sensibility: The Ecopsychology of Perception*. New York: Tarcher/Putnam.

*W*orking in a hospice or a similar environment often confronts us with amplified emotional challenges that can frequently cause us to close our ears and even our hearts as well. In this selection
from Lessons from the Dying, *hospice director and Buddhist teacher Rodney*
Smith offers deep wisdom earned at many a bedside on ways and means for
keeping both organs open, especially at times of greatest duress. Sometimes
the most compassionate thing we can do for another person is to leave them
alone—which paradoxically is one of the greatest fears of the dying. Rodney
guides us to vigilant practice, helping us to come to true understanding of
another, an understanding that enlarges the heart sufficiently to make gen-
uine room for another. It is this deep understanding that is tantamount to love.

Listening from the Heart

Rodney Smith

Siddhartha listened. He was now listening intently,
completely absorbed, quite empty, taking in everything.
He felt that be had now completely learned the art of listening.
He had often heard all this before, all the numerous voices
in the river, but today they sounded different. He could
no longer distinguish the different voices....
They all belonged to each other: the lament of those that yearn,
the laughter of the wise, the cry of indignation and the groan
of the dying.
~Hermann Hesse, Siddhartha

WHEN WE ARE COMMITTED to learning for its own sake rather than accumulating knowledge, every experience becomes a teacher. Learning from our interpersonal relationships becomes a priority because much of our lives is spent with other people. In fact we are always in relationship regardless of whether we are with people or alone.

The greatest gift we can offer is the gift of our understanding. Each of us in our hearts seeks to be understood, for to be understood is to be loved. Understanding requires the total participation of the mind and heart of the listener. There can be no evaluation or judgment, just listening with caring attention. The speaker can then grow naturally in whatever way is most appropriate.

Working with the dying shows us how we can learn to listen more effectively. When people die they often reach out for somebody to make the journey with them. Most people prefer companionship to isolation. Dying alone is more feared than dying in physical pain. To be with a person who is dying requires listening beyond our usual means. It means crossing from our territory into his and being with him in his aloneness. Often this requires extra effort, for we must pierce our own resistance to being alone.

In the Thai language, the word for understanding can be literally translated as "entering the heart." Allowing a person to enter the heart means that our heart is large enough to contain more than our self-interest. When we understand something, we allow it to be itself. We place no demands upon it and ask nothing from it in return. Listening requires such an effort. Our heart becomes vulnerable to the pain of another. We feel her suffering, and her pain affects us. We do not try to take it away because we are listening; we are participating, without reacting.

It is very difficult to listen because we keep getting in the way of what we hear. In hospice work, for instance, the dying patient may choose not to take medications. Everyone on a patient's hospice team wants that person to be physically comfortable, but unless we try to understand why the patient chooses to be noncompliant, our efforts will frequently be met with more rigidity from the patient. The patient may want to feel pain because it reminds him that he is still alive. Or the pain might allow him to feel he is atoning for the sins of a lifetime.

In either case, sitting with the person and building a trusting relationship will allow the exploration of these issues. But if the issues are explored with the intent to bhange the dying person's mind, listening becomes a form of manipulation. We pretend to be neutral on the outcome of the discussion, but in fact we usually want the patient to die our death. We hope to push him subtly toward our definition of salvation. But if we remain vigilant about our own prejudices, we will not contaminate and disturb the listening.

Usually we listen from our own agenda. No matter what the occasion, we judge and evaluate what the person is saying in relationship to our own opinions, to our own standards and measurement. We listen through the screen of our own intentions, waiting for the person to stop speaking so we can assert our own point. Our motivation is often to persuade rather than understand. Frequently we treat the speaker as an adversary rather than a welcome friend. So we may hear little of what is said, and understand even less. In dismissing a person's words, we dismiss the person.

But escaping our biases is not easy. Our opinions influence our listening in subtle ways. No one benefits when we ignore our prejudices or pretend that we have transcended them, for they still color our listening. The only way a prejudice can be neutralized is by owning it as part of our consciousness. It is possible to hear *through* our opinions, much as we are able to focus our vision on an external object and still be aware of the background.

I was once visiting Lisa, the spouse of a patient who was very close to death. She was an astute and sensitive woman who was very honest and open with her feelings. We had met several times, and each time Lisa grieved intensely. We were sitting facing each other, and I started our conversation by leaning toward her with my arms resting on my legs. I was expecting Lisa to continue her grief work. Lisa looked at me and said, "You know, when you sit like that you force me to grieve. Today I am not feeling sad. I want to talk about other things." In that moment I was clearly not being present with Lisa. All our past sessions together were coloring my availability to her in that instant. I was taken by how subtle my habitual actions may influence and persuade a person in some unconscious way.

PROJECTIONS

Most of us think of reality as an external objective truth. Reality for us is the same as reality for everyone else. It is simply the way we perceive events. Few of us consider that our perceptions could be distorted. We believe that everyone hears or sees in the same way. This limited view of reality is dangerous precisely because we believe it is objective. We do not even realize that we are looking at life through our own prism.

Our perceptions are actually colored by our experiences, opinions, history, and values. For example, when we walk into a dying patient's home, and he is in pain, we bring with us our history of bruised knees and dental appointments. We react out of our personal struggle with pain rather than from the clarity of seeing things the way they are. We end up perceiving only what our mind allows us to see. Instead of letting perceptions come to us, we go out and distort them. We actively influence our reality to fit our preconceived notions and then assume that our embellished version is true. Only when we acknowledge our distortions and prejudices do we begin to free ourselves from their influence.

We are controlled by what we do not include. Most of us have parts of ourselves which we dislike. For some it is our anger or rage; for others it is jealousy and lust. It does not matter what the trait is, it is what we do with it that makes it a problem. Disliking these qualities does not make them go away, it just obscures their influence. When we are averse to these qualities, we attempt to drive them from our consciousness. We deny ownership of them by projecting them onto other people. They are still in us, but by casting them onto someone else, we can react and dislike the other person rather than ourselves.

I worked with Tom, the son of a hospice patient, who I initially thought was a very concerned and loving caregiver. He would appear constantly at the side of his dying mother, catering to her every wish. As I got to know Tom, this constant attention seemed too solicitous. Something did not ring true. It was revealed through our conversations that Tom was a battered child and was harboring enormous hostility toward his mother. He was never able to admit to his anger because it would have been too overwhelming. Tom also became suspicious when other family members spent a lot of time caring for his mother. He felt they would not treat her as well as he did and occasionally accused them of mistreating her. He was, I thought, disowning his anger, displacing it onto other family members, and then overcompensating with excessive caring behavior of his own.

So long as we project our traits onto other people, we remain bound by their power. Battling to escape their control over us, we expend enormous energy to maintain the illusion that these qualities are "out there" rather than originating within us. Touching those disliked areas of ourselves with the same kindness that we show the dying patient is the all-important first step on the road to recovering these rejected parts. Allowing ourselves to see and feel these qualities within our consciousness gives us the freedom to recognize their existence and act differently. Although we may fear being overwhelmed if we allow them access to our consciousness, by not owning them, as we have seen, we imprison ourselves within their energy. Awareness liberates us from their power and makes us whole and total. We can then listen from our heart rather than react from our mind because we have owned all parts of ourselves.

I was teaching a recent workshop for people who were interested in the issues of death and dying. One of the participants, a hospice nurse, expressed guilt and shame for her inability to be present for her patients day after day. I suggested she treat herself as kindly as she treats a dying patient. I asked if she would ever offer the dying the same unforgiving attitude she was inflicting on herself. Later she wrote me the following note: "Thank you deeply for your suggestion to treat myself as a hospice patient. I have intuitively treated hospice patients with a spaciousness and allowance that I do not extend to myself. Are we not all a heartbeat away from dying? Why wait? Why not accord ourselves and every person that same compassion while we are fully engaged in life? Yes!"

LISTENING TO THE DYING

When we sit with the dying we need all our skills to keep from being swept away by the drama in front of us. Dying accentuates almost everyone's problems. Mild emotions grow more volatile and extreme, small incidents become overblown. This is true for the patient, the family and friends, and the caregiver. Death squeezes our unresolved issues to the surface. Because it is the complete and total ending of life, one of the predominant emotions for many people who are dying is fear. Our unreconciled life issues are laced with the intensity of our fear of dying. The compounding of fear and unresolved issues creates a situation of intense unpredictability.

The hospice staff come into this situation not only with their own historical issues around death, but with the additional task of trying to provide a calming reassurance to the patient and family throughout their ordeal. A more experienced caregiver has probably been through several hundred deaths, and though these deaths have imparted a familiarity with the process, they have also left their toll on the worker's accumulated grief. Through all of this inward and outward emotional residue, the worker's job is to start afresh with each new family.

Listening to the dying involves listening to the person and simultaneously listening to our own reactions. The two are easily confused, since the intensity of the situation causes a heightened form of projection and bias. Our fear of dying, our aversion and denial, color and filter the reality. So many traps lie along the path to clear listening that it is a wonder we ever connect at all beyond our own needs.

Elisabeth Kübler-Ross tells the story of a young mother who was dying. Every person who came into the room entered with the reactions and feelings they had about the death of a young mother: pity, anger, fear, and sadness. The young woman complained that everyone was entering her room to be with their preset feelings. Few came to be with her.

We all know people who have physical or psychological traits that provoke a reaction in us. For some of us it is the disfigured burn patient, for others the person caught in his rage. We usually turn away because we are repulsed by the idea of ourselves being like this person. We react because the issue that confronts us outwardly exposes us to our worst fears. Dying is such a condition. As long as the person is much older we can tolerate being with her. Her age confirms that death is far away from us. But what about the dying patient who is of the same age as us or shares the same life circumstances? Such patients often create the most intense reactions.

Other patients can activate issues we may have with our own family. We can easily fall into the trap of trying to work out our concerns while attending to the patient's. We find ourselves so enmeshed in caregiving that we lose objectivity or perspective. We desperately want to help the patient because in doing so, we hope thereby to untangle our own internal confusion.

Listening to the dying takes us to the edge of our own fears, for when we open our hearts to someone, we open ourselves to their death. Death will come in with a force equal to the resistance we have to it.

The reaction we feel when confronting death is death confronting us. Our resistance comes from the tenacious hold we have on personal safety in the face of an event that represents the complete elimination of security. We are never on psychologically safe ground when we deal with death and dying. Our need for self-preservation can force us away from creative responses. We find ourselves responding with a cliché or saying something completely inappropriate.

We may approach the dying patient with a genuine desire to help but feel totally inadequate to do so. The truth is that we are inadequate at stemming the tide of a terminal illness. We do not need to force an answer to a problem that has no solution. We feel uncomfortable with not saying anything in the face of so much pain, so we endeavor to make death palatable by offering trite responses that frequently cause more difficulty than they solve. "It's God's will." "You need to get on with your life." "He's better off now." To the dying and the bereaved these phrases are confirmation that we are troubled by their pain but uninterested in them as individuals. Such comments are cues that there is no listening going on here at all. They are attempts to move away from our feelings of deficiency and the vulnerability of our own mortality.

If listening is to occur, it is imperative to become aware of our inner voice of protest. Only when we are unencumbered by our own history are we free to act spontaneously and appropriately within the context of the moment. One hospice nurse confided in me that, against everything she had learned in nursing school, she had once climbed in bed with a patient and snuggled next to her. It had felt like the appropriate response for this patient, who had voiced the fear of dying alone. The patient died half an hour later in the nurse's arms.

The more open and honest we are in facing our reactions, the less likely we are to rush in to fix situations without discovering what the patient actually wants. The more softly and gently we treat ourselves, the more available and compassionate we will be to those in need. We do unto others as we do unto ourselves. There are no demarcations between our inner psychic world and external circumstances except the ones we artificially impose.

The most difficult part of listening is learning to leave the other person alone. We try to apply our standards universally to resolve problems, but listening is not about problem-solving. It is about the gift of our attention. Listening bestows on each individual her own uniqueness; free from our demands, it fully acknowledges that person's worth by validating her. When we demand something from someone, we are requesting them to change or be altered. Listening does not demand anything, it allows everything to be just as it is. When a person is not pressured by the opinions of the listener, he no longer evaluates himself on external criteria and is therefore free to look within. Less external judgment frequently leads to less internal judgment and therefore to a natural growth of consciousness. With self-judgment temporarily abated, a person is able to move into areas within himself that call for his attention. He grows where he needs to grow merely by paying attention to those areas without aversion or criticism.

Growth has its own time frame. The patient's natural timing may make us impatient, but that is not the patient's problem. The listener moves at the speed of the patient, not the other way around. Through being heard we develop an inherent trust in our own growth process. Unburdened by criticism, a person's growth moves naturally toward greater openness. We become more at ease and have greater faith in the process of growing.

TRUE AND USEFUL

The Buddha stated clearly that saying only what is true is not sufficient for skillful speech. Speaking skillfully also requires saying what is useful for the listener to hear. One has to speak what is true and what is useful.

Honest feedback at first appears to be simply a matter of saying what is true, communicating what one actually sees as straightforwardly and reliably as one can. This, however, is not the full meaning. Viewing honest speech as simply a statement of fact leaves the impact of that fact out of consideration. Honesty needs to be tempered with timeliness. To tell someone that they are offensive in some way or other may be the truth, but it is an act of unkindness if that person is unprepared for such bluntness. Honesty without sensitivity can be a weapon. To say what is true and useful involves the full-hearted sensitivity of the listener. When a hospice patient asks if he is going to die, the truth is, "Yes, of course, why else would you be in hospice care?" Usually that is far too coarse a response. A more appropriate answer might be, "What is your body telling you?" This allows the patient to come to his own truth through the experience of his body. For truth to have an impact on a person's growth it is necessary for the patient to hear it within the context of his own perceptions.

If the timing is wrong, the patient's perceptions can cloud and twist the truth into something entirely different. If the truth is not useful, it will be distorted into a false perception.

Usefulness is the compassionate aspect of honesty. Truth can be a genuine gift or a weapon of destruction. It can cut and slice, or heal and mend. The determining factor is the context of the communication, which is as important as the truth of what is said. The context includes both *when* something is spoken and *how* it is said. The when and how of honesty allow the listener to grow from the feedback rather than recoil from it. This is the art of truthfulness.

The art of truthfulness can be applied to speech if the speaker first becomes aware of all the circumstances, both the external factors and the internal motivation for responding. Poor communication can occur if either one of these two cues is ignored. As long as our response includes an understanding of our own motivations, it will not come out of our own selfish needs. With full awareness of the external and internal cues of listening, our response flows from the situation itself without imposing an agenda. The wider the scope of our attention, the more love there will be in the reply. When our speech comes from a clear comprehension of the entire setting, our heart governs our communication. Attention is like a camera lens: the smaller the opening, the less light of understanding illumines the event; the wider the aperture, the better we see what is needed.

For example, it is impossible to be angry at someone and to understand them at the same time. When we are angry our responses come from our self-righteousness. Our view is narrowed to our own opinion. To understand someone, we have to be willing to listen to that other person free from our perspective. This means that we have to expand our point of view to include theirs. Anger cannot sustain itself when we drop our self-righteousness.

I worked with Ellen, the hostile spouse of a patient close to death. She was deeply dependent upon her husband for almost every form of security. Poorly educated and illiterate, Ellen had left the responsibility for all their paperwork to her husband. He had not had time to teach her about these matters before he became too weak to do so. Feeling her vulnerability, Ellen railed at him and screamed at me. It was a house I enjoyed leaving. During one of my visits, Ellen happened to see an old photo of her husband. It depicted the two of them together, healthy and strong, on vacation. She started to tell me about their earlier life together. Her eyes softened, and she began to sob. Ellen went over, lay down beside him, and cried for a long time in his arms. Her anger could not continue in the face of the love she held for him.

INTIMACY

Most of us do not know how to die. It is not something we have rehearsed or practiced. We have a mind full of ideas about what will happen, but little if any actual experience with the process. We need to have someone who knows, guides, teaches, and reassures us, someone we can trust, someone who will stand naked with us, who will not be overwhelmed. The dying need much more than pat answers or good feelings. Their hearts call for someone who can open into the unknown, someone who will travel the road of fear with them. To find such a companion is a very rare and precious occurrence.

Dying strips away everything that has kept us distant from each other. In this open vulnerability and shared pain there is little room to hide and nothing to protect. Our life as we have known it is essentially over. We have little need to defend ourselves. As Bob Dylan once sang, "When you ain't got nothin', you got nothin' to lose." From that void comes a willingness to expose ourselves to another.

Offering our attention during this time allows the dying companionship and a shared intimacy. Intimacy is the joining of human hearts, allowing both participants to momentarily step out of their self-concern. People are more likely to live in isolation and die in company. We keep ourselves well protected until our time has run out. Then, in pain and with little to protect, we reach out for companionship.

As a hospice worker I was always astonished by the level of intimacy expressed to those of us who were strangers to the family. Almost all of the families welcomed us. They shared their quiet and heartrending stories in the most personal ways, allowing us to stand with them in the midst of their pain. The relationships seemed richer and more poignant because the usual formality of new acquaintances was eliminated. This raw trust brings out the best in us. Frequently, during the wake or funeral of the patient, a family member will rush past long-standing friends or relatives to hug and acknowledge the hospice worker. The hug symbolizes the level of human involvement during the death.

Most of us have known this level of intimacy only once or twice, perhaps when we first fell in love or when someone allowed us to share our pain with them. It is common to obtain this level of involvement when working with the dying. Over the years I have heard many hospice people attempt to describe what they receive from their work. Frequently they speak of how the families open their lives and how vulnerable and exposed they seem. A tenderness is communicated in these descriptions, a tenderness that indicates a high level of mutual respect and love.

Allowing ourselves to be vulnerable is not a display of weakness but of courage, the courage to meet someone in intimacy. The healing potential of the human heart is available only through intimacy. Reaching out with our listening, allowing others to expose their personal and family shadows, their grief and helplessness, their anger and fear, does not dull or dissolve these emotions. It simply provides a space for our human condition to be heard and acknowledged. When a person is able to stand in front of someone else and be granted permission to be just who he or she is, life meets life through the human heart. Life recognizes itself, and the effect of such a meeting is a gentle and joyous reunion.

The development of intimacy requires infinite patience and freedom from time constraints. There is no goal to the relationship. With goals, there are expectations and judgments all along the way. Patience requires no forethought of where the intimacy might take the speaker or the listener. It is an unguided journey deep into the hearts of both participants.

On several occasions, absorbed in intimate dialogue with a dying patient, I completely lost track of time. Often the patient and I would come out of that shared moment together and be amazed at the elapsed time. In the intimacy of that space there was no reference to time because neither of us was going anywhere. The feeling we came away with was that the moment was total and complete in itself. This was the result of both people dwelling together in their hearts.

The willingness to be intimate allows us to share the one thing we all value, genuine human warmth. Our time is their time, and we meet in the timeless. The speaker ingests the listener; and the listener, the speaker. Each of our roles becomes blurred, and it is no longer certain who is helping whom.

A spiritual teacher once said, "Love will not let us rest." The moments of love experienced through intimacy keep us working on ourselves so that we can abide for longer periods of time in that state. Initially at least, hospice workers associate this deep heartfelt contact with their work with the dying. The unknown and mysterious qualities of death keep us attentive, clear, and open in our relationship to the dying. The sadness is that we normally do not use the same quality of attention in all of our relationships. Many of us feel most alive when we are relating to death. Our other relationships seem to pale by comparison.

As many hospice workers come to eventually understand, these moments of openness are not dependent upon the dying at all. They are related to our ability to drop our own barriers and live free of fear. Hospice work is a tool by which we access our own potential. That potential is present in every relationship and in every moment. We can use our work with the dying as a portal through which we can step into universal intimacy. It takes a single step to walk over the threshold to love.

LISTENING AND SPEAKING

Reflect upon what it means to understand someone. Think of a time when you were involved in an intimate conversation with another. Your heart was open and you both shared and listened with deep affection. What allowed you to understand the other person? What was the relationship between understanding and intimacy, understanding and affection?

The next time you find yourself angry, be aware of how you listen to the other person's point of view. When you are angry, do you ever really listen to the other person? Now, in the midst of your anger, try to listen attentively and then see what effect your listening has on the anger. What does this teach you about listening and personal opinions?

Reflect on a meaningful and affectionate relationship that you have. What blocks you from listening to that person even more than you do now? Why are you only partially available? Reflect on what keeps you from participating fully and intimately.

Practice listening to a close friend or loved one without responding in any way. Do not give advice, opinions, or solutions. Do not judge or criticize this person or what he or she is saying. Watch your tendency to formulate a response rather than to listen. Be aware of nodding your head in agreement. Listen, through all your internal noise, to the other person's words and their impact on you. Connect with his or her pain or joy. How does your heart respond to this person's emotional life?

Reflect on your areas of prejudice. Where does prejudice still hide in your heart? Do you pretend to be tolerant even as you harbor intoler-

ance? How does your prejudice manifest? Prejudice is hard to own if it does not fit your self-image. What part of your self-image feels betrayed by having this prejudice?

This exercise is difficult. The question to consider when approaching it is, do you want to die with your prejudices or begin to understand them while you live? Merely thinking about them is not sufficient. You need to connect with them while they are active. If you can be aware of both your prejudice and the fear that drives it, you will make significant inroads toward understanding how and why it operates. Sit down and have a heartfelt conversation with someone about whom you harbor a prejudice. Watch how your mind wants to fix and hold that person in a predetermined way. Can listening occur in the middle of this projection, or are you constantly asserting your old ideas about who he is? Can you connect with the person's humanity? Can you access his pain? Are you able to own the anger that you project onto him? Accept the prejudice as coming from you and not as being true in itself? Owning your prejudice is the first step toward healing.

Reflect on a time when you were visiting someone who was very sick or dying and you felt powerless to change the situation. Did you try to comfort the patient with false hope, or did you steer the conversation away from anything meaningful? Do you find yourself avoiding such situations, not knowing what to say? What is causing this reaction? What fears arise when you see someone dying?

Another difficult exercise: Intentionally seek out an opportunity to be with someone whose illness or infirmity causes you to feel uneasy. Can you be with both your reactions to the disease and the person at the same moment? Attempt to connect with the person and let the infirmity be just as it is. Work toward allowing the person and your reactions to be just as they are, without trying to change either one. See if you can listen through your reactivity without acting upon it. Try to bring the same quality of listening to your fear as you do to the person speaking.

Reflect on how sometimes you speak the truth but do so hurtfully. Is there a better way to say it? What else could you say that would allow others to hear your useful criticism? What are the limitations of just saying what is true? Notice what occurs when you do not consider the usefulness of your speech. Are you in touch with your heart? How does the other person respond?

When you say something true without considering the other person's readiness to hear, you may do more harm than good. Practice giving feedback only when you include the other person's feelings within your response. Offer your feedback from genuine care and concern. What effect does this have on the other person's ability to hear?

*M*uch as the accomplished writer completely lets go of conscious concerns about grammatical rules and transcends
conventions in the service of her literary art, all concern about our listening
techniques disappears when the intention to be of genuine service to another
human being's spiritual development becomes the paramount consideration
underlying every interaction. In this selection, Zen teacher Cheri Huber takes
such a transcendent step and presents us with clear distinctions between simply pandering to the needs of ego and authoring more authentic responses
aimed at sincere spiritual development and growth. Such an approach is not
for the faint of heart, since it often requires courageous and skillful ways of
dealing with negative projections and the shadow aspects of ego that frequently emerge.

Fierce Listening

Cheri Huber

As THE TEACHER-IN-RESIDENCE at the Zen Monastery Practice Center in Murphys, California, I am often called upon to listen to students and colleagues and visitors. I listen differently depending upon the person, the place, and the context. In what follows, I'll outline and discuss the various approaches I take and offer examples as well.

When I listen to you talking about some problem, I will always try to help you see how you cause yourself to suffer. When I'm working with you, we will get very quickly to the understanding that you already know everything you need to know and do. You know what's important to you, what you value, what you love, what you feel good about, what you feel bad about—I can't contribute to that. But if I listen to you and I accurately reflect what you are saying back to you, you have a chance to actually hear what you're saying. Many of us talk and don't deeply listen to ourselves, but when we do, we find we are provided access to our own wisdom. This is a gorgeous thing because it demonstrates that we ourselves have first access to the wisdom that we're seeking. It's active and living inside each one of us.

When I work with people who are coming to a training to listen in this way for the first time, what often gets in the way of them being able to listen and accurately reflect what they're hearing is the belief: "If I'm going to make you feel heard, I need to paraphrase what you're saying so that you'll know that I really understand." But *my* words don't make *you* understand; only *your* words make you understand.

Helping people understand that point and then encouraging them to practice giving and getting accurate communication from people is what is really helpful. And one of the unexpected benefits which students soon learn is that people develop the belief that those who listen well are wise. So by accurately reflecting back their own thoughts and experience to someone for an hour, they come away thinking you're a sage—and all you've done is accurately reflect what they're saying clearly back to them!

Consider the following example: A young man at a weekend retreat spoke up and said, "Well, you know I try to be compassionate to all the voices in my head—even cruel, judgmental voices, whatever they may be saying." And in response, I said, "Well, that's fine, if that's what you want to do. But I can tell you, it's unnecessary. Those are the voices of self-hatred. They hate you. In no way do *any*, even the good ones, have your best interest at heart. And feeling sorry for them or coddling them is a waste of time, and it's only going to prolong your suffering." I said it very calmly, very politely, but also very straightforwardly.

Nevertheless, this simple declaration threw this young man into great distress. After the workshop I got a six-page email in which he told me that he hated me. I'm sure that many of the things I say often have that effect on a lot of people and I never hear from them again. But this young man took the time and made the effort to let me know. But then he let my words work on him a little bit. He grappled with what I'd told him and he actually got to a place in his own experience where he could see that what I was saying held some small potential to be true—and then he hated me even more! But again, he continued to let things simmer, continued with the incubation process until he went past that painful place, past the resistance of ego, until he finally got to an even deeper realization about what I was telling him.

Years ago I did a job where I talked to the public and I was actually in charge of something that was called "manner." What it entailed was instructing employees on how to deal with the people who called in to the company complaining. One day, a person called in and his call was answered by a friend sitting next to me. Immediately he just started in loudly attacking and condemning and demanding. And since my friend has just gone through the training in "manner," she was giving it her polite, professional best: "Well, I'm sorry that that happened, sir. Is there anything I can do to help you?" and so on. Finally, at the end of an exchange that went on way too long for her, the guy burst into tears. And then, through the sobs, he said, "I am so sorry. I just buried my mother, and I am absolutely beside myself." What allowed this to happen? I believe it was her skillful responses and her nonreactivity. She could have hung up on him, she could have done all kinds of less skillful things—but she didn't. She assumed that he was coming from a basically good place and treated him that way.

When you have people speaking to you who are angry and upset and you can treat them kindly and with respect, you place yourself in a position to graciously excuse them and help them. My Zen teacher used to say, "When somebody backs themselves into a corner, look the other way until they get themselves out. And then, act as though it never happened." Often that can be a great kindness to offer to somebody who most likely is in a place of pain and suffering that has nothing directly to do with you.

My role as a teacher also presents other unique challenges in listening. The pesky problem of projection onto "the Zen teacher" sometimes causes people to distort what I say, what they say, and what they hear. I'm recorded a lot in what I do, and sometimes I'll say to people who are projecting distortions, "You've got to take the tape home and listen to it." Because it's clear they haven't really heard *either* of us and that they can't get past what they're projecting onto me and what they believe I'm saying to them. And of course, almost everybody thinks that I'm saying to them what they already believe about themselves and the world—and very often I'm saying exactly the opposite. We see and hear what we already think, and we believe that other people see and think exactly the same as what we see and think. Even the people who understand intellectually that we are constantly creating the world we live in can have trouble accepting it emotionally. It's not that when people see things differently than we do they are seeing things the wrong way and just being stubborn or stupid; it's that we each do live in completely different realities. The problems of the world would disappear if we could truly and deeply understand our role as creators of our own reality.

But that's really difficult to comprehend. Why? Because we don't listen to one another. We don't take time to listen, to deeply *get* another person's reality. We don't take time for conversation. We want email. We want voicemail. We want finite little periods of time in which essential information can go back and forth. But listening absolutely demands time, which is one of the central foundations of something like Buddhism. We need to be willing to sit down and sit still. We need to be willing to be in solitude. We need to learn to have a different relationship with the voices in our heads. For a surprising number of people, it's first discovering that there actually *are* different voices in our heads. My relationship with myself, those voices in my mind, is primarily what I project out onto my relationship with you and beyond that, onto the entire world I live in. So if I can't listen to *me*—if I'm not interested in who I am, in what I feel and what I think—how can I hope to have any interest in who you are or how you feel or how you think? If I don't have time for myself, I'm certainly not going to be able to make time for you.

But making time to listen, making time for conversation, is just the beginning. Once we do that, here come the projections and our own values that we so readily and unwittingly ascribe to other people. Eventually though, through meditation and other teachings, people become more skilled at attending to their minds and at recognizing those patterns.

Sometimes certain people might announce that they've received "divine guidance." Then, of course, I have the unhappy task of pointing out that by the time this guidance has made it into the mind as a thought that can be turned into language and perceived as thought, we've entirely missed the divine. The divine is long gone and what we're usually doing is running that inspiration through our conditioned belief system so that the ego can take ownership of it. Conditioning then compares that inspiration to everything else that we know, so that we can be internally consistent, so that it's not anything that's too disturbing to us—nothing that's going to change or upset our lives particularly. By the time we go *"Aha!"* we're past the moment and we're in rehash mode.

Part of the purpose of meditation practice is being able to stay in this moment, not getting pulled off either into a voice that's just our habitual voice: *"Oh God, why are people such bad so-and-so's?"* or *"Wow! That experience was amazing. If that's true, then..."* And of course, people love both those experiences because they feed the ego.

It becomes useful to distinguish between the person who tells the story and the person who had the experience. It's not possible for the experiencer to actually authentically relate the experience. Time and selective perception have inevitably altered it.

To elaborate further, if you were to walk out on the street and, God forbid, be attacked and mugged and then later you tell me about the experience, the person who's talking to me now is somebody who survived it. Perhaps, if you're really tuned in, you could intimately recreate what it felt like while the person was hitting you, mugging you—good actors have cultivated that ability to a degree—but now it's a whole new, albeit similar experience, happening for the first time. The really tragic thing about those kinds of traumatic experiences is that some essential part of the person has been left behind and that part is having that painful experience over and over until it gets to the point where it has to be addressed.

And I don't think there's anything wrong with anything that happens to anybody. This is something that makes people crazy when I say it. Such a notion can be deeply disturbing. But again, I look at my own life, and some pretty grisly things have happened. And every one of those things has been a benefit to me, grisly grist for my own personal mill.

Many people will look back at some past event and say, "Oh, yes. I can see how that was a turning point. That was one of the most powerful, significant things that ever happened to me." But if they look at their lives now, invariably they'll say, "Oh no. I don't want anything painful like this to ever happen to me again." Still, through all this, I don't have the experience that there's anything wrong with anybody. And while it's true that people have some horrifying, grisly experiences, adding the dualistic judgments of right and wrong brings little to the healing equation.

I'm reminded of a friend, a death row attorney, and nonduality is the role she takes. Whenever she's defending a person she always attempts to bring in the family of the victim or victims. She tries to help them see, to help them heal, if they're at all ready and open to it. And she makes it clear: she is *not* saying: "What my client has done is okay. I condone this." She's not minimizing or diminishing their loss in any way. But if there's a possibility for healing and forgiveness to take place, she wants to do what she can to facilitate it. And of course, that perspective, that possibility is so foreign in this culture. There is a *right* and a *wrong*. Pure and simple. If you are being supportive of the murderer, then you are automatically assumed to be disrespectful, hateful, and minimizing and discounting the suffering of the victim and the victim's family. And of course, what my lawyer friend is showing is, "No. It's possible to stand in a place where it's all very, very sad for everyone concerned, and we don't have to decide who's to blame and who's wrong, and who's right, and we don't need revenge, and…" It's an extraordinary perspective—much like Jesus' or the Buddha's.

When I first began teaching I would listen to those kinds of dramas much differently than I do now though. For me now, hearing the *content* of any interaction is extraneous. It's irrelevant. I don't think there's anything wrong with anybody. I almost never, at this point, listen to what anybody says, to the content they bring me. I mostly listen to their energy. And I'm often listening for what they're *not* saying—because very often people talk about the opposite of what's actually of concern. This goes counter to the idea of actually listening, technically listening to content that a person presents.

Also, now there's much less of me, of my ego, involved in the way I listen. These days I have absolute faith in everyone's ability to diligently work out their own salvation. Essentially I'm mostly superfluous, although tracking people and being authentically present with them frequently makes them feel more comfortable. They appreciate knowing there's somebody else on the path with them.

Listening is actually a very large part of the practice we do at the Monastery. Every Tuesday evening people visit from the surrounding community and join the monks, who do what's called "Process Mapping." What Process Mapping involves is listening to a person, accurately reflecting them, and charting what they say. So when they leave at the end of the evening, they have an actual, physical, tangible map of what they talked about. We write down exactly what they say on Post-Its and put them on a large piece of paper so they can have a record: "I said that. And then I said that. And then I looked at that. And then I talked about that. And then I...." And what often emerges is people discover that none of the talking is random. We think we're so spontaneous, but we're really quite programmed. We're automatons. And to some people their own *robot-ness* is quite frightening.

One area that's a growing edge for me as a listener is when a person is really caught in their story, really believing it, immersed in the whole panoramic drama, and I get the sense that I'm the nine-millionth person who has been trapped in this soap opera, and that no matter how long I listen, all that's going to happen is that I'm going to get used up and then they're going to go on to the next person and tell the same story all over again. I don't have a lot of patience for never-ending stories. I understand that sometimes it's necessary to tell the story, but I figure that's why God made therapists. Let them pay somebody to listen to their story. Don't be perpetually inflicting it on other people.

I try to be present to people with "Beginner's Ear." I come with the notion that, in fact, I don't know what this interaction's going to be like, how this conversation's going to unfold. I don't know who this person is or what they're going to say. This is a brand new moment. Even if the exchange is just "Hi, how are you?" They've never been this person who is asking the question in this moment. I've never been the awake-and-alive person receiving the question. So, if I'm aware of it, it's a brand new "beginner's" experience for both of us. It's a brand new now. Ideally, I am able to sense the newness of each moment, the fresh quality of each moment, rather than being in my old ear, my old-timer's ear, where I know it all, and I've heard it all, and I've been there, and there's nothing new happening here…which is what happens to us when we're not in Beginner's Mind. But, when you're in Beginner's Mind, accessing Beginner's Ear, you're not gathering information. All you're doing is listening with freshness. You're not listening so that you can then know something or understand something, or add something to your arsenal of weapons against humanity! It's just for this moment. It's just for now. We're not going anywhere. We're not getting anywhere. This is it. This is all of life, right now.

So, however we are with our senses in that way, here's the catch: People think, "Well, okay, then if I were to have Beginner's Eye, well, I want to be somewhere really beautiful." *No!* If I have Beginner's Eye, where I am *becomes* really beautiful. It's astounding. It's amazing. Wherever I am. But we don't see it, because we go to preference, which is what keeps us from Beginner's Ear as well. We go to preference. "Well, I don't wanna talk to that person. They're not interesting. I don't wanna have that conversation. That's boring."

Of course, all conversation is simply an excuse to exchange energy. At an essential level that's all that's going on. We're rarely going to exchange words that will supremely significant. But even if they are, what's still going on is the energy that happens between us. Mostly the words are just something to do because it would be too uncomfortable just to sit together. But if we listen with our Beginner's Ear, then we're really listening for "Who are you? What are you about? I want to connect with you. I want to exchange energy with you." And then it doesn't much matter what we say.

*T*his book has repeatedly emphasized that learning to listen skill-fully takes ongoing, disciplined practice. This contribution, my own, details a number of elements that might go into such a practice. It also presents a discussion of some of the challenging aspects of learning to listen—aspects frequently encountered as a result of even some small bit of improvement.

What I've Learned
from Listening

Mark Brady

*Listening is an attitude of the heart, a genuine desire to be with
another which both attracts and heals.*
~ J. Isham

IN THE PROCESS of compiling this anthology, I have learned more than
I ever could have imagined about listening. In what follows, I'll do my
best to share a small part of what I've learned and also offer some specific
skills that I've taught others over the years. My hope is that these skills and
practices inspire you to creativity and enable you to reap the surprising benefits inherent in the skillful practice of listening—sooner rather than later!

THE WORST LISTENER IN THE WORLD

One thing I love most about what I've learned is this: The more we listen skillfully, the better listeners we become. It's much like learning to
write: I may not always be able to write the perfect sentence, the perfect
paragraph, the perfect chapter, but through study and practice, I can
often recognize flawed writing, particularly my own, when I read it. I
know what's amiss, and possibly what to do to correct the flaws. Similarly,
I can become better at listening by simply recognizing unskillful listening when I'm practicing it.

As I've become a more skillful listener, knowing more clearly what actually constitutes good listening beyond the mechanics, it becomes easier and easier to recognize when I am *not* listening well. At such times I must make conscious choices to either listen more attentively, and with more presence, or to explain to the person who's talking why I am not able to listen fully right now, and then suggest other possibilities for our interaction.

Indeed, the most significant accomplishment in this regard I've managed over the years is a fairly regular recognition of when I'm listening poorly. Often, without excessive prompting, "judging mind" will certify that I might very well be the worst listener in the world—especially given that I've made listening a subject of such in-depth study and practice. If I'm paying close attention, the recognition that I'm listening poorly sometimes comes from the response reflected back to me. A speaker may speed or slow their rate of speech, go flat in affect, or simply stop talking altogether. Other times I am suddenly aware when my mind is racing, itching to interrupt, or forcing my eyes to one distraction or another.

With awareness, I can make choices that will improve my ability to be with another, to listen more skillfully. As I try to listen for instance, to my colleague Pete as we sit together in a restaurant, with awareness I can recognize that when the noise and people on the periphery interfere with my ability to listen, I can make choices that will enable me to listen better. I might sit closer or move us to a quieter table. When I know what internal distraction feels like, when I am aware of my mind abuzz with some new discovery and there's no room for what my daughter Amanda longs to tell me, or what my friend Nancy might yearn to confess, I have greater awareness of that condition, and I can practice temporarily holding my own excitement in abeyance and await a more fitting moment. When I recognize the discomfort caused by my own words spilling over onto Jane's, cutting her short and indirectly telling her that I think what I have to say is more important, I can stop myself. I can apologize and gently urge her to continue. Greater awareness gives us all more choices, improving communication skills as we go.

When my students ask for a single rule of thumb for good listening, I often tell them: "Set the intention. Fire the desire. Find ways to feed the impulse to become a better listener." It's out of the recognition of the real power inherent in skillful listening, and the desire to acquire such skills, that the real creative juice of this practice flows. And being at ease with the possibility of being the worst listener in the world is an important aspect to integrate into such a practice!

A recurring intention to be a good listener can drive the engine of skillful listening. And the *MeMind,* the ego-centered, discursive thinker that seems to rule both my own private world and the larger planet as well, impels us toward unskillful listening.

But the MeMind is a poor emperor: as a result of its worldwide rule over the last century, we have seen more people maimed and murdered than any other 100-year period in human history—more than 100 million human beings.[1] And so the MeMind needs to be reined in, trained, and put to better use.

In one of his early talks, J. Krishnamurti taught, "You are the world."[2] Learning to become a more skilled, more tolerant listener is one way I can deploy such training, embrace that metaphor, and become a unique facet for positive change in the world I want to be.

But the MeMind can be a formidable adversary—at least early on in the practice. Ego is not something that willingly steps aside. Rather, once it sniffs out attempts to rein it in, it resorts to craftiness and subtle cunning. And so paradoxically, developing creative ways to *embrace* this adversary as a worthy opponent can be quite successful. Such an opponent might be like the *uke* in aikido, the attacker who functions as a sharpening stone upon which we can hone our skills. The worthy opponent can be like a trusted and respected friend who leaps from the rafters without warning and uses his crafty imagination in all manner of ways to launch sneak attacks on us, much like Kato would attack Peter Sellers in the *Pink Panther* movies (for those of you young enough to remember them!). Kato attacks with increasing determination, just as we can employ the MeMind in the service of making us better practitioners of our craft, working with the wild distractions as they arise during our attempts to become more skillful listeners.

LISTENING THROUGH THE DROSS

Margaret Fuller, the nineteenth-century intellectual, said: "What a woman needs is not as a woman to act or rule, but as a nature to grow, as an intellect to discern, as a soul to live freely and unimpeded to unfold such powers as are given to her."[3] It's my experience that this is true for all of us, women and men alike.

But to grow as a nature, to unfold as a discerning intellect, and to somehow find a way to live freely requires considerable creative, investigative work. Rarely do the first thoughts that come floating through the MeMind reverberate with the thrilling timbre of divine inspiration. More often, such courageous realizations only come about by attending to the dull and confused things which we may first struggle to formulate into words.

To return to my analogy of listening and writing: First thoughts—the dross that comes skimming off the unplowed, unfertilized fields of my own walking-daily-through-the-world mind—are like first drafts. They need the editing and revision that a skillful, trusted listener can provide by reflecting back what I've said, clarifying my assumptions, and inviting expanded expression. Thus skillful listening can help clarify the expression of the one being listened to in the same way as an engaged reader can clarify muddled writing by accurately and succinctly reflecting what is being thought, felt, and said.

I have become a better listener by expanding upon the elementary menu of feelings taught by Transactional Analysis almost forty years ago. Thus: mad, sad, glad, excited, and scared have become frustrated, melancholy, jazzed, energized, contracted, and myriad other creative variations. The repertoire granted by this expanded menu allows us to make finer observations and discriminations about what people are thinking and feeling, which helps us in turn be more skillful listeners. Going one step further, putting such observations in the words another might actually use frequently stimulates delicious resonance, with compassion and authentic connection often being the result.

With practice, the heart and art of what longs for expression can then find its way most fully from the inside out. In this respect, a skillful listener works to facilitate the life-affirming practice that Jesus, in the Gnostic Gospel of Saint Thomas, described this way: "If you bring forth what is within you, what you bring forth will save you. If you do not bring forth what is within you, what you do not bring forth will destroy you."[4]

BRINGING THE INSIDE OUT

By listening to my own inner wants, wishes, and rhythms over many years, I've learned that whether I'm aware of it or not, whether I believe it or not, whether I trust it or not, life continually orients towards healing and wholeness. By listening deeply to the world around and within me, I've learned that what causes suffering in me, causes suffering in others as well, and that such suffering can become a lesson in *shunyata* or *kenosis* or any of the many other words for such experience. There are many words for the lessons. They refer to the emptying out of my whole barrel of intellectual, material, and moral achievements, disposing of the proud offspring of MeMind—sometimes presented in Buddhism as "gaining mind."[5]

From listening, I've learned that the MeMind can be trusted to scan the immediate horizon and respond to perceived threats to my survival. But, I've further learned that the MeMind is best regularly cleansed of whatever truths, whatever past or recent history it attempts to cling to whenever dangerous moments of "understanding" and "intelligence" attempt to take up permanent residence. I've learned that theory, more often than not, fails miserably, or at least needs significant reworking, when confronted with the reality of the ever-changing, present-moment-ness of the world. I've learned that what I might say in response to another is only of secondary importance, that it is the *state of my mind and the quality of my heart* that is truly of primary significance.

I've grown to not only realize but accept that listening is a practice that takes practice. Part of the practice that can often take us out to the furthermost tips of our growing edges may be simply listening to those we love—and even more importantly, to those we don't. It's important to listen to people like us and people different from us, to listen to them as if we are permitted to enter into the secret garden of their deepest core. Such listening, if done heartfully, with skill and compassion, will invariably lead us in the direction of "making relatives" of the world's peoples, rather than enemies of them. Gene Knudsen, the founder of The Compassionate Listening Project puts it this way: "An enemy is someone whose story we haven't really heard." It's important for someone significant—a partner, teacher, family member, friend, or therapist—to listen to every heart in the world, to feed and grow them through "persuasive listening" so that we might all uncover the common field of our own broken hearts. I've learned that such listening helps people blossom and, like a dried sponge responding to the first drops of moisture, makes them unfold and expand and become full of life, brimming with constructive possibilities. By learning to listen with genuine affectionate interest, with positive curiosity rather than judgment or criticism or correction, something essential in us feels deeply met, lovingly touched, sweetly received. Together, fearlessly, as "relatives" now, we at least hold the possibility to birth something new and true and clear and good into the world.

PRACTICE MAKES SKILLFUL

There are a number of practices I offer students to help with listening. As mentioned above, cultivating *kenosis* is one such practice. Best described as "emptiness of self," similar in certain ways to *shunyata* in Buddhism, *kenosis* can be found in many spiritual traditions. The manner in which I employ it as part of a skillful listening practice is to first recognize when the wild, urgent ramblings of the MeMind have taken over the thought-space and are preventing me from paying full attention. After several deliberate breaths, I might call up a vision of my kitchen sink filled with soapy dishwater after the dishes are done. On an outbreath I simply pull the rubber plug and breathe easy as the flood of sludgy thoughts begins to gently whirl and spin down the drain. The space behind is left empty, clean, and shining, restoring a ready receptivity to the person before me.

Often, as a child in grammar and middle school, I would spend many hours listening with such an empty, open mind—not at all clued in to the fact that the acceptable way to demonstrate to teachers that I was listening was to ask discerning questions or make critical comments! It was not acceptable to simply take in what was presented, openly with little judgment; one had to question analytically and critically.It has taken me years to undo that learning and make progress in the restoration of "original mind."

In my classes I also teach a technique I call "Beginner's Ear," which is related to the Buddhist concept of "Beginner's Mind" popularized by Shunryu Suzuki in his book *Zen Mind, Beginner's Mind.* Beginner's Ear is the practice of holding oneself open in relationship to the words and sounds I am hearing, very similar to how I imagine a young child might attend to the sounds of new music, or of a cat purring, or of water as it whirls down the toilet bowl. There's a certain curious interest that draws me, a desire to remain present until the sound is completely finished.

Another useful practice on the road to becoming a skillful listener is *tonglen,* the silent, internal practice of taking and giving. This practice has been spoken and written about at length by Tibetan Buddhist nun and popular author Pema Chödrön. I will offer an example: As a friend is speaking to me of the pain of growing up in a family of three sisters and four brothers, and of being forced to compete fiercely for the available scarce resources, I can breathe in and fully receive that pain as it is impacting her in the present moment, perhaps by imagining a channel of jagged energy flowing from her heart to my own. Then, in its stead, I can silently send back to her relief in any of many imaginary forms I might conceive. I might send her luscious vegetable stews to fill her aching stomach, or I might send her a stylish summer outfit to wear to work, or I might send her a tube of superglue to mend her broken heart. What I imagine sending is not as important as my intention to be of service while she is telling me what hurts. Whatever I can imagine sending in the service of relief, I am then free to send in *tonglen* practice. It is a gentle and focused way to keep the mind present and the heart engaged in the presence of someone in unremitting pain.

VIRTUOSO LISTENING

Virtuoso listening, like virtuoso piano-playing or virtuoso crocheting, requires discipline, practice, and a recognition that mistakes will happen—wrong notes will be struck, stitches will be dropped, and the MeMind will invariably take me away from the direct experience of the speaker's message. Although knowing what skills are lacking is essential, it takes more than that to become a virtuoso.

It takes time and and it takes active energy. Active energy is required for sustaining the discipline and practice necessary to develop as a skillful listener. It is this active energy that can be characterized as the crucial difference between passively hearing and listening with attentive engagement. Social workers, counselors, psychiatrists, clergy—anyone engaged in the helping professions—will all attest to the energy necessary to be effective, and if they are being at all honest, many will be able to recount endless failures at this singular task. Distractions happen. It is how we respond to those times when we do not connect, when the MeMind takes over and sends us out to the grocery store or off on our summer vacation before we've ever left the office, that makes the greatest difference in the quality of our listening practice. Listening is perhaps like batting in baseball: connecting solidly one time out of three is good enough to achieve excellence and be voted into the Hall of Fame!

Another aspect of virtuoso listening is sometimes difficult to demonstrate in practice: being tolerant and forgiving of self and others when listening falls short of expectations. We must avoid the litany of "shoulds" that can tyrannically fill our heads: I shouldn't be so easily distracted; Susan shouldn't interrupt me with her self-referential non-sequiturs, no matter how far off on a tangent I fly; Amanda shouldn't have her eyes roaming all around the room while I pontificate on a subject of little interest to a teen; Pete should be able to concisely and accurately summarize with unfailing zest everything I've been droning on nonstop about for the last half hour. But recrimination is never the most skillful response at such times as these. Rather, a gentle recognition, an awakening awareness, recalls the resolve to keep playing, to keep practicing until improved skillfulness becomes the inevitable result. *That's* virtuosity.

In our culture listening is *not* the most valued role, and transcending that societal bias is important. It is speaking, teaching, and preaching that hold center stage in what passes for much of human discourse in the world today. It was the writer Brenda Ueland, author of *Strength to Your Sword Arm,* who realized by learning to become a charming and curious listener herself, that the poetry of relationship most readily becomes birthed into being through skillful listening. As this fiery confidante of Carl Sandberg realized, it is in the listening place, that hard-won bastion of inner silence, where much of life's poetry is born. Working to become a fearless listener does deliver strength to one's sword arm, as well as to one's mind and heart. Ueland's method for drawing out and encouraging the self-expression of others was simple and straightforward. It came alive for her and others in the sweet, elegant phrase, "Tell me more."

LISTENING DANGEROUSLY

Finally, I've learned that listening skillfully, like most things achieved in life, has a cost. Sometimes the "still, small voice," which is infinitely worthwhile to cultivate a capacity to uncover, isn't so still and isn't so small. Sometimes it's loud and large and makes great demands of us. It's helpful to know ahead of time what such a price may be before we can legitimately be asked to pay it. One price is this: the more skillful a listener you become, the higher the probability that you are transforming yourself into someone to whom painful, tender truths will be told, someone open to hearing things even a devout personal practice or professional training and experience may not have adequately prepared you for, something that sooner or later is going to break your heart wide open. But it's also important to realize that a broken heart is not necessarily a bad thing because, as writer and poet Stephen Levine reminds us, a broken heart is an open heart. When we take a heart that's been broken wide open out into the world, we take much that is pure and innocent and good and truly compassionate out there along with us.

Integral to the skill of listening with our hearts open is the inevitable requirement to respond in some way that deeply honors those things with which you have been entrusted. And as we find ways to truly honor those truths in others, we are inevitably led to the other dangerous dimension of skillful listening: learning to listen deeply and authentically to our own tender heart.

In the mid-1980s Patricia Hopkins and Sherry Ruth Anderson spent eighteen months traveling around the country interviewing a hundred women of spiritual accomplishment, women like Jungian analyst Marion Woodman, activist Joanna Macy, and psychiatrist Jean Shinoda Bolen.[6] Out of that research they discovered a common thread running through each woman's journey: they were all virtuoso listeners—to self and others. With respect to themselves, they each asked two recursive questions in one form or another. The two questions these women asked over and over were: "What's true for me?" and "What do I want?" And then they waited, sometimes fearfully, sometimes with excitement, but prepared somehow to honor whatever quivering answers they received. We too must be prepared to ask such questions and to listen patiently for the answers.

LISTENING AS ART

At the end of the classes I teach in listening, I frequently close by holding up a card that has only one word on it printed in big black letters. The word is "HEART." What I tell the students as I prepare to send them back out into the world, hopefully as significantly improved listeners, is this: "All the important words of my message are contained in that single word: Skillful listening is:

The ART of HEARing with the EARs of the HEART."

REFERENCES

1. Cooper, Robert (2001). *The Other 90%*. New York: Crown Publishers.

2. Krishnamurti, Jiddu (1976). *You Are the World*. Ojai, California: Krishnamurti Foundation of America.

3. Fuller, Margaret (1997). *Woman in the Nineteenth Century*. New York: W.W. Norton & Company.

4. Pagels, Elaine (1989). *The Gnostic Gospels*. P. 126. New York: Vintage.

5. Suzuki, Shunryu (1997). *Zen Mind, Beginner's Mind*. New York: Weatherhill.

6. Anderson, Sherry Ruth and Hopkins, Patricia (1991). *The Feminine Face of God*. New York: Bantam Books.

Conclusion

S
O THERE WE HAVE IT. Nineteen diverse and learned voices have spoken with passion and personal authority about the promise, practice,
and power of listening. Some echoed the experience of Dean Rusk, a
member of JFK's cabinet in the 1960s who deployed what he described as
"persuasive listening" as an integral part of U.S. foreign policy. Other perspectives aligned with Seva Foundation's Mirabai Bush and her prescrip-
tion for action: "When we begin to act by listening, the rest follows
naturally." And yet others with the point of view so succinctly expressed
by Jungian analyst Jerome Bernstein: "All things, animate and inanimate,
have within them a spirit dimension. They communicate in that dimension to those who can listen."

Whatever perspective each of the contributors to this collection has
offered, if there is a central theme that shines through, it is this: Listening is a skill that can be greatly improved upon for most of us, and it may
indeed be one of the most important skills we can cultivate in our lives.
It is a skill out of which great questions and world-preserving creative
responses can find a safe place to come into being.

I had the great privilege of witnessing two of the contributors to this
anthology several years ago demonstrate the power and promise of skillful listening. As I recall, Ram Dass and Joan Halifax were part of a group
of people presenting at a conference in upstate New York on the topic of
conscious aging and conscious dying. Suddenly, out of the sanctity of the

container that had been created over a number of days, and as a result of the quality of the exchanges that were taking place and the willingness of most people present to consider a variety of diverse viewpoints, Joan was inspired to ask Ram Dass a daring and memorable question.

"Do you think people become enlightened at the moment of death?" she asked.

I had never considered such a question before, but my own immediate, instinctive response was, "Yes. Of course." So I was quite surprised when I heard Ram Dass reply firmly, "No, I don't." And then, as if sensing Joan's divergent point of view, he returned the question: "How about you? Do you think people become enlightened at death?"

"Yes, I do. Absolutely," came back her reply. "I have seen it over and over again."

Pin-drop silence filled the room. Here were two greatly loved and highly respected teachers (possibly recalling images of Mom and Dad for many!) expressing directly opposing opinions. Finally, after several moments, Ram Dass broke the tense silence. In a friendly, warm, and affectionate voice, he said simply, "Interesting. Perhaps I will need to revisit my perspective."

I have revisited my own perspective on that and other questions and perhaps they each have as well, and perhaps so will you. But the point of their exchange and the lesson I came away with is the power and the possibility that a lifetime of listening as a personal practice permits. Such a practice not only allows us to ask questions we might ordinarily never have the wild mind or the courageous heart to ask, but it allows us to cultivate a mind that can entertain thoughts that would otherwise be unable to even find their way into conscious awareness. It is my firm conviction that a practice designed and intended to help us become more skillful, compassionate listeners is one way to facilitate movement toward the higher level of consciousness necessary to solve the growing problems in our shared world.

About the Contributors

A. H. ALMAAS is the pen name of A. Hameed Ali, the originator of the Diamond Approach.® Born in Kuwait, his academic background is in physics, mathematics, and psychology. Ali is the founder of the Ridhwan Schools in Boulder and Berkeley as well as the author of *The Pearl Beyond Price, Essence with the Elixir of Enlightenment,* and *Diamond Heart, Book 1: Elements of the Real in Man.*

MARK BRADY, PH.D. is a senior faculty mentor at the Institute of Transpersonal Psychology in Palo Alto, California. A long-time student of meditation, he teaches classes in Deep Listening through the University of California Extension. Contact: paideia@casbs.stanford.edu

RAM DASS (Richard Alpert, Ph.D.) is a spiritual teacher who has contributed significantly to the integration of Eastern spiritual philosophy into Western thought. He is the founder of the Prison-Ashram Project and the Seva Foundation. He is the author of *Be Here Now* and *Still Here: Embracing Aging, Changing, and Dying.*

PAUL GORMAN is the vice president for public affairs and communication at the Cathedral of St. John the Divine in New York City. He is the co-author with Ram Dass of *How Can I Help?*

JOAN HALIFAX, PH.D. is a Buddhist teacher and an anthropologist. She founded the Ojai Foundation, where she lived and worked until 1990. She then founded Upaya in Santa Fe, New Mexico, where she now practices, teaches, and works in the New Mexico State Penitentiary with maximum-security prisoners on death row. She also works with individuals who have catastrophic illnesses. She is the founder of the Project on Being with Dying, and founding teacher in the Zen Peacemaker Order. She is a Soto Priest and teacher.

MARGARET TRUXAW HOPKINS is a chaplain and the bereavement coordinator at Heartland Hospice in Santa Clara, California. She is the co-founder of the Electronic Hospice and a director of the Death Education Institute in San Jose, California.

CHERI HUBER has been practicing in the Soto Zen tradition for over 30 years. She is the founder and teacher-in-residence at the Zen Monastery Practice Center in Murphys, California, and travels throughout the world, conducting workshops and retreats. Cheri is the author of *Nothing Happens Next: Responses to Questions about Meditation, Suffering is Optional,* and *When You're Falling, Dive.*

MICHAEL S. HUTTON, PH.D. is on the faculty at the Institute of Transpersonal Psychology, where he is head of the Ecopsychology Program. In addition to being a licensed psychotherapist in private practice, Michael volunteers with many environmental groups, and is a co-recipient of the first Woodfish Award in 2001, given for projects involving reciprocity between Euro-American and Native American peoples.

CHRISTINE LONGAKER is the former director of the Hospice of Santa Cruz, California as well as the founder of the Rigpa Fellowship, for which she has developed the Spiritual Care and Education Training Program with

Sogyal Rinpoche. She is the author of *Facing Death and Finding Hope*.

MICHAEL P. NICHOLS, PH.D. is a professor of psychology at the College of William and Mary. He is the author of *The Lost Art of Listening*, and co-author with Salvador Minuchin of *Family Healing*.

TONI PACKER is the founder of the Springwater Center in Springwater, New York. She is the author of several books, including *The Work of This Moment, The Light of Discovery*, and *The Wonder of Presence*. Toni no longer calls herself a teacher and makes no claim to special authority.

FRAN PEAVEY is a long-time social activist who travels around the world learning from and advising other activists. Among projects she has initiated, the work of cleaning up the Ganges river in India is perhaps most significant. She is the author of many books, including *By Life's Grace: Musings on the Essence of Social Change*.

MARSHALL ROSENBERG, PH.D. is the founder of the Center for Nonviolent Communication. He is the author of *Nonviolent Communication* and teaches the principles and practices of nonviolent communication all over the world.

NANCY MANGANO ROWE PH.D., C.E.T. is a faculty mentor at the Institute of Transpersonal Psychology and has a heart-centered expressive therapy practice in Woodstock, New York. Her practice and life have been significantly influenced by Pema Chödrön, John Welwood, and other Buddhist teachers.

ANNE SIMPKINSON is an award-winning journalist and was the cofounder and editor of *Common Boundary* magazine. She currently works as an editor for *Prevention* magazine.

CHARLES SIMPKINSON is a clinical psychologist and founder of the Family Therapy Networker. He was also the cofounder, with Anne Simpkinson, of *Common Boundary* magazine.

KATHLEEN DOWLING SINGH, PH.D. is a student of Venerable Geshe Kelsang Gyatso and a teacher within the Kadampa Buddhist tradition. She is the author of *The Grace in Dying: How We Are Transformed Spiritually As We Die* and has published numerous articles on the spiritual dimensions of dying. A therapist, workshop leader, mother, and grandmother, she is at work on a new book which offers Dharma insights and practices for caregivers and others in the helping professions.

RODNEY SMITH is the director of Hospice of Seattle. A Senior Teacher for the Insight Meditation Society, he teaches Vipassana meditation throughout the United States. He is the author of *Lessons from the Dying*.

KATHLEEN RIORDAN SPEETH, PH.D. is a licensed psychotherapist and teacher. In addition to personal hands-on expertise across many esoteric spiritual disciplines, she grew up in a household of Gurdjieff students and subsequently became a Gurdjieff scholar. She is the author of *The Gurdjieff Work* and *Gurdjieff, Seeker of the Truth*.

KAREN KISSEL WEGELA, PH.D. is a psychologist in private practice and the director of the M.A. Program in Contemplative Psychotherapy at the Naropa Institute in Boulder, Colorado. She is the author of *How to Be a Help Instead of a Nuisance*.

Acknowledgments

Grateful acknowledgment is made to the following publishers and authors for permission to include material from their books and articles.

"Listening with Presence, Awareness, and Love" by Christine Longaker. Copyright 1997 by Christine Longaker. Reprinted by arrangement with Doubleday, New York, N.Y.

"The Theory of Holes" from *Diamond Heart: Elements of the Real in Man* by A.H. Almaas. Copyright 1987 by A. Hameed Ali. Reprinted by arrangement with Shambhala Publications, Inc., Boston, Mass.

"Feeding One Another" from *Soul Work: A Field Guide for Spiritual Seekers* by Anne Simpkinson and Charles Simpkinson published in Copyright 1998. Reprinted by arrangement with HarperCollins Publishers, New York, N.Y.

"American Willing to Listen" and "Strategic Questioning" by Fran Peavey. Copyright 2001 by Fran Peavey. Reprinted by arrangement with the Crabgrass Foundation, San Francisco, Calif.

"On Therapeutic Attention" by Kathleen Riordan Speeth. Copyright 1982 by the Transpersonal Institute. Reprinted by arrangement with the Transpersonal Institute, San Francisco, Calif.

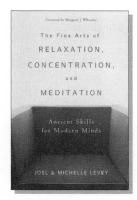

The Fine Arts of Relaxation, Concentration, and Meditation
Ancient Skills for Modern Minds
Joel and Michelle Levey
Foreword by Margaret J. Wheatley
304 pages, 0-86171-349-4, $14.95

"An inviting and highly practical manual for those who want to enhance 'health and performance, master stress, and deepen their appreciation of life.' Many of the strategies found here are clear, step-by-step procedures; others are scripts suitable to record and play back during a relaxation, concentration, or meditation session. The authors continually emphasize the depth and sacredness associated with these 'inner arts', resulting in a useful handbook that will appeal to a wide range of readers seeking increased tranquility in and mastery over their lives."—*Publishers Weekly*

"A skillful blend of time-proven antidotes to the stress of modern life."
—Daniel Goleman, author of *Destructive Emotions: A Scientific Dialogue with the Dalai Lama*

How to Meditate: A Practical Guide
Kathleen McDonald
224 pages, ISBN 0-86171-009-6, $14.95

What is meditation? Why practice it? How do I do it? The answers to these often-asked questions are contained in this down-to-earth book written by a Western Buddhist nun with solid experience in both the practice and teaching of meditation.

"As beautifully simple and direct as its title."—*Yoga Today*

Mindfulness in Plain English
Revised, Expanded Edition
Bhante Gunaratana
224 pages, ISBN 0-86171-321-4, $14.95

"Mindfulness in Plain English is just that: a wonderfully clear and straightforward explanation of mindfulness meditation. Venerable Gunaratana has done a valuable service in writing this book. It will be a great help to all who read it."—Joseph Goldstein, author of *One Dharma*

"Extremely up-to-date, and approachable, this book also serves as a very thorough FAQ for new (and not-so-new) meditators....Bhante has an engaging delivery and a straightforward voice that's hard not to like." —*Shambhala Sun*

Zen Meditation in Plain English
John Daishin Buksbazen
Foreword by Peter Matthiessen
ISBN 0-86171-316-8, $12.95

"Buksbazen, a psychotherapist and Zen priest, offers practical and down-to-earth advice about the specifics of Zen meditation: how to position the body; how and when to breathe; what to think about. Helpful diagrams illustrate the positions, and Buksbazen even provides a checklist to help beginners remember all of the steps. This is a fine introduction to Zen meditation practice, grounded in tradition yet adapted to contemporary life."—*Publishers Weekly*

Beside Still Waters

Jews, Christians, and the Way of the Buddha
Edited by Harold Kasimow, John P. Keenan, and
Linda Klepinger Keenan
Foreword by Jack Miles, Pulitzer Prize-winning
author of *God: A Biography*
288 pages, ISBN 0-86171-336-2, $14.95

Authors such as Sylvia Boorstein, Norman Fischer, Ruben Habito, and John B. Cobb relate the impact that Buddhism has had upon their sense of religious identity.

"Presented with honesty, intellectual integrity, and humor, the stories in this wonderfully assembled collection will surely encourage those who grapple with divergent perspectives and seek meaning from multiple sources."—Marcia Falk, author of *The Book of Blessings: New Jewish Prayers for Daily Life, the Sabbath, and the New Moon Festival*

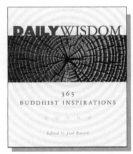

Daily Wisdom

365 Buddhist Inspirations
Edited by Josh Bartok
384 pages, ISBN 0-86171-300-1, $16.95

Daily Wisdom draws on the richness of Buddhist writings to offer a spiritual cornucopia that will illuminate and inspire day after day, year after year. Sources span a spectrum from ancient sages to modern teachers, from monks to lay people, from East to West, from poetry to prose. Each page, and each new day, reveals another gem of *Daily Wisdom*.

Meditation for Life

Martine Batchelor

Photographs by Stephen Batchelor

168 pages, ISBN 0-86171-320-8, $22.95

"This exquisite book combines stories, instruction, and practical exercises from three Buddhist traditions: Zen, Theravadin, and Tibetan. Along with chapters on meditation, ethics, and many other aspects of the path, Batchelor has included chapters on inspiration, the role of a teacher, and bringing meditation into our daily lives. She has written this guide to basic and more advanced practices in language accessible to anyone, including non-Dharma practitioners. Complementing the text are photographs that help us discover the beauty of things as they are, by Martine's husband, Buddhist teacher and writer Stephen Batchelor. Highly recommended."—*Turning Wheel*

Blue Jean Buddha

Voices of Young Buddhists

Edited by Sumi Loundon

Foreword by Jack Kornfield

288 pages, ISBN 0-861781-177-7, $16.95

"From committed, articulate contributors—including activists, health-care workers, students, teachers, monks, and a nun—come thirty frank and thoughtful tales of striving to reconcile Buddhist practice with the demands of school, work, family, and relationships."—*Booklist*

"A down-to-earth and inviting collection about Buddhism as practiced by young people in the West. These stories resonate."—*Shambhala Sun*

"A bellwether anthology."—*The New York Review of Books*

About Wisdom

W ISDOM PUBLICATIONS, a nonprofit publisher, is dedicated to preserving and transmitting important works from all the major Buddhist traditions as well as related East-West themes.

To learn more about Wisdom, or browse our books on-line, visit our website at wisdompubs.org. You may request a copy of our mail-order catalog on-line or by writing to:

WISDOM PUBLICATIONS
199 Elm Street
Somerville, Massachusetts 02144 USA
Telephone: (617) 776-7416
Fax: (617) 776-7841
Email: info@wisdompubs.org
www.wisdompubs.org

Wisdom is a nonprofit, charitable 501(c)(3) organization affiliated with the Foundation for the Preservation of the Mahayana Tradition (FPMT).